The Bible Tells Me So

A Year of Catechizing Directly from Scripture

Christian LeBlanc

ISBN-10: 1-4752-9665-7

ISBN-13: 978-1-4752-9665-5

Nihil Obstat
Sister Pamela Smith, SS.C.M.
Censor Deputatus

Imprimatur
Robert E. Guglielmone, D.D.
Bishop of Charleston, SC
September 17, 2012

Cover image of the *Coronation of Mary* fresco by *Il Bergognone* in San Simpliciano, Milan, Italy

Cover design by Gabrielle McGrath Graphic Design
gabrielle@gabriellemcgrath.com

Contents

Unit # 3: The Mass

Afterword

Images

Acknowledgments

In writing *The Bible Tells Me So,* I'm indebted to many people over many years. I especially want to thank the following individuals:

- Sister Helena, who pounded English grammar into my callow head.

- Fr. (Msgr.) Robert Berggreen, who used the Bible instead of a textbook in Religion class.

- Fr. Charles Day, who asked me to be a catechist.

- Joann Miller, my DRE, who has supported all of my adventures in catechism.

- Pat Perkins and Karen Joseph, my fearsome class bouncers, who maintained order in the classroom and allowed me to think only about teaching.

- Lisa Mladinich, who invited me to write articles for her Amazing Catechists website, which prompted me to start writing this book.

- All the dear children whom it has been my greatest privilege to teach.

- And my wonderful wife Janet, who on hundreds of Wednesday nights patiently endured a recounting of each and every class, and provided valuable feedback and advice during the writing process.

Christian LeBlanc

April 2012

Preface

Centuries ago St. Jerome wrote, "Ignorance of Scripture is Ignorance of Christ." And since Vatican 2, the Church has explicitly emphasized Bible literacy. The Church is right: there is no substitute for a Catholic faith that is firmly grounded in Scripture. Not just a Bible story here, a verse or two over there; but understanding the Catholic faith and the Bible *at the same time as a unified whole.*

The Bible Tells Me So recounts one year of Bible-based teaching for 6th-graders, featuring both Bible-sourced Catechesis and the give-and-take between teacher and students. The text is edited from recordings of the classes, plus my lesson plans and accumulated class notes. It's intended to provide a firm Scriptural foundation for today's Catholic children and catechists, giving them an invaluable familiarity with the Bible and their faith at the same time. Because the text is written as a dialogue between the teacher and the students, the reader will learn not only *what* has been taught, but *how* it's been taught.

I've taught 6th-grade Catechism for eight years now; The *Bible Tells Me So* is drawn from that experience. As an age group, I've found 6th-graders to be ready to learn, ready to think, and ready to know more about God and Faith. They have an as-yet unjaded view of life, and a natural disposition to take God seriously. They grasp big ideas quickly, adjust to new information, and leap to conclusions in a single bound. Their brains are more nimble than an adult's, and they come to class with much less baggage. They like to be respected as people, not just as children. They will meet high expectations and enjoy doing it.

Now is the perfect time for these young minds to acquire a Bible-Catholic framework, a *cadre*, which will serve them for the rest of their lives.

Introduction

I have no formal training as a teacher in general, or as a catechist in particular.

My critical exposure to Scripture in the classroom was at St. Joseph's Cathedral Prep, a minor seminary in Baton Rouge, La. Our Religion class was taught directly from the Bible by Fr. (now Msgr.) Robert Berggreen.

Years later, at Clemson University's College of Architecture, I was educated via a distinctive type of instruction, in which the professor directed the learning through a combination of direct teaching, asking questions, drawing, and guiding discussion. Several years after graduating, I taught in the architecture studio myself as a visiting assistant professor, using the same engaging method I'd experienced as a student.

In the spring of 1999 our pastor, Fr. Charles Day, asked my wife (an Art History professor) and me to teach RCIA; the year before we had managed an adult class in which the topics were determined by consensus. We were interested in doing RCIA, and our adult class, which had not gone through any formal faith instruction since the 8th grade, agreed to attend as well. We soon decided, however, that the RCIA course wasn't ideal for Catholics in the Bible Belt: it worked mostly with the Catechism, and documents from Vatican II. Our catechumens would need to learn their Catholicism directly from the Bible in order to better explain (or defend) the Faith to their Evangelical and Fundamentalist neighbors and family members. In other words, the Catechism would be a resource, and the Bible would be the textbook. After we outlined a new syllabus, Fr. Day allowed us to design a new curriculum. The catechumens, candidates, and Catholics all learned a lot that year; and the classroom style owed much to how I'd been taught in architecture school and at Cathedral Prep.

Then one year I was needed as a 6th grade catechist. I did not want to deal with kids: what do they care about the Council of Nicaea? But God does work in mysterious ways. I was wrong to think I'd have to dumb things down for them, and the substantial and orthodox textbook wasn't the least bit coddling.

But the 31-chapter textbook was designed for a 180-day school year; we have at most 30 evening classes. It would be impossible to slam through a week's content in 55 minutes. I decided to cover the material that the book expected the kids to learn, but in a way that worked within our time constraints. Each Thursday I began to write out a scratch lesson plan on a legal pad for the next Wednesday's class. Because I was accustomed to using the Bible as the textbook, I included Bible references. But unlike adult class, where I could just give a verse or two, and rely on the individuals to already know, or check, the bigger passage on their own, the kids needed more context. For example, if I were discussing baptism with adults, I could just summarize Naaman and Elisha; but with the kids, I needed to tell the whole story. In fact, I wound up *acting* the story as much as telling it, which was great fun, and the little brains soaked it right up. At the end of that first year, I noticed how often Catholic concepts were communicated through Bible storytelling. Some stories, such as the Healing of the Paralytic, came up several times during the year.

Over the next few years I continued to catechize through increased storytelling, acting, using props, and directed Q & A. I also continually revised and added to my lesson plans. Parents often sat in the back of class, and told me how much *they* were learning.

Increasingly, the textbook's content was covered by acting out and discussing Bible stories more than by direct reference to the textbook, which by that point the kids did not bring to class. By 2008 (my 5th year of teaching 6th graders) I was using over 50 Bible stories (or topics involving multiple stories), and for my own benefit was writing down what happened in each class. In 2009, I began writing a custom syllabus that would make the Bible be the spine of the catechetical year. The kids would learn their Catholic faith, but they'd be doing it directly through Scripture. In the Spring of 2010 my DRE, Joann Miller, approved my reorganization of the curriculum around a 27-lesson chronological overview of the Bible, followed by 3 lessons on the Mass, which draw from the prior 27 lessons. *The Bible Tells Me So* is the condensed recounting of that year of catechesis. Because the book is as much about *how* faith is taught as *what* faith is taught, the content is presented as a series of live discussions. When the children speak, *their words are in italics.*

Units 1 and 2 treat the Bible chronologically from Genesis to Revelation, emphasizing the Catholic understanding of Scripture. These classes were taught directly from a highlighted Bible. Unit 3 then examines the Mass in lessons which draw from the knowledge gained in the preceding units, using the same highlighted Bible and a highlighted Missalette. Most chapters roughly correspond to class meetings. Some are shorter due to the subject matter, and won't take an entire class. Besides, I don't expect catechists to march straight through the year the same way I do, but to use this book as a supplement to what they're already teaching.

In covering the Bible and the Mass in a year, I've skimmed over, or omitted entirely, some popular or well-known parts of the Bible. That doesn't mean they aren't worth learning; it only means I had to pare the Bible down to what I saw as Catholic essentials (barely mentioning David and Goliath), or what had particular value in laying a foundation for the Mass (including the story of Manoah and the Angel).

Between 52 and 55 minutes of actual teaching is achieved in a typical 60-minute class period, but readers will soon notice that none of the chapters take 55 minutes to read. That's because in class the children naturally need to hear new concepts restated and re-explained, and old concepts reviewed; have stories elaborated on, acted out, and drawn on the board; and contribute their own observations, all of which take time. When the kids are fired up, they also ask lots of questions; plus they love to digress. If it's a good digression, we'll explore it; if not, I deflect it. Leaving all that out, the book condenses each class period to less time than it takes to teach the material live.

Because the lessons are taught from the Bible, not a particular textbook, any catechist can easily use this information in the classroom. Most Bible quotes in English are from the Revised Standard Version- Catholic Edition. A few come from the 1611 King James Version, and they are noted as such. No materials are required in my classes beyond the contents of this book, a Bible, a Missalette, inexpensive props, and a whiteboard. The students don't bring a textbook to class (some bring Bibles), and have no paper, pencil, or anything else to distract them except for the occasional handout.

Most of the handouts are of fine art, with a bit of Scripture at the bottom to give some context. Images help children learn, and I like to use fine art rather than something specifically pitched at 11-year-olds. The kids can learn from a "grownup" fresco as well as they can a cartoon; and fine art is simply a richer experience, spiritually, culturally, aesthetically, you name it. Some of the handouts are in the Image appendix, while others are mentioned as they come up in the chapters.

While I use the Catechism as a reference in my lesson-planning, I rarely read from it in the classroom, except to answer specific questions such as, "What if a baby dies before it's baptized?" When the Catechism has a pithy answer it can't be beat.

Finally, let me quote St. John of the Cross: "If I should misunderstand or be mistaken on some point, whether I deduce it from Scripture or not, my intention will not be to deviate from the true meaning of Sacred Scripture or from the doctrine of our Holy Mother the Catholic Church. If this should happen, I submit entirely to the Church, or even to anyone who judges more competently about the matter than I."

On to Unit 1, the Old Testament.

Unit 1

The Old Testament

Chapter One:

Adam's Nose (Genesis part 1)

Introduction to the Bible 1: Old Testament and New Testament. Introduction to the Bible 2: Genesis in the front; Revelation at the end; everything else in the middle. Genesis chapters 1-2: God creates, lower to higher life forms. Adam, a unity of body & soul. Adam's authority/ dominion over animals shown by naming them, but not eating them. Marriage: Rib-bone vs. toe-bone vs. heart; is Eve God's last creation? Adam and Eve together continue creation.

Getting Acquainted

Hey y'all, welcome to 6th grade Wednesday Night Sunday School. This is your textbook. I don't want to see it again. *What?* Take it home, there's no time in class to be reading from the textbook; I'll let you know each week what you ought to read for next week's class, as in: *read it at home.* You'll enjoy class better if you read the assigned bits, and these chapters won't take you 5 minutes to read. Yes? *But we aren't supposed to take it home.* Well darlin', this year is the opposite of last year. Don't worry, you'll get used to it.

Now, who likes parties and crafts and games? *I do! Me, too!* OK, you are going to be miserable this year. We won't have any time for that stuff, there's too much to learn. Yes? *No parties?* Nope. Look, here's what I want y'all do this year [on the board]: SUFFER. *Suffer!?* Yes, suffering is good, and I'm the meanest teacher in Sunday School. Yes? *My brother says he really didn't suffer last year and he had fun.* Oh. Well, he was *supposed* to suffer. If you do have fun in here it'll be a miracle, but keep it to yourself. Don't spoil the suffering of others. Hey there daughter, stop smiling! *I can't!* Well, try harder. No smiling; and *definitely* no laughing. Stop laughing! Wednesday Night Sunday School is not funny!

But I don't want y'all to just suffer. I want y'all to prepare for class by actually, *you know,* reading the week's chapter if there is one, pay attention, and participate in class. If you participate, the time will pass more quickly and you'll think that you suffered less. By the way, I know many of you are tired at 6:30 on a weeknight. If you are shot and want to put your head down that's ok. The thing to never do is to interfere with other kids' learning.

Oh, and my name is... *oops.* I have a special Sunday School name like Lady Gaga. Is that her real name? *No.* Well, my Sunday School name isn't real either [on the board]: Stratopops. Yes? *What kind of name is that?* It's a secret name; don't tell anyone outside class. Yes? *I already knew your name was Stratopops.* Well, pretend you didn't. This way you don't have to call me Mr. Labink or whatever my real name is. Stratopops is easier.

15

OK, time's a wastin', let's get started!

Two-Minute Cadre

[I hold up the Bible with my finger separating the Testaments.] Y'all tell me, what's this book? *The Bible.* Yes, it has two sections. The first is the Old Testament, which was written mostly in Hebrew before Jesus was born. If the first section is the...? *Old Testament*, yes, then what's the next one? *The New Testament?* Yes. It was written mostly in Greek. If the Old Testament was written *before* Jesus was born then the New was written....? *After Jesus was born!* Yes.

Testament comes from the verb *testify.* When people testify in court, what do they do? *They say what they saw somebody do.* Yes, what happened; and they swear to tell only... *the truth!* So the Testaments do what? *They say what people did.* Yes, what happened. Did God sit down and write the Bible? *No, other people did.* Right. Did God dictate the Bible word for word to them? *I don't think so.* Right, they used their own words to communicate God's message: we say that the Bible is *God-breathed.* ¿Quién aquí habla Español? Who speaks Spanish? *Me. Me, too.* Tell me please how we say 'breathe' in Spanish. *Ummm... respirar?* Yes [respirar goes on the board]. What's an English word like respirar? *Respiration!* Yes, good, it means...*breathe!* Yes. Now watch the magic finger [I erase respiration down to -spir-]. Some of y'all are learning roots or stems in school, right? *Yes, I do. Me too.* OK, who knows what *-spir-* means? Yes? *It means 'breathe' in Latin.* Yes, good. What does *inspire* mean? *Ummm, like you feel excited?* Yes, sort of; it usually means our *spirit* is lifted. *Spirit* comes from the Latin word for breathe. So we say that God 'in-spired,' *breathed into* the writers the gift of writing only the truth. God also breathes *on* people on some special occasions in the Bible, so pay attention when that happens.

[Now I hold up the Bible divided into 3 parts with my fingers.] The Bible tells the hi*story*, the story of God and us; the story has 3 basic parts. The little part in front, Genesis, tells about when Adam & Eve lived body and soul in perfect friendship with God in Eden until they sinned. This last little bit is *Revelation*, which *reveals* to us that in the future we will once again live body and soul in perfect friendship with God, as Adam and Eve once did. All these 1,500 pages in the middle is the story of us getting there. We're living in the middle part right now.

Now, quick review: two sections, the Old and...*the New!* The New Banana? *No, the New Testament!* Which was written in Greek when? *After Jesus was born!* Yes, and the first part of the story is about...*Adam & Eve before they sinned.* And the end? *When we are with God again.* And the middle? *When we try to be in heaven.* You explained it pretty well. Good children, y'all learn fast.

Creating Stuff

Sons & Daughters, what's the first book in the Bible? *Genesis!* Right you are, and what happens in Genesis? *That's when God makes everything.* Yes. The first two chapters of Genesis are about Creation. Genesis (γένεσις) is the Greek word for *origin, birth, beginning, creation.* It's related to words such as *gender* and *generation.* We're going to look at Creation, especially the last thing God created, because it's not obvious, but it's very important.

Trick question: in the beginning of the first chapter of Genesis, what are the first three words? *Umm, God made everything?* Not a bad guess, but no. *God made Adam?* No again. The first words in the beginning of the first chapter of Genesis are: In... The... Beginning! I win! *Awwww...no fair!* Yes fair!

So, we read: "In the beginning God created the heavens and the earth. The earth was without form and void..." (Gen 1:1+) What's a void? *Nothing, it's empty.* Yes, that's how Genesis explains that there wasn't anything yet...not even space or time. There wasn't even nothing, which is hard to imagine. Yes? *What color was it?* Nobody knows. I imagine it was infinite clear, neither light nor dark.

Then God said, "Let there be light"; and there was light. And God saw that the light was good." This is important to remember: the things God creates aren't neutral, they're *good*. Even rocks. You have to remember that so that you get a point the story is going to make later. Remember, the Bible was written in two languages: Hebrew and Greek. What's the other language the Church uses, especially at Mass? Come on, [I sing] "Agnus Dei, qui tollis peccata..." *Oh, Latin!* Yes, Latin. In Latin we say 'Fiat Lux' for 'Let there be light' [I write *Fiat Lux* on the board]. ¿Como se llama 'light' in Español? How do you say 'light' in Spanish? *I know, it's 'luz'* [which I write under 'Lux.']. See, Spanish is close to Latin; it's one of Latin's beautiful daughters. Who's heard of Chrysler? Yes? What does Chrysler do? *They make cars!* Yes. An Italian car company owns Chrysler; its name is Fiat, just like in 'Fiat Lux.' In Latin, *fiat* means "Let it be done" or "Let it be made." It's the sort of word used by a king... or God. I believe the car company is named Fiat because it "lets cars be made." Italians familiar with God saying 'Fiat Lux' at the start of creation would find Fiat a very grand name for a carmaker. And let's remember, Italian is yet *another* one of Latin's beautiful daughters.

So, God says 'Fiat Lux' and there's light on the first day. What does God 'fiat' next? *Earth?* Good guess, but not yet. He fiats the sky on the second day. On the third day? *Earth?* Yes! And the sea, and plants. And he saw that it was.... *good.* Trick question: God made light, darkness, earth and sea. Then he made plants. What makes plants different from those other things? *Plants are alive!* Yes. And what's more like God, things such as the earth, or living things like plants? *Living things.* Yes. On day four, God creates the sun, moon, stars and planets. And he saw that it was...? *Good!* Yes. On the fifth day God creates birds and fish. On the sixth day God makes all the animals. What's more like God, plants or fish? *Fish!* Yes. Fish or animals? *Animals!* Yes. They have what in Latin is called an *anima* [goes on the board], a life force that plants don't have. So things that have an *anima* are...*animals!* Yes, genius, they're *animated!* So as creation moves along, the things created are more and more like... *God!* Yes. The things created later are *closer* to God. And God saw.... *that it was good!* Yes.

Creating Adam

Now I want us to slow down. What's left for God to fiat? *People!* Yes, people. And as creation developed, the later something was created, the closer it was to God. So God created man last, in his own image, in the image of God. Man is as close to God as creation gets. And remind me please, God saw...*that it was good!* Yes.

But let's look at how God made man. He didn't just say, "Let there be man." He didn't *fiat* a man. How'd he make a man? *He used dirt!* Yes, Genesis says: "then the LORD God formed man of dust from the ground, and breathed into his nostrils the breath of life; and man became a living being." (Gen 2:7) The way God made man was very personal. The Latin word for breath is *spiritus,* so man has a *spirit*, not just an *anima* like animals do [*breath, respiration,* and *spiritus* go on the board]. God's breath, his *spirit,* is in us. Notice that as God was making Adam's body, he blows his spirit into him. Adam's body and soul go together, neither part by itself is Adam. Yes? *But what about when your soul goes to heaven?* Well, if a soul is in heaven that's great, but the *complete* human being isn't there. We'll see how God takes care of that later on this year.

I forgot, what was the name of the first man? *Adam!* Yes...trick question: why is his name Adam? OK, this is a hard one. Genesis is in which Testament? *The old one!* Yes, and so it was written in... *Hebrew?* Yes! Now, the Hebrew word for the earth, the ground, is *Adama* [goes on the board]... *He's Adam 'cause he's made from the ground!* Yes, genius! Adam was made from Adama, earth! His name helps tell the story. There are other names in the Bible that help tell stories, we'll see more of them later on.

So God made Adam carefully, and made just one of him. And being the last thing God made, Adam was closest to God, most like God. Then God put Adam in Eden to be happy. And of course, all of this was *very good.* But then God noticed something was *not* good...how could that be? Somebody tell me what was not good. *Adam doesn't have Eve yet.* Yes. So even though the whole universe was good, if Adam is alone, that's...*not good!* That's right! It's awful! God said, "It is not good that the man should be alone; I will make him a helper fit for him." (Gen 2:18) And what did he do then? *Make Eve!* No, not yet. First he brought all the animals to Adam, "but for the man there was not found a helper fit for him." No kidding. I can imagine God suggesting I'd be happy with a dog instead of a wife...no thanks. So what now? *God makes Eve!* Yes, from what? *Adam's rib!* Yes!

Creating Eve

Now we need to slow way down. The next few lines of Genesis are to me, the most beautiful in the Bible. [I read and act out] Genesis says: "So the LORD God caused a deep sleep to fall upon the man, and while he slept took one of his ribs and closed up its place with flesh; and the rib which the LORD God had taken from the man he made into a woman and brought her to the man. " Trick question: why did God take a rib and not, say, a toe? No guesses? How about an ear? Or a hunk of Adam's butt? *Ewww, that would be gross.* Yes, Eve should come from a dignified part of Adam, and a part that wouldn't disfigure him or kill him to lose it. For example, since we know Adam will love Eve, what would be a good part of Adam to use to make Eve? *His heart?* Yes; but if God took Adam's heart and closed him back up, what would happen? *He'd die.* Right again. We might say he'd 'ex-spire' give up his breath, his...*spirit!* Yes. So God used a rib from Adam's side, in part because Adam and Eve would be equals, side by side; and losing a rib won't make Adam die, or be ugly like if God had used his nose to make Eve. And can you guess what side of Adam the rib came from? What's by my ribs on my right side? *Your lung?* Yes, and on the left side? *Your other lung.* Yes, and something more important...*oh, your heart!* Yes, so what side do you think the rib came from? *The heart side, Adam's left side!* I think so too. Genesis doesn't say either way.

Also notice after God takes the rib, He closes Adam back up, so we know He didn't replace the rib. Is Adam complete without his rib? *No!* Right, Adam's missing his rib.... how can he have his rib again? *By having Eve!* Yes, he can hug her against himself like this [I pretend to hold my wife close to my left side] right next to...*his heart!* And when Adam does this, is he missing his rib? *No!* Right, with Eve by his side, Adam is complete. But when Eve is away, he always misses her.

Speaking of Eve, was Adam made last after all? *No, Eve was last.* Yes, and Adam was made of....*dirt!* And Eve from...*Adam's rib.* Which seems better, to be made from dirt or someone's rib? *A rib!* And in the creation story the later you're created the closer you are to God, right? *Yes, but.... aren't they equal?* Yes, I think so; Eve was made from Adam, so they are one flesh, but on the other hand, women get to have the babies! I think they may have a little advantage there.

Let's look now at the last line of this passage: 'God brought her to the man.' I like this line because God brought my wife to me, too, like a wonderful gift. I know just how Adam feels when he says, "This at last is bone of my bones and flesh of my flesh." I think of my wife the same way. She's a part of me now just like my arms, legs, and heart.

Creating Everyone Else

Then we read: "Therefore a man leaves his father and his mother and cleaves to his wife, and they become one flesh."

'Cleave' is an old word; here it means to cling or stick to, like this [I press my hands together as if in prayer], and that's what married people do. They become one. And we know when married people become one, the result is...*babies?* Yes, more people. All creation didn't stop on the sixth day. So I think that the last thing God created wasn't Adam...what was created last? *Eve!* No, Eve wasn't last either. The *last thing* God created was *Adam and Eve being together, being one,* which we call what? *Marriage!* Yes, the last and highest of God's creations is marriage. Marriage allows God's creation of the creatures most like him, who are...? *people, us!* made in his image and likeness, to continue into the future.

Quick review, who were Adam and Eve? *They were the first man & woman.* Yes...Eve was made from...*Adam's rib!* Yes...so, was she his daughter? *No!* Hmm, were they cousins? *No, there weren't any cousins yet.* Oh, yeah, I forgot. Were they brother & sister? *No, they were married! They were husband & wife!* That's right!

Here's a question: what's the First Commandment? *Love the LORD thy God & have no other Gods before him.* Yep. And what was the first commandment for Adam & Eve? *Well, we said it already: Love-the-LORD-thy-God-and-have-no-other-Gods-before-him!* Ha! Wrong! Trick question! Whom did God give the Commandments to...Adam? *No, umm...* C'mon, God gave someone the stone tablets in *Prince of Egypt!* Oh, *Moses!* And who came first, Moses or Adam? *Uhh, Adam!* So did Adam know anything about however-many Commandment thingies? *Umm...no, they didn't exist yet!* Right! So back to the trick question... what was the first commandment for Adam & Eve? *I know I know! Don't eat the fruit!* Ha-Ha, I am the *King* of

Trick Questions! No! That came later! But that's a good answer.

OK, let's read a bit from Genesis. When you hear the first commandment God gives Adam & Eve, say it out loud. Then God said, "Let us make man in our image, after our likeness; and let them have dominion over the fish of the sea, and over the birds of the air, and over the cattle, and over all the earth, and over every creeping thing that creeps upon the earth. So God created man in his own image, in the image of God he created him; male and female he created them. And God blessed them, and God said to them, "Be fruitful and multiply, and fill the earth and subdue it; and have dominion over...*IknowIknowbefruitful&multiply!* Yes, be fruitful & multiply... what an odd commandment. How would Adam & Eve grow fruit off themselves or need to know how to multiply? *It means to have babies!* Oh yeah, that's right...why didn't God just say so?

So, Adam & Eve are in Eden, they just got created...have they disobeyed God yet? *No!* And if they're obeying God's first commandment they must be...*having babies?* Sure, unless you can imagine Adam & Eve saying, "God we'd like to be obedient'n'all, but we wanna lie around on the beach, check out the pizza buffet, relax some...since we can't die we'll be fruitful later on, in 50 years or so...what's the rush? Don't worry, we're gonna obey ya!" *Ha, that's silly.*

Yes, so my guess is Adam and Eve had kids in the Garden before they sinned and were thrown out. They were just being obedient... up until they *weren't* being obedient. And after they sinned and were being thrown out, God said to Eve, "I will greatly multiply your pain in childbearing," which sounds to me like she had already birthed some kids *without* lots of pain.

The Church hasn't firmly decided about Adam & Eve having kids in Eden, and the Bible isn't specific, either. It's an interesting question, but it doesn't affect our lives either way. On the other hand, the Church and the Bible *are* clear about whether married people, like Adam & Eve, should be fruitful & multiply, though. What's *that* decision? *They should have babies?* Yes. The Church says marriages must be *open* to having children... but everyone doesn't necessarily wind up with kids.

Eating Meat

And let's learn what Adam and Eve had to eat...speak up when you know. "And God said: Behold I have given you every herb bearing seed upon the earth, and all trees that have in themselves seed of their own kind, to be your meatAnd God said: Behold I have given you every herb bearing seed upon the earth, and all trees that have in themselves seed of their own kind, to be your meat:" (DR, Gen 1:29) *Well, they could eat fruit I guess?* Yes, and vegetables. What couldn't they eat? *Meat?* That's right, no meat. What's wrong with them eating meat? *Nothing's wrong with eating meat.* Let me put it this way: what would be wrong with eating meat in the Garden of Eden? If Adam wanted some bacon, could he just cut a pig's leg off, and hope the pig would grow another leg? Would that be OK? *No.* Why not? *It would be mean.* Yes. In Eden eating an animal wouldn't happen. *But we eat meat now!* Yes, and we'll come back to that later.

This brings us to the end of Chapter 2 of what book? *Genesis.* Yes. This last bit of Chapter 2 is as great as it gets in Eden: all of creation is made, God sees it's all...*good!* yes, including the last, and best part of God's creation, which is...? *Adam and Eve.* More specifically please: Adam and Eve separately [I show my two hands unfolded]? *No, together!* Yes, [I fold my hands] together, which makes what? *A marriage!* Yes, which makes what? *More people!* Yes. Good class!

Are any of y'all altar servers? *I am.* Tell us the prayer y'all say outside of church after Mass. *Oh, Father Newman says, "Praised be Jesus Christ;" and we say, "Now and Forever."* Yes. That's going to our closing prayer. Here we go: Praised be Jesus Christ! *Now and Forever.*

C'mon, say it like you're *in-spired!* Praised be Jesus Christ! *Now and Forever!* That's it! Are y'all suffering yet? *Yes! No!* Work on that! Class over!

Chapter Two:

Smarter Than God (Genesis part 2)

Creation before sin; friendship with God; no sacrificing yet, why not? Gen 3-4: The Fall, free will, and pride: everybody thinks they know better than God. All creation messed up by sin: death, tornadoes, germs, you name it. Adam & Eve driven out of Eden, now guarded by a cherub. People physically separated from God. Cain and Abel, now sacrificing. Why sacrifice?

Let's see, what book in the Bible are we learning about? *Genesis!* Yes, we're up to the end of Chapter 2, and Adam & Eve are in Eden. Somebody tell me about life in Eden. *Nothing was bad!* Yes. Could Adam & Eve get sick? *No.* Get zits? *No.* Get hit by lightning? *No!* Die? *No!* Right. In fact, life was so good in Eden that Adam & Eve hung out with God in a physical way, not just spiritual...does God the Father have a body? *No.* Right. But listen: "...they heard the sound of the LORD God walking in the garden in the cool of the day"...so, even though God didn't have a body, he was still with them in a way we don't understand. He wasn't far-off in Heaven, but right there. Now somebody tell me about Adam's rib. *He misses his rib and wants her back!* That's right! How many ribs did God take from Adam? *One.* Yes...so how many wives should Adam have...three? *Ha, no, one!* Yes. God didn't take a bunch of ribs for Adam to have a wife *posse*, just one rib. Now all of us men, and boys, who are future men, inherited that sense of missing something. Honorary son, let's say God took *your* rib and made *her* out of it, and you over there, *your* rib became *this* girl, and my wife came from *my* rib. Now if you're missing *your* rib, do you want *his* rib? *Ha, no I want mine!* Right. You don't just want *any* rib...you want *your* rib. Well that's how my wife is to me, not just *a* woman that God made, but what? *The woman God made for you?* Yes, just for me. I don't want another woman any more than I want someone else's rib.

Free Will

[I pull out a rubber ball] What's this? *A ball.* Yes... watch this. I throw it down, it bounces up. I throw it up, it bounces down. OK, watch closely this time, it's gonna decide not to bounce down...nope, it came down. Let's try again; I'll decide for the ball not to come down...huh, it came down again! Why does the ball always come back down? *Gravity!* Yes, the Law of Gravity. Can we decide not to obey the Law of Gravity? *Huh?* If I jump like so, [jump] can I decide not to come down? *No!* Right. It's a physical law, I can't decide to ignore it. The Laws of Physics are part of God's Creation, and we don't have any choice about observing them. Can someone think of one of God's laws that we *can* choose to ignore? Yes, tell it. *Don't steal?* Yes, someone else, another one. *Don't kill?* Yes. Why can we decide to ignore those laws? *They're moral laws?* Yes, good. But why would we break them? *Because we have free will?* Yes, what's that mean, to have free will? *It means you can be good or bad.* Yes, that you can *freely decide* to be good or bad. If I grab your wrist & swing your hand to hit someone, are you being bad? *No, you are bigger than me.* Right, you have to make a free decision to be bad...or good. Hmm... can a bear decide to be good or bad? *Ha, no!* Right. Bears and other creatures aren't made in God's image & likeness like we are. God loves us so much he allows us to choose between good and evil on our own. He doesn't force us to be good, doesn't treat us like babies.

Speaking of babies, what was the first commandment to Adam & Eve? *Have babies!* Yes, be fruitful and multiply. And the second commandment? *Don't eat the fruit!* Yes. Let's look at that now. Chapter 3 of Genesis says, "Now the serpent was more subtle (subtle means *sly*) than any other wild creature that the LORD God had made. He said to the woman, "Did God say, 'You shall not eat of any tree of the garden'?" And the woman said to the serpent, "We may eat of the fruit of the trees of the garden; but God said, 'You shall not eat of the fruit of the tree which is in the midst of the garden, neither shall you touch it, lest you die." But the serpent said to the woman, "You will not die. For God knows that when you eat of it your eyes will be opened, and you will be like God, knowing good and evil." Tell me, who's the snake? *The devil.* Yes. How is the snake tempting Eve about the fruit? No guesses? Is he saying it's tastier than the rest? *No...?* OK, listen again, "God knows that when you eat of it your eyes will be opened, and you will be like God, knowing good and evil." Guesses? *That she'd be like God!* Yes. And if Eve could be *like* God, in the sense of being *equal* to God, would she have to obey him? *No, she could do what she wanted to.* Yes. Show me hands, who likes to be told what they can or can't do? Nobody? Don't feel bad, I don't like it either. Neither did Adam & Eve. We're all proud of ourselves; we're the smartest things on Earth, we don't need to be ordered around, right? We don't like to be subject to anyone else's authority. And in Eden there was only one little thing that was forbidden; why wouldn't Adam & Eve leave it alone? *Well...they just wanted to see what would happen; they wanted to know for themselves?* Yes, they wanted to be as smart as God; smarter, even. When I was kid, I asked my parents, "What's in that cabinet? *That's the liquor cabinet.* What's liquor? *It's something grownups drink, like whiskey.* Can I have some? *No it's for adults, not children."* So what did I most want to taste in the whole world? *Whiskey!* That's right!

Who can tell the story about Pandora's Box? *She had a beautiful box that she wasn't supposed to open, but she opened it anyway and bad things came out.* Yes, that's a Greek myth, and it makes the same point: people's pride, mostly pride in their intellect, their brains, gets them in trouble. Who's someone who never sinned? *Umm, Jesus?* Right. And was Jesus proud, or humble? *Humble!* Yes, perfectly humble. And who is a huge sinner? *The devil!* Yes, Satan. And if Jesus is *humble*, then Satan...*has a lot of pride?* Yes. And that's one reason he knew he could appeal to *Eve's* pride: "Oh *Eeeve*, God doesn't want you to know what he knows, you wouldn't have to listen to him anymore...like me. I decide for myself."

So Adam & Eve's sin was simply to disobey God because of their pride. All their descendants, which include us, still have this problem with our pride. We like to think we're as smart as God. Or smarter.

After they ate the fruit, "the man and his wife hid themselves from the presence of the LORD God among the trees of the garden. But the LORD God called to the man, and said to him, "Where are you?" And he said, "I heard the sound of thee in the garden, and I was afraid, because I was naked; and I hid myself." Why did Adam hide? *Because he was embarrassed?* Yes...but God knows Adam's naked, God doesn't care. Why'd he hide, give me another reason. *He felt guilty!* Yes, he disobeyed God and he feels guilty and ashamed. When I was a kid and would get in trouble in school, what did I do when I got home? *Go hide in your room!* You bet I did!

Then God said, "Who told you that you were naked? Have you eaten of the tree of which I commanded you not to eat?" The man said, "The woman whom thou gavest to be with me, she gave me fruit of the tree, and I ate." Then the LORD God said to the woman, "What is this that you have done?" The woman said, "The serpent beguiled (tricked) me, and I ate."

I love this. First Adam says, "It ain't *my* fault, *you* gave me Eve, and *Eve* gave me the fruit." Then Eve says, "It ain't my fault *either,* that *snake* made me do it." See, pride hates to admit guilt, because it's humbling. It's easier to say someone else is guilty. Show of hands, who likes to apologize for bad stuff you do? Me neither; but we should whether we like it or not.

So what happens to Adam & Eve? *God makes them leave Eden.* Yes. God doesn't get rid of Eden, he...*gets rid of Adam & Eve!* Right. "He drove out the man; and at the east of the garden of Eden he placed the cherubim, and a flaming sword which turned every way, to guard the way to the tree of life." Hey, who knows what a cherub is? *They're like little baby angels.* Yes, you see them on Valentine cards, things like that, they're chubby and silly. But a real cherub is not chubby and silly...what language do you suppose cherub is if I'm reading from Genesis? *Umm...Hebrew?* Yes, genius! In Hebrew it's spelled like this: K-E-R-U-B [on the board], kerub. Kerub means "near one," someone who is close to God. When the President goes out in public there are usually some tough guys who stay near him all the time, why's that? *They keep people from bothering him.* Yes, what do you call those guys? *Bodyguards?* Yes. The kerubs, the cherubim, are God's bodyguards, and they are serious as cancer. Did you know we have two kerubs in our church? *We do? Where?* Mmm, I'm not telling tonight, but we'll find out later this year. In the meantime keep your eyes open in church.

Cain & Abel

So Adam & Eve are out of Eden. Could they get sick? *Yes!* Get zits? *Yes.* Get hit by lightning? *Yes!* Get sucked up by a tornado? *Yes!* Be a snack for tigers? *Eww, yes!* Die? *Yes!* Right. Their sin didn't just mess up their souls, it messed up Creation. The consequences of sin are almost always bigger than we can imagine. God said, "cursed is the *ground* because of you; in toil you shall eat of it all the days of your life; thorns and thistles it shall bring forth to you... In the sweat of your face you shall eat bread till you return to the ground, for out of it you were taken; you are dust, and to dust you shall return." Yuck: one sin and even the *ground, the Adama,* is cursed.

But Adam and Eve still obeyed God's first commandment, and so...? *They had babies!* Yes, who? *Cain & Abel!* Yes, and what was Cain's job? *He was a farmer?* Yes, and Abel? *He was a shepherd.* Yes, good. Genesis says, "Cain brought to the LORD an offering of the fruit of the ground, and Abel brought of the firstlings of his flock and of their fat portions." (Gen 4:4) Question: what's an offering? *When they gave something to God?* Yes, good. Cain gave God some of his wheat and fruit, I suppose, and Abel gave what? What's a "firstling of the flock?" *Umm, a baby sheep?* Yes, what's a baby sheep? *Oh, a lamb.* Yes, and the firstlings would be the best ones.

Y'all tell me how a lamb is offered to God...did Abel say, "This firstling lamb is for you, God; now I'm going to make it into lamb chops just for you and then eat them just for you?" *Ha, no, he had to kill it but not eat it!* And then what, leave it sitting there for buzzards to snack on? *Umm, no...he had to burn it?* Yes, and Cain did the same with his offering. When people kill lambs & offer them to God what's the word for that kind of offering? *A sacrifice?* Yes, good. Did Adam & Eve offer sacrifices in Eden? *Umm, no?* Right, they did not...why not? Why were they thrown out of Eden? *'Cause they ate the apple?* Yes, the fruit; the Bible doesn't say what kind of fruit...what's the bigger reason? *They sinned!* Yes. They disobeyed God. So where there's no sin there's...*no sacrifice?* Yes, and where there *is* sin...*there's sacrifice!* Yes. What is it about sin that makes people offer sacrifice? OK, if you break your mom's nicest flower vase, what should you do? *Fix it?* Yes, what if it's too busted up to be fixed? *Well, I guess buy another one?* What if it's too expensive? *Umm, say I'm sorry?* Yes. Suppose you didn't break it in the first place? *Then I wouldn't have to do anything.* Right. So what's the point of sacrifice? *Making it up to God?* Yes, partly; making up for what? *Well, just sinning?* Yes. And it can also be a way of saying thank you. Abel is saying, "thank you God for all these sheep, I'm giving the best back to you."

Back to their offerings: "And the LORD had regard for Abel and his offering, but for Cain and his offering he had no regard." Abel offered God his "firstlings," but Cain probably offered some good fruit, some bad. God could tell that Cain would rather keep the best stuff for himself.

"So Cain was very angry. The LORD said to Cain, "Why are you angry, and why has your countenance fallen? If you do well, will you not be accepted? And if you do not do well, sin is couching (lying in wait) at the door; its desire is for you, but you must master it." Why didn't God look with favor on Cain's offering as he did Abel's? *Cain didn't give God his best stuff.* Right, and if Cain is upset about it what can he do? *Give his best stuff like Abel does.* Yes. It's clear, but Cain wants to keep his best for himself and is angry that Abel isn't as selfish.

So "Cain said to Abel his brother, "Let us go out to the field." And when they were in the field, Cain rose up against his brother Abel, and killed him." What had Abel done to Cain to deserve being killed? *He didn't do anything to Cain.* So why did he kill Abel? *Because Abel was so good?* Yes. Cain couldn't stand being made aware of his own selfishness by constantly comparing himself to Abel. It's the same in school: slackers and misbehavers can't stand a good student.

This is the first time in the Bible, but not the only time by any means, that an innocent person is killed just because sinful people can't stand to have him around. We'll learn about those other people later this year. Think of one right now...an innocent person...killed because he aggravated people...*umm, Jesus?* Yes. And because Abel resembles Jesus in that way, we say Abel is a *type* of Christ.

After Cain killed Abel, Cain was driven away. But Adam had other sons and daughters; who knows one? *Seth!* Yes. Seth fathered Enosh, who fathered Kenan, and so on. In each case, the Bible says "and he died." One man in that line of fathers & sons was named Enoch. About Enoch, the Bible *doesn't* say "and he died." Instead it says, "Enoch walked with God; and he was not, for God took him." (Gen 5:24) What would that mean, "Enoch walked with God; and he was not, for God took him?" *That God took him straight to Heaven?* Yes, more or less. Remember, Jesus hadn't opened Heaven yet. But Enoch still 'walked with God' in some special way. And Enoch isn't the only person that went to be with God without dying, as we'll learn about later on.

By the way, Enoch was Methuselah's father; who was Methuselah? *He lived the longest!* Yes, the Bible says he lived longer than anyone. What's more interesting about Methuselah is that he was Noah's grandfather. We'll discuss Noah next week. This brings us to the end of Chapter 5 in Genesis.

Praised be Jesus Christ! *Now and forever!*

Class over!

Chapter Three:

Carnivores (Genesis part 3)

Genesis 6-9: Noah and the Ark, morality after the Fall. 40 days. God allows eating meat now, why? [Lent] The rainbow: God works through the physical world [Sacraments].

Noah's Container

Hey y'all, last week I said a bit about the guy who lived longer than anyone else in the Bible...who was that? *Umm...Matthew?* No, not Matthew, but his name does start with an 'M'...*Methuselah!* Yes. And we're going to talk about Methuselah's grandson tonight...Noah. Yes, what? *He built the ark!* Yes. Remind me please, was Noah in Eden eating grapes? *No, he's in the world.* Yes, where there is...*sin!* Yes. In fact there is so much sin that Genesis chapter 6 says, "The LORD saw that the wickedness of man was great in the earth, and that every imagination of the thoughts of his heart was only evil continually. And the LORD was sorry that he had made man on the earth, and it grieved him to his heart. " I suppose generations of people were bad all the time unless they were asleep, and then they were *dreaming* about being bad.

And then: "So the LORD said, "I will blot out man whom I have created from the face of the ground, man and beast and creeping things and birds of the air, for I am sorry that I have made them." Trick question: could those animals sin? *No!* Right. Can we? *Yes!* Because we have what? *Free will!* Yes. Then doesn't it seem like God would just wipe out the people who commit the sins, and leave the animals alone? *Yes.* Tell me, in Eden would a lion eat a lamb? *No!* How about after Adam & Eve's sin? *Yes!* So even though the lamb hadn't done anything to deserve it, it might get eaten because of...*Adam & Eve's sin!* Yes, which didn't just mess up the two of them, it messed up...*everything!* Yes, all of Creation. So all of Creation, even cute squirrels and chipmunks and babies suffer. Yes? *We suffer too!* Yes, 6th graders suffer *extra.*

Well, thank goodness that "Noah found favor in the eyes of the LORD," which means Noah wasn't so bad...he was still a sinner, like me, but Noah had God's favor. So tell me what happened. *God told Noah to make a boat and put the animals in it!* Yes, good. And what was the boat called? *The Ark!* Yes. Ark is an interesting word, well aren't they all...what's it mean? *Boat!* No! That was a trick question- it just means a *container*. Sometimes in the Bible an ark is a box. But if the container has to float, then...*it's a boat!* Yes. And in the Bible arks are sturdy because they protect precious things. Not precious like cute bunnies, but precious in the sense of something very valuable.

And what went in the ark? *Two animals of each kind?* Yes, like...two male pandas and two female camels? *No, one boy and one girl.* Why's that? *So they could breed and make more.* Right. And Noah's family got in too. Then what? *It rained for 40 days!* Yes, 40. How long is Lent? *Umm...40 days?* How long did the

Israelites wander in the desert? *40 days...no, 40 years!* And how long did Jesus fast in the desert? *40 days!* Yes. In the Bible, the number 40 means "a lot." It also signifies a time of preparation. So when we have 40 days of Lent what do we prepare for? *Easter!* Yes. By the way, how many thieves did Ali Baba have? *Who?* Never mind... he had 40 thieves.

So after 40 days of rain then what? *Noah sent a bird out but it came back.* Yes, a dove. And after 7 days he sent it out again, and...*it came back with a branch.* Close, an olive leaf. Then after 7 more days he sent the dove out and...*it didn't come back.* Because...*the land was ok.* Yes. Why did Noah let the dove out every 7 days? *'Cause it's a week?* Sort of... what day did God rest on? *The 7th day!* Yes, so 7 is a holy number, a Godly number.

Covenants vs. Contracts

New topic. Who can tell me what a contract is? *When you sign a paper to make a deal.* Yes, great answer! Well, God made a contract with Noah, a particular type of contract we call a *covenant.* If I buy a house, it's a regular contract. It may be twenty pages long, all kinds of details, stuff to sign. People often have long, picky contracts with people they don't know, because if they don't really know each other, it's hard to trust each other. But a covenant is different, it's more like a marriage. Trick question: how many pages long is my marriage contract? *None!* Wow, that's right! All we signed was a marriage license about the size of my hand. And the priest signed it too. So we didn't have a contract with conditions like, "I agree to unclog the toilets and clean up the kids' vomit if you agree to change the code brown diapers and cook spaghetti on Saturdays." That'd be a 50/50 deal. Instead, we essentially said, I give myself to you without worrying about the details because I love you and you love me. That's a covenant, not 50/50, but 100/100. It's based on love, and it's personal.

Well, after everyone got out of the Ark, God made a covenant with Noah: "I establish my covenant with you, that never again shall all flesh be cut off by the waters of a flood, and never again shall there be a flood to destroy the earth." And God said, "This is the sign of the covenant which I make between me and you and every living creature that is with you, for all future generations: I set my bow in the cloud, and it shall be a sign of the covenant between me and the earth." (Gen 9:11-13) What's "a bow in sky"...for God to shoot giant arrows? *Ha, no, it's a rainbow!* Oh, yeah, you must be right. I like the rainbow because it shows how God uses Creation, the world he made, to communicate with us, to send us things. Somebody tell me how God worked through Creation to make sure the Wise Men didn't get lost on the way to Bethlehem. *They followed the North Star!* That would've worked if Jesus was an Eskimo; but yes, a particular star did appear that they followed across the desert to Las Vegas...why are you laughing? *It was Bethlehem!* Oh, yes. Bethlehem.

And "God blessed Noah and his sons, and said to them, "Be fruitful and multiply, and fill the earth." Have you heard that before? *God said it to Adam & Eve!* Y'all are too smart! God is starting over with Noah and his family, and this new covenant is like the one he made with Adam & Eve. But then God says, "The fear of you and the dread of you shall be upon every beast of the earth, and upon every bird of the air, upon everything that creeps on the ground and all the fish of the sea; into your hand they are delivered. Every moving thing that lives shall be food for you; and as I gave you the green plants, I give you everything." Sounds awful doesn't it? All the animals will be in fear of Noah. Why? *Because Noah can eat them?* Yes, he and his descendants can kill and eat animals now. Why's that ok now? *Because they haven't planted any food yet?* Well, maybe. Tell me this: why is it that there are any animals at all, why didn't they all drown? *Because Noah put them in the Ark!* Yes, they didn't do anything themselves, it was all Noah's work. So if not for Noah, they'd all be...*dead!* Yes. So the animals owe Noah...what do they owe him? *Their lives?* Yes, so God is acknowledging that since the animals and all their descendants owe Noah their lives, God won't forbid people to kill and eat them. Now just because God no longer *forbids* eating animals, does that mean he *approves* of it? *No.* Right. God didn't say, "Eat a bunch of chickens, Noah and I'll bless you." But sin has made the world a hard, fearful place, and God doesn't blame us individually for that.

¿Quién aquí habla Español? Who speaks Spanish? *Me!* OK m'ija, digame, cómo se llama "carne" en Inglés? How do you say *carne* in English? *Meat!* Yes, C-A-R-N-E means meat, flesh. How about 'voracious,' do y'all know that word? *No...no...no.* No worries, sometimes 6th graders surprise me. How about 'devour'? *To eat real fast?* Yes, like a possum? *No, a lion!* Yes. If we put the Latin roots of *carne* and *devour* together we get *carnivorous;* anyone know that word? *Yes, it means to eat meat!* Yes; ever since Noah we've been carnivores, like lions. So animals are afraid of us- even the carnivorous ones.

Lent and Meat

Tell me about the 40 days before Easter. *Lent?* Yes, Lent. Sometimes during Lent we don't eat something...*meat!* Right. Is it better to be in Eden or in the world of sin? *Eden!* Yes, where nobody would kill or eat animals; and so they weren't afraid of people. Well, during Lent the Church encourages us to not eat meat, as though we were in Eden, at least as far as animals are concerned. I like eating meat, but I admit that if I have a hamburger, someone kills a cow. In fact my eldest son has been a vegetarian for years because of this, and he's perfectly healthy eating veggies. I admire that, even if I don't follow his example.

Tell me please, what's a generation? *Like a father and son?* Yes, from father to son is one generation. From grandmother to granddaughter is how many? *Two!* Yes. Well, it's 10 generations from Adam to Noah, and 10 more from Noah to the person we're going to learn about next: Abraham.

(continued in the next chapter)

Chapter Four:

Laughter (Genesis part 4)

Genesis 14: Abraham & Melchizedek. Genesis 17, 18 & 21: Sara, marriage, and the miraculous conception of an only-begotten son. The joy of children; Ishak (Hebrew, laughter). Gen 22: Isaac and the Ram: firstborn sacrifice by father/elder. Moloch, child sacrifices. God allows substitution. Genesis 27: Isaac, Jacob & Esau; the permanence & effects of laying of hands [Confirmation].

Abram not Abraham

Who knows what Mesopotamia is? *Me! Me too! I do!* Wow, y'all all know! Yes? *Mesopotamia means "land between the rivers."* Yes, good! Yes, what? *The Tigris and the Euphrates rivers!* Yes! Hey, did you know Mesopotamia's a Greek word: *Meso* means middle, *potamus* means river. *I do.* You 6th graders are too smart! Tell me smarties, where's Abraham from? *Mesopotamia?* Yes, that was a gimme question. Well, one day in Mesopotamia, *Abram* was standing on a ziggurat having a beer and minding his own business when God spoke to him. Yes? *They had beer?* Yes; I think that's great! I love beer. *Do you get drunk?* Of course not.

I'm reading now from Genesis chapter 12. God told Abram: "Go from your country and your kindred and your father's house to the land that I will show you. And I will make of you a great nation, and I will bless you, and make your name great, so that you will be a blessing." Yes, what? *Who's "Abram?"* Oh, his name isn't Abraham yet...God changes it later on. So God tells him to drop everything and take off into the desert, and God'll let him know when to stop. And off Abram goes! Now that's faith. If God told me tomorrow to move down to Charleston, I'd probably say, "What? I can't hear you!" I'd think of reasons not to go. But Abram took off with his wife Sarai, and his extended family. Eventually Abram came to the land of Canaan, where Israel is now. God said, "To your descendants I will give this land," which is odd, because Abram & Sarai were old, and had no children. Then Abram "built there an altar to the LORD, who had appeared to him." What's an altar for? *To pray?* Good guess, but we can pray without an altar...another guess? *To sacrifice?* Yes, you need an altar for that. If I'm going to offer a thanksgiving sacrifice of say, a lamb, I suppose I could throw the lamb on the ground, put my foot on his neck and jab it with a sharp stick 'til it was dead. Then I'd set it on fire, say, there you go God, thanks, and walk away. *That would be weird.* Yes, it's not dignified. Raising the sacrifice up on the altar shows respect, plus it moves the sacrifice away from Earth and toward...*Heaven?* Yes, toward God. It's even closer to God if you put the altar on a... *mountain.* Yes, and if you live in the flat plains of Mesopotamia and there's no mountain, you build... *a ziggurat!* Yes, good. Now there are two main things we offer sacrifices for: to atone, to make up for sin, and to give thanks. My guess is Abram offered a thanksgiving sacrifice because God finally let him stop walking.

Once Abram arrived in Canaan, you'd think he could settle down, but *nooo*, people were already living there. Imagine I'm a pagan Canaanite, I'm minding my own business in Canaan. Abram comes walking in from the desert, finishes the last of his beer, and says, "Hello, God gave me this land." I'd say, "Oh yeah? God didn't bring me the news, and this is *my* land. Get off it." So Abram had to fight a lot of other tribes, and even today, Abram's descendants, the Jews, are still fighting for that same land.

Melchizedek

After one particular battle, Abram was victorious. Who might he thank for that? *God?* Yes, and how would he thank God? *By sacrificing?* Yes, what kind of sacrifice? *A thanksgiving sacrifice?* Yes. Genesis 14 says, "And Melchizedek king of Salem brought out bread and wine; he was priest of God Most High. And he blessed him and said, "Blessed be Abram by God Most High, maker of heaven and earth." Who has heard of Melchizedek before? *Me!* Where from? *I forgot.* OK, anyone else? *No?* Well, if you've ever been to Mass you've *heard* his name, but if you weren't *listening* you wouldn't remember. Pay attention at Mass. Melchizedek's a priest, what's a priest's job? *To pray?* Yeah...he does that, but he does something more particular...at altars...*oh, he sacrifices!* Yes, so instead of *Abram* sacrificing...*Melchizedek does?* Yes...but he doesn't kill a lamb, what's he offer? Listen again: "Melchizedek king of Salem brought out bread and wine; he was..." *Oh, bread and wine!* Yes. And what do we bring up at the Offertory at Mass? *Bread and wine!* Yes, the same. And then "Abram gave him a tenth of everything." Abram is giving money, camels, goat cheese, whatever to Melchizedek in thanks, the same way we do at the Offertory at Mass, although we skip the goat cheese nowadays.

[A good visual aid for discussing Melchizedek is the Abel and Melchizedek mosaic in San Vitale church in Ravenna, Italy.]

Melchizedek shows up again near the end of the Bible and also in the Mass, so remember him.

Tell me, what do we call the deal God made with Noah? *A covenant.* Yes. Now that Abram is in Canaan, God makes a covenant with him, too: "I will make my covenant between me and you, and will multiply you exceedingly...you shall be the father of a multitude of nations. No longer shall your name be Abram, but your name shall be Abraham...I will make you exceedingly fruitful; kings shall come forth from you. And I will establish my covenant between me and you and your descendants after you throughout their generations for an everlasting covenant...And I will give to you and to your descendants...all the land of Canaan, for an everlasting possession..." (Gen 17)

First off, how many kids does Abram have? *None!* Right; so being a "father of a multitude of nations" seems impossible. But God says Abram will "be fruitful and multiply," just like who? *Adam & Eve!* Yes, and? *Noah!* Yes. And God changed Abram's name to *Abraham,* which is what language...*Hebrew!* Yes, it means "father of multitudes;" how convenient is that? And God changes Sarai's name to *Sarah,* which means "princess." So they both got an upgrade in the name department. As the year progresses we'll learn about other people in the Bible whose names are changed; a name-change usually means more authority and higher status.

Miracle Baby

Well, name changing is fine as far as it goes, but Abraham and Sarah are still old and childless. But one day they were visited by 3 strangers, whom Abraham invited to stay for lunch. Now how many strangers are there? *Three.* Yes, but here is how they talk (Gen 18): "The LORD said, "I will surely return to you in the spring, and Sarah your wife shall have a son." When the 3 of them speak, it's the LORD speaking. They don't speak as individuals. If it's God speaking, why are there 3 persons? *Umm...because it's the Trinity?* Yes, Christians believe that the Trinity visited Abraham. Look at this picture; it's called "The Hospitality of Abraham."

[I hand out half-size (8x5) color copies of the *Hospitality of Abraham* fresco from the Hermitage of St. Neophytos in Cyprus. I have also used the mosaic of the *Hospitality* in San Vitale church in Ravenna, Italy, but the following discussion is based on the Cyprus image.]

Can you tell where Sarah is? *That's easy, she's the woman.* Yes, and Abraham? *The old man.* Yes, and the other three...*the Trinity.* Yes who are...*Father, Son and Holy Spirit!* Yes. How can you tell they are more holy than Abraham & Sarah? *They have wings?* Yes, and something else...look at the haloes. *Oh, their haloes are nicer!* Yes, each one has 3 crosses on it, to emphasize the 3 persons in the Trinity, and why crosses? What do they remind you of? *Jesus being crucified?* Yes. And what are they all holding? *Scrolls?* Yes. Why? *Umm...they're bringing a message?* Yes, which is...*Sarah will have a baby?* Yes, good. We'll look at other art during the year, I want y'all to learn to notice the details, they're important.

Back to lunch: when Sarah heard she would have a baby, she laughed, because she and Abraham were so old. But God said, "Is anything too hard for the LORD? At the appointed time I will return to you, in the spring, and Sarah shall have a son." So what do you think happened in the spring? *She had a baby!* Yes she did. And they named their son Isaac, which is Chinese for...*Chinese? It's Hebrew!* Y'all are too smart, yes it's Hebrew for 'laughter;' why'd they name him Laughter? *Because they were so happy to have a baby!* Yes. When my kids were born I laughed too, it was so wonderful. Sarah said, "God has made laughter for me; everyone who hears will laugh over me." (Gen 21) Isaac was their firstborn and only child. We might call him their only-begotten son. Where've you heard "only-begotten son" before *...at Mass?* Yes, and it refers to...*Jesus?* Yes. Like Abel, Isaac's a *type* of Christ.

So Isaac grew up, and they were a happy family. Now y'all remember, Abraham had to fight lots of nearby pagan tribes to get his piece of Canaan. Those other people didn't worship God. They worshiped false gods with names such as Moloch and Ba'al. Abraham's neighbors were so afraid of their gods that they sacrificed their firstborn children to them. Can you imagine how awful that would be? Fortunately, God didn't ask that of Abraham when Isaac was born. But then years later when Isaac was older, God said, "Take your son, your only son Isaac, whom you love, and go to the land of Moriah, and offer him there as a burnt offering upon one of the mountains of which I shall tell you." (Gen22) I can't imagine killing and burning one of my children, I don't even like to think about what Abraham went through. Who can tell the story? *He put Isaac on the altar but an angel grabbed his arm so he couldn't kill him!* Yes. So God doesn't make Abraham give Isaac back to God. But that doesn't mean that Abraham doesn't have to give *something* back. C'mon, y'all tell me. *Abraham saw a lamb to sacrifice.* Yes, a ram, a grown-up lamb, whose horns were caught in some brambles so Abraham could catch it. God accepted the ram instead of Isaac. What's more valuable, the ram or Isaac? *Isaac!* Yes, God loves Abraham so much that he accepts the ram as a *substitute* for Isaac. And God continues to do this with his people; they won't have to kill their kids, but can substitute something less precious in the place of their children, or in place of themselves.

Spiritual Tattoos

Eventually Isaacs' parents died. Isaac married a woman named...*Rachel?* Close...*Rebekah?* Yes; but they couldn't get pregnant. Who does this remind you of? *Abraham and Sarah!* Yes! But "Isaac prayed to the LORD for his wife, because she was barren; and the LORD granted his prayer, and Rebekah his wife conceived." (Gen 25) She became pregnant with twins. They would jostle each other in Rebekah's tummy; they didn't get along even before they were born. [I take two rubber fetuses out of my prop bag.]

Hey, who're these babies? *Umm, Jacob and Esau?* That's right, and they already don't get along. Look, I'm Rebekah, here they are in my womb, fighting [I bang them into each other in front of my stomach like Punch & Judy puppets, accompanied by grunting sounds]. "There ain't enough room in this womb for the two of us! Then *you* get out! No, *you* get out!" And Rebekah is groaning, "Oww, y'all settle down in there!" *That's weird!* What's weird? *Those things.* What things? *Those babies, they're weird looking.* Oh yeah? I think they're cute [I give 'em a kiss], they look like my kids when they were growing in my wife...would you like to kiss them? *No!* Hey now, don't get squeamish on me, this is what *you* looked like when you were a couple of months old and still in *your* momma....and I bet she loved you even if *you* thought you were *weird-looking*.

Later on, when the first baby was being born, they saw he had more hair than most babies, so they named him Esau, which is Hebrew for 'hairy.' *Ewww, gross, a hairy baby!* C'mon, he wasn't hairy like a *gorilla*, some people just have more hair. Well, as Esau came out, they saw another little hand grabbing onto his ankle...that baby was named Jacob, which means "heel-holder." Yes, what? *Umm, how does that work?* What exactly? *You know...babies?* Oh- you mean how does sex work? *Yeah.* Ask your parents, this is a religion class, not a plumbing class.

So: who was the firstborn? *Esau.* But they were twins! *But Esau came out first!* Yes, right. And if you grab someone's heel what happens? *You trip them!* Yes. Jacob's going to trip up his brother, let's see how.

In those days the firstborn son usually inherited from the father all the goodies: tents, camels, goat cheese, iPads, along with the father's authority. When the father gets too old to run things, he blesses the firstborn son by laying his hands on him; that's how the son gets all the stuff and becomes the new boss of the family. But Esau wasn't too sharp, and Jacob tricked him by swapping some bean stew for Esau's inheritance when Esau was hungry. Esau lived for the moment; he didn't like to plan ahead. But since Isaac still had to lay hands on Jacob instead of Esau, Jacob and his mom, Rebekah, also had to trick old Isaac, who couldn't see very well. They disguised Jacob to be like Esau, and confused Isaac laid hands on Jacob, and blessed him. But Isaac *thought* he was blessing Esau. So although in *spirit* he blessed *Esau*, with his *hands* Isaac blessed *Jacob*. [all acted out with the kids' help and narration]

Esau found out about the trick, and said, "Bless me, even me also, O my father!" (Gen 27:34) But Isaac said, "Your brother came with guile, and he has taken away your blessing." Isaac couldn't give Esau the blessing! And he couldn't take it back from Jacob, either! Isaac said, "Your brother came with deceit and has taken away your blessing." Then Esau said to his father, "Have you but one blessing, my father?" But Isaac couldn't give the firstborn blessing more than once. So even though it doesn't seem fair, Isaac's misplaced blessing was permanent. Not even Isaac could undo it.

Some blessings are like Isaac's: so special that they make a permanent difference. They're like a spiritual tattoo: they don't ever come off. You can usually tell a blessing is permanent when someone with authority puts his hands on the person being blessed. In the next year or two, who will lay hands on you? *The Bishop.* Yes. It'll be like Isaac's blessing, but better.

That's it for tonight; next week we'll learn a bit about Joseph, and a lot about Moses.

Praised be Jesus Christ! *Now and forever!*

Class over!

Chapter Five: Big House

(Exodus part 1)

Exodus 1-3, Moses: Pharaoh kills firstborns, Nile ark through killing Egyptian. Burning Bush, shoes off, showing respect physically. Exodus 4-11, Moses returns to Egypt: Plagues, Passover (Pesach, Hebrew) Pharaoh (Hebrew: Big House). Exodus 12-13, Passover in detail: killing & eating Paschal Lamb. Sprinkling blood, why?

Y'all remember last class we were talking about Mr. Laughter, what was his name? *Isaac!* Yes, and his two sons, Mr. Hairy...? *Esau!* Yes, and the Heel-grabber...*Jacob!* Yes, good. And Jacob tricked his Daddy and his brother so he got...*the inheritance!* Yes. Well, years passed, Isaac died, and Jacob became a grown man. One night he was attacked by a stranger, and he wrestled all night with him. At dawn the stranger tried to get away, but Jacob wouldn't let him go until he identified himself. The stranger said he was an angel sent by God; and because Jacob had wrestled with God's messenger, his name was changed to I-s-r-a-e-l, which is Hebrew for "struggles with God." The "el" on the end means *God.* Anytime you see a Bible name like Michael, Gabriel, or Daniel the *el* means "of God, with God," that sort of thing, and the first part of the name means something else. Do you remember who has already had a name-change in the Bible? *Sarah?* Yes, and her husband...*Abraham.* Yes. And when a name changes in the Bible that person gains authority and status...like getting a promotion from God. And it can't change back.

Israel had 12 sons. We're not going to learn all their names, but their descendants became 12 tribes of a particular nation...? *Umm, Egypt?* No, but a good guess. These 12 tribes were the descendants of.... *oh Israel!* Yes, the whole nation was named... *Israel.* Yes. How about that for a name-change? Well, Israel had a lot of sons, and his second-youngest son was Joseph; and being little, Joseph was also cute. Most of his older brothers were grown men with beards and not cute. Old Israel loved Joseph so much he gave him a very nice present...a garment...*a coat with colors?* Yes, and his brothers were jealous, they couldn't stand how their father doted on the kid while they had to work all day. So what did they decide to do? *Make him a slave!* Almost. First they decided to kill him but figured that was too mean, so they threw him into a pit. Later on a slave-merchant came along, bought Joseph, and took him to...*Egypt!* Yes, good. Then his brothers took his colorful coat, put some goat's blood on it and told Israel that an animal had killed Joseph. What did Joseph do to deserve being hated? *Nothing.* Right. What did Abel do to deserve being hated? *Nothing.* Right again. In both cases they were innocent victims...like lambs that are sacrificed.

Joseph was a useful slave in Egypt, and as an adult was such a good manager that he became the Pharaoh's right-hand man, what we might call the prime-minister.

Then one year there was a great famine began in Canaan, where Israel and his extended family lived. What's a famine? *When people starve 'cause there's not enough to eat.* Yes, what usually causes a famine? *It doesn't rain?* Yes, there's a shortage of water. So Israel's family moved to Egypt. Why Egypt? No guesses? Let me put it this way: why would there be water in Egypt even if there's no rain? *The Nile river is there!* Yes. So all the family, the nation of Israel, came to Egypt, and met with Joseph, who ran things for the Pharaoh. They didn't recognize him, but Joseph knew who they were, his rotten brothers and their families. But he let them live in Egypt. Eventually they all made up, and Israel was so happy to his son Joseph back. I bet he was as happy as Abraham when he didn't have to sacrifice...*Isaac!* Yes. By the way, who has seen the movie *Prince of Egypt*? *Me. Me too. I did.* But not all of you. The movie covers what we're going to be talking about for the next couple of classes, in case you want to watch it for homework. Be sure not to enjoy it.

Almost the 2nd Commandment

Now we're finished with Genesis and are on the second book in the Bible... any guesses? *Exodus!* Yes, good. What's Exodus mean? *To exit?* Yes. Why is that the name of this book? *'Cause the people exited from Egypt?* Yes. Let's learn the story.

For generations after Joseph, the Israelites lived in Egypt, but as slaves. Everyone worked for the Pharaoh. Hey, if you saw *Prince of Egypt*, what was the bad guy's name? *Ramses.* Yes...what was his job? *He was the Pharaoh.* Mmmm, that was what people *called* him. What was his *job*? *Being the king, ruling Egypt.* Yes. Now if we were speaking to the king could we say, "hey Ramses, howya doin'? Sure is hot today in Egypt isn't it, Ramses?" *Ha, that wouldn't be right.* Why not? *Well, he's the king.* Yeah, so? *So you have to show respect.* OK, so one way we show respect for someone's *authority* is to show respect for his *name.* By the way, Pharaoh doesn't actually mean King. Egyptians had another word for king: Nisut. "Pharaoh" means "Big House." Why would Ramses be called Big House? *Because he lived in a big house, a palace.* Yes. And the point is that the Egyptians and the Hebrew slaves had so much respect for Ramses that they wouldn't call him Ramses, or even call him King, but only refer to him by where he lived. Even nowadays we don't call our parents, or priests, or other people with authority by their first names. Somebody tell me the second commandment. *Don't take the LORD's name in vain.* Yes, we have respect for God's name, too. We'll learn more about that in a minute.

Well, the Israelites were so fruitful that...*they had a lot of children!* Yes, they multiplied so much that Pharaoh got nervous. He was afraid the Hebrews might take over Egypt. While the Israelites are in Egypt the Bible calls them *Hebrews.* So Pharaoh commanded that all the Hebrew boy babies be thrown into what river? *The Nile,* yes...which is the only river in Egypt, so that was easy. What had those babies done? *Nothing.* Right. Who can tell me another time that a King killed a whole lot of baby boys? *Oh, King Herod!* Yes, good, we'll talk about Herod later this year. All these babies were...innocent...*innocent victims!* Yes, like sacrificed...*lambs!* Yes.

When Pharaoh gave this command, one Hebrew woman hid her newborn baby. But babies grow, and get too big to hide, so what did she do? *Put him in a little boat in the Nile, and a lady found him.* Yes, but the

Bible doesn't say *boat*, it says...*ark?* Yes, a container for valuable things; in this case...*a baby!* Yes, a container for a baby. It was a basket with tar on the outside to make it waterproof. Who found the baby? *The Queen?* Close, the Pharaoh's daughter, a princess. She adopted Moses, and he grew up as part of Pharaoh's family.

One day when Moses was a young man, he saw an Egyptian beating a Hebrew slave. Moses got upset, and killed the Egyptian. When Pharaoh found out, Moses had to flee Egypt. He got a job in the desert tending sheep, and married his boss's daughter, Zipporah (I like that name). But all the Hebrew slaves were still stuck in Egypt: "the people of Israel groaned under their bondage, and cried out for help, and their cry under bondage came up to God. And God heard their groaning, and God remembered his covenant with Abraham, with Isaac, and with Jacob. And God saw the people of Israel, and God knew their condition." (Ex 2). And a covenant is a contract, but more like...*a marriage!* Yes, good.

So Moses was tending sheep one day, minding his own business, when "...the angel of the LORD appeared to him in a flame of fire out of the midst of a bush; and he looked, and lo, the bush was burning, yet it was not consumed. And Moses said, "I will turn aside and see this great sight, why the bush is not burnt." (Ex 3) I'd be the same, I gotta see that! "God called to him out of the bush, "Moses, Moses!" Then he said, "Do not come near; put off your shoes from your feet, for the place on which you are standing is holy ground." Moses had to take his dirty shoes off to show respect. And God said, "I am the God of your father, the God of Abraham, the God of Isaac, and the God of Jacob." God is reminding Moses that God has a long history with Moses' forefathers. Then God says, "The cry of the people of Israel has come to me, and I have seen the oppression with which the Egyptians oppress them. Come, I will send you to Pharaoh that you may bring forth my people, the sons of Israel, out of Egypt." Then Moses said to God, "If I come to the people of Israel and say to them, 'The God of your fathers has sent me to you,' and they ask me, 'What is his name?' what shall I say to them?" God said to Moses, "I AM WHO AM." And he said, "Say this to the people of Israel, 'I AM has sent me to you." Now that's an odd name: I AM WHO AM. More or less it means God is who always was, is and will be. We recall that when we pray a Glory Be: "As it was in the beginning, is now, and ever shall be." In Hebrew, God's name is spelled YHWH [on the board]. *That's weird.* Yes, Hebrew doesn't have written vowels. Anyway, remember that people had so much respect for Pharaoh's name that they'd never say it. Well, once they learned God's name from Moses, the Hebrews wouldn't say that name, either. They might carefully write it down in the Bible, but they would say "the LORD" or the "Blessed One" to avoid saying His name, just in case they might *accidentally* show disrespect, such as by belching in the middle of saying it. Imagine Moses saying, "All praise & honor to thee, oh Yah...brraAAACK...weh, oops, sorry." The Church still has that same respect for God's name so we won't pronounce YHWH in class either.

Back to the story. Moses wasn't happy about God disturbing his life. "Oh, my Lord, I am not eloquent... I am slow of speech and of tongue." Then the LORD said to him, "Who has made man's mouth? Who makes him dumb, or deaf, or seeing, or blind? Is it not I, the LORD? Now therefore go, and I will be with your mouth and teach you what you shall speak." But he said, "Oh, my Lord, send, I pray, some other person." That's what I'd say too. So God decided to give Moses some help: tongue-tied Moses could let his brother Aaron do the most of the talking in Egypt.

Moses goes to Egypt. He and Aaron visit his childhood friend Ramses, who is the Pharaoh now. They say, "Thus says the LORD, the God of Israel, 'Let my people go, that they may hold a feast to me in the wilderness." But Pharaoh said, "Who is the LORD, that I should heed his voice and let Israel go? I do not know the LORD, and moreover I will not let Israel go." Having thousands of slaves is a good deal for Pharaoh, he's not giving that up. Now it'd be easy for Pharaoh to just kill Moses, but he wants to show his power. So he orders his bosses to make things harder for the Hebrews at work. Then the Hebrews will blame Moses and Aaron for their problems.

Moses is unhappy, and tells God, "O LORD, why have you done evil to this people? Why did you ever send me? For since I came to Pharaoh to speak in thy name, he has done evil to this people, and you have not delivered thy people at all." That doesn't mean delivered like a pizza...what's it mean? *Taken away from Pharaoh?* Yes, delivered *away.* (Exodus 5)

 So God worked through Moses to bring 10 plagues on Egypt, who knows some of them? *The river became blood?* Yes, and? *Frogs?* Yes...any more? *Hail?* Yes, more? No? Well, there was a plague of gnats, one of flies, diseases, boils, which are big pus infections that hurt like crazy- all kinds of gross stuff, but Pharaoh wouldn't let the Israelites go after 9 plagues. So God sent a tenth plague: "Yet one plague more I will bring upon Pharaoh and upon Egypt; afterwards he will let you go; when he lets you go, he will drive you away completely...About midnight I will go forth in the midst of Egypt; and all the first-born in the land of Egypt shall die, from the first-born of Pharaoh who sits upon his throne, even to the first-born of the maidservant who is behind the mill; and all the first-born of the animals. And there shall be a great cry throughout all the land of Egypt, such as there has never been, nor ever shall be again." (Ex 11)

Something's Already Dead Here

But does God plan to kill all the *Hebrew* firstborn? *No!* Right, Moses tells the Hebrews: "Select lambs for yourselves according to your families, and kill the passover lamb. Your lamb shall be without blemish, a male a year old...eat the flesh that night, roasted; with unleavened bread and bitter herbs they shall eat it." (Ex 12) Notice each family has to kill an unblemished lamb...what's unblemished? *Umm...no zits? Nice skin?* Sort of. It means flawless: no broken bones, healthy, not mangy. The sort of lamb Abel would sacrifice, not Cain. Cain would get a cheap, scrawny lamb. So they get a good lamb, kill it, and eat it. By eating it, they make the sacrificed animal part of themselves.

Then Moses instructs: "Take a bunch of hyssop and dip it in the blood which is in the basin, and touch the lintel and the two doorposts with the blood which is in the basin; and none of you shall go out of the door of his house until the morning. For the LORD will pass through to slay the Egyptians; and when he sees the blood on the lintel and on the two doorposts, the LORD will pass over the door, and will not allow the destroyer to enter your houses to slay you." What's a basin? *A big bowl.* Yes, about handwashing size.

When you kill a lamb like this [I act all this out], the blood runs into the basin. Then the Hebrews had to spread it on the doorposts with a bunch of hyssop. Hyssop's a plant; if you tie a bunch of hyssop together it makes a broom or a brush. Question: why did they have to spread the blood on the doorposts? *God told them to.* Well, yes. But imagine you're the destroyer, the angel of death, floating over the houses going into each one and killing all the firstborn. Then you fly over a house with blood all over the doorway...what does that tell you? *That something's already been killed there!* Yes, genius! So what do you do? *Go to the next house?* Yes. You *pass over* the houses where something has already been killed. What is this event called? *The Passover!* Yes! Jewish people still observe the Passover every spring. And tell me, who else in the Bible was able to spare the firstborn by sacrificing a substitute animal? *Abraham!* Yes, good. But suppose instead of sprinkling blood, the Israelites just stayed inside and prayed hard...would that work? *No!* Suppose they didn't want to mess the doorway up and left the basin full of blood on the porch? *No!* Killing a calf instead of a lamb? *No!* Paint the doorposts red? *No!* Right. For God to help the Israelites, they had to...*help themselves?* Yes, they had to *cooperate* with God. Could they cooperate however they wanted to? *No, the way* God *wanted them to.* Yes, it's still like that, we have to work with God, to cooperate, *his* way, not *our* way.

So around midnight, "Pharaoh rose up in the night; he, and all his servants, and all the Egyptians; and there was a great cry in Egypt, for there was not a house where one was not dead. And he summoned Moses and Aaron by night, and said, "Rise up, go forth from among my people, both you and the people of Israel..." And so the Israelites prepare to leave Egypt after many years. What's "exit" mean? *To leave.* Yes, to go out. Next we'll see what the Israelites did when they exited Egypt.

Praised be Jesus Christ! *Now and forever!*

Class over!

Chapter Six: Media

(Exodus part 2)

Exodus 14-16: In the desert for 40 years, Manna and Quail [miraculous food]. Exodus 17: Water from the Rock (using a stick as a prop), physical conduits of God's power [Sacraments]. Ex 32 & 33: Hebrew bad habits in Egypt, Egyptian idols, false gods, Golden Calf, intercession, 40 days.

So the Israelites were thrown out of Egypt. Pharaoh didn't just say, ok y'all can leave, he said *get out!* Why was he so angry? No guesses? He wasn't just Pharaoh, but a father. *Oh, because his son was killed!* Yes, his firstborn. And the Israelites were prepared to leave, so within the day they were gone. Remind me why this book in the Bible is called Exodus. *Because the people were leaving Egypt.* Yes.

And by the time they got to the Red Sea, [I draw a quick map of the Nile, the Red Sea, Sinai & the Mediterranean coast] Pharaoh was having second thoughts: "What meant we to do, that we let Israel go from serving us? So he made ready his chariot, and took all his people with him. And he took six hundred chosen chariots, and all the chariots that were in Egypt: and the captains of the whole army. And the Lord hardened the heart of Pharaoh, king of Egypt, and he pursued the children of Israel; but they were gone forth in a mighty hand." (Ex 14, DR)

And when the people saw Pharaoh's army coming, they started complaining to Moses: "And when Pharaoh drew near, the children of Israel lifting up their eyes, saw the Egyptians behind them: and they feared exceedingly, and cried to the Lord. And they said to Moses: Perhaps there were no graves in Egypt, therefore thou hast brought us to die in the wilderness: why wouldst thou do this, to lead us out of Egypt? Is not this the word that we spoke to thee in Egypt, saying: Depart from us, that we may serve the Egyptians? for it was much better to serve them, than to die in the wilderness." (DR) Now I know what Moses is thinking: *stop WHINING!* But God tells Moses: "But lift thou up thy rod, and stretch forth thy hand over the sea, and divide it: that the children of Israel may go through the midst of the sea on dry ground." (DR) [I do this with my rod]. What happens? *The water splits apart!* It does! Would it have parted if Moses hadn't used his rod? *No!* If Moses had prayed real hard? *No!* Supposed he smacked the water with his hand? *No!* Right. Moses had to actively, physically cooperate with God...Moses' way? *No, God's way!* Right. God's power goes through something physical, a part of his creation; in this case the rod, the stick. Tell me the rest. *They cross over and the soldiers chase them but the water comes back and they drown.* Yes, Good.

Miracle Bread

Now the people of Israel are heading back to Canaan, the land God gave to...*Abraham,* yes, their forefather. But they wander around for a long time, which the Bible says is...*40 days!* That's not so long. *40 years!* There you go. Well, within a month or so of leaving Egypt, they ran out of food: "And all the congregation of the children of Israel murmured against Moses and Aaron in the wilderness. And the children of Israel said to them: Would to God we had died by the hand of the Lord in the land of Egypt, when we sat over the fleshpots, and ate bread to the full: Why have you brought us into this desert, that you might destroy all the multitude with famine?" (Ex 16, DR) What's Moses thinking right now? Stop...*whining!* Yes. But God told Moses: "Behold, I will rain bread from heaven for you; and the people shall go out and gather a day's portion every day..." What's that bread called? *Manna?* Yes, manna. Question: if God didn't want the people to be hungry, couldn't he just think, "they shall not be hungry," and have that work? *Well, God can do anything.* Yes...so why did he go to the trouble of putting miracle bread on the ground every morning? *So they would know where it came from?* Yes, God wanted them to believe not just spiritually, but...*physically!* Yes, 'cause we're a...*body'n'soul!* Yes, and they had to *cooperate* with God: pick up the bread and chew it and eat it. God did most of the work, but the people had to do something, too. And "the taste of it was like wafers made with honey"...sounds pretty good!

Miracle Water

But if they ran short of food in the wilderness you can bet they also ran short of...*water!* Yes. Exodus chapter 17 says: "...there was no water for the people to drink. Therefore the people found fault with Moses, and said, "Give us water to drink." I love that: it's all *Moses'* fault! Stop...*whining!* Yes! And Moses said to them, "Why do you find fault with me? Why do you put the LORD to the test?" But the people thirsted there for water, and the people grumbled against Moses, and said, "Why did you bring us up out of Egypt, to kill us and our children and our cattle with thirst?" *Waah, waah,* like spoiled brats. "So Moses cried to the LORD, "What shall I do with this people? They are almost ready to stone me." And the LORD said to Moses, "Pass on before the people, taking with you some of the elders of Israel; and take in your hand the rod with which you struck the Nile, and go. Behold, I will stand before you there on the rock at Horeb; and you shall strike the rock, and water shall come out of it, that the people may drink." And Moses did so, in the sight of the elders of Israel." And so? *Water came out!* Yes. And why did the elders have to watch? *So they could tell the people that Moses did it.* Yes. So the people couldn't say the water flowed all by itself.

Suppose Moses didn't do the rod thing, but say, slapped the rock? *No water!* Yes...trick question: is the rod magic? *Umm...yes...no! No!* Right; think about TV. If someone is funny on TV, do you think, "Wow, the TV sure is funny?" *Ha, that's silly!* Oh yeah, why? *Because the* people *are funny, not the TV.* Right. The TV is just an invention that lets you see and hear the comedian. We call the TV a *medium.* A medium is something which connects two other things. [I draw] Here's the comedian in the studio; over here are...*the people watching the TV?* Yes, so between the audience and the comedian is...*the TV!* Yes, it's the *medium*, it just carries the information.

Think about a light bulb and a power station, what's the medium there? *Umm...wires?* Yes, the wire transmits...*electricity?* Yes, power. When Isaac blessed Jacob, what was the medium? *His hands!* Yes. Sometimes we talk about the *news media*, which means magazines, newspapers, the net, radio, TV. If there is more than one medium, we say *media*. God uses Moses' rod as a medium, and this year we'll see more examples of God using physical things, stuff, as *media* to transmit his power and grace.

Once the Israelites quit whining about being hungry and thirsty, they stopped for a while at the bottom of Mount Sinai, which nowadays is in Egypt. Moses went up to the top to visit with God...for a long time but not 40 years, which is *too* long...*40 days!* Yes; and why on the mountaintop? OK, where is God usually? *In heaven?* Yes, which is under the ground? *No, up in the sky!* So then? *Oh, the top is closer to God!* Yes. Remind me about Mesopotamia, please. *They built the ziggurats to get closer to God.* Yes.

Apparently the Israelites got bored with twiddling their thumbs for 40 days, which reminds me of a saying: "Idle hands are the Devil's playground." Exodus chapter 32 says: "When the people saw that Moses delayed to come down from the mountain, the people gathered themselves together to Aaron, and said to him, "Come, make us gods, who shall go before us; as for this Moses, the man who brought us up out of the land of Egypt, we do not know what has become of him." And Aaron said to them, "Take off the rings of gold which are in the ears of your wives, your sons, and your daughters, and bring them to me." So all the people took off the rings of gold which were in their ears, and brought them to Aaron. And he received the gold at their hand, and fashioned it with a graving tool, and made a molten calf; and they said, "These are your gods, O Israel, who brought you up out of the land of Egypt!" Oh dear: does God the Father have a body? *No.* Is he a calf? *Ha, no!* But Egyptians worshiped make-believe gods, what sort of bodies did they have? *One was a bird.* Yes, Thoth had a bird-head...another? *Umm...a crocodile?* Yes, Egyptians had all sorts of animal-body gods. So the Israelites, having picked up some bad habits in Egypt, decided to make up an animal for YHWH.

After the calf was made, Aaron "built an altar before it; and Aaron made a proclamation and said, "Tomorrow shall be a feast to the LORD." And they rose up early on the morrow, and offered burnt offerings and brought peace offerings; and the people sat down to eat and drink, and rose up to play." Uh-oh, like the Devil's...*playground!* Yes! God saw them, and was angry that they would treat him like some bogus animal-god. He told Moses he would wipe them out and start over, but Moses pleaded with God not to. "You promised they would have the land of their forefathers, Abraham, Isaac, and Israel, give them another chance." We would say that Moses *interceded* for the people. So God agreed not to kill them. As Moses came down the mountain he saw the calf, and the drunk people running wild, and participating in adult misbehavior. *What's adult misbehavior?* Ask your parents. So Moses was angry, and threw something down, which was...*the Ten Commandments!* Yes, which were written on...*two stone tablets!* Yes, they were shattered.

Next we'll see how God and Moses dealt with all this idol-worship and sinning.

Praised be Jesus Christ! *Now and forever!*

Class over!

Chapter Seven: Sprinklers

(Exodus 3, Leviticus)

Exodus 32: after the Golden Calf, the Levites. Leviticus, typical sacrifices, blood and water. Imperfect atonement.

Last week when Moses came down from the mountain with the 12 bananas, *10 Commandments!* yes, right, he was so angry with the Israelites' misbehavior that he threw the tablets down and shattered them. Then he lays into Aaron: "What did this people do to you that you have brought a great sin upon them?" And Aaron said, "Let not the anger of my lord burn hot; you know the people, that they are set on evil." That is: *it ain't my fault!* And of course the people are running wild, out of control. Remind me please, how many sons did Israel have? *12?* Yes. And from each son came a tribe; there were 12 tribes. One of Israel's sons was named Levi; his tribe, his descendants, were called *Levites.* Not Levi's, which are jeans. Aaron was a Levite, not a pair of pants. Well, "Moses stood in the gate of the camp, and said, "If any man be on the Lord's side, let him join with me. And all the sons of Levi gathered themselves together unto him. And he said to them: "Thus saith the Lord God of Israel: Put every man his sword upon his thigh: go, and return from gate to gate through the midst of the camp, and let every man kill his brother, and friend, and neighbor. And the sons of Levi did according to the words of Moses, and there were slain that day about three and twenty thousand men." Man, that's harsh! But in those days just because God didn't require people to sacrifice their firstborns didn't mean he was a pushover. So the only tribe that was on God's side of this idol-worship were...*Levites!* Yes. "And Moses said: You have consecrated your hands this day to the Lord, every man in his son and in his brother, that a blessing may be given to you." (Exodus 32:26-29, DR)

Class, remind me please, who was going to sacrifice Isaac? *Abraham.* Yes, and who killed the ram instead? *Well, wasn't it still Abraham?* That's right...just checking. Who sacrificed Abel's lamb? *Abel?* Yes. And who killed all those lambs at the first Passover? *Moses?* Wow, Moses ran around all night killing lambs? *Oh...was it the fathers?* Yes, an elder in each family. Remind me please, if you offer sacrifice, you're a...*priest?* Yes. So being a priest wasn't a special job. If I fix a toilet at home, I'm not called a plumber; it's just something I do as the eldest man in the house. But if I make a mess, and water sprays all over the place, my wife will say: "You made such a mess I don't feel good about you fixing leaks anymore...I...want...a....? *Plumber!* Yes, who I have to pay!

And it was like that for the Israelites after they made such a mess by worshiping an idol. God said, "All you Calf-worshipers can't be trusted to make a proper sacrifice anymore. From now on y'all have to pay the Levite men to do your sacrificing for you." That's why the book of Leviticus is full of blood'n'guts: from then on, the Levite elders offered sacrifices for a living. That's the blessing they received from God. All the other 11 tribes had to work to support the Levites.

About a month or so before Israel decided to worship the Calf, Moses sacrificed some bulls to honor God's covenant with the Israelites. Exodus says, "Then Moses took half of the blood, and put it into bowls; and the rest he poured upon the altar. And taking the book of the covenant, he read it in the hearing of the people:

and they said: All things that the Lord hath spoken, we will do, we will be obedient." (Exodus 24, DR) Like the rest of us, the Israelites were ready to be obedient as long as they were in a good mood.

"And he took the blood and sprinkled it upon the people…" [I walk around the class, and pretend to sling blood on all the kids while I talk] I suppose he used a hyssop brush like on Passover. So you Israelites are in the desert, and it's dry, and Moses is going to sprinkle you from a bowl full of hot bull blood…why do you want to be sprinkled with that hot sticky stuff? No guesses? Why did the doorposts in Egypt need blood sprinkled on them? *So the firstborns wouldn't be killed.* Yes, the blood marked the houses where a substitute had been sacrificed. So, Moses sprinkles the people to show…*that the bulls were substitutes for the people?* Yes. And the blood marks the people as part of the covenant, which is not like a contract, but like…*a marriage!* Yes. Trick question: if someone overslept that day, and didn't get sprinkled, would they be included in the covenant? *No!* Right. They had to get the blood on their bodies. If people have blood all over them what do you usually assume? *That they're dead?* Yes. So by getting a dead animal's blood on them the people share in the death of the animal. It marks them just like what other blood? *The blood on the doorposts in Egypt!* Yes.

While Moses sprinkles, he says, "This is the blood of the covenant, which the Lord hath made with you concerning all these words." (Ex 24:8, DR) Does this sound like anything in Mass? *The priest says that about the wine!* Yes, good, he *almost* says this. The priest actually says what Jesus said at the Last Supper. He quotes Jesus. And who do you think Jesus referred to when *he* talked about the blood of a covenant? *Moses?* Yes genius, and we'll learn more about this later on.

Speaking of wandering in the desert, remember that wanderers are…*nomads,* yes, who live in…*tents,* yes. So the Israelites made a very deluxe tent for God to live in among his people: the Meeting Tent, which in many ways is like our church. Well, to get things off to a clean start with the Tent, there was a purification event. Tell me, what tribe didn't worship the Golden Calf? C'mon…L-E-V- *Levites!* Yes, descendants of Isaac's son Levi. And because they behaved, God put them in charge of sacrifices and all the business of the Meeting Tent. And there was one high priest, Moses' brother Aaron. So we have the high priest, the Levites, and the people, who are all sinners. To have a clean start, do they need to take a big bath together? *Huh?* Do their bodies need cleaning? *No, their souls.* Yes, cleaned from…*sin.* Yes, good. Here's how that was done: the LORD said to Moses, "Take the Levites out of the midst of the children of Israel, and thou shalt purify them… Let them be sprinkled with the water of purification… And when they shall have washed their garments, and are cleansed." (Num 8: 6-7, DR) Anybody know what *expiation* means? No? That's OK, 6th graders don't know everything. It means to make up for something, to atone. So their clothes are clean…souls clean too? *No.* Right. But they're just getting started. "And thou shalt bring the Levites before the tabernacle of the covenant, calling together all the multitude of the children of Israel.

"And when the Levites are before the Lord, the children of Israel shall put their hands upon them: And Aaron shall offer the Levites…" So all the Israelites lay hands on the Levites…why? *To bless them?* Good guess, but no. Priests can bless the people, fathers bless sons, but not so much the other way around. Here's the next bit: "The Levites also shall put their hands upon the heads of the oxen, of which thou shalt sacrifice one for sin, and the other for a holocaust to the Lord, to pray for them." (Num 8:12, DR) Why are the bulls killed…to atone for...*sin!* Yes. So the people were trying to get rid of their...*sins!* Yes! How'd they move their sins away from themselves? *Umm, they laid hands on the Levites?* Yes, and how'd the Levites move their sins and the people's sins off of themselves? *They laid hands on the bulls!* Yes, geniuses! Then they killed the sin-full bulls and thus atoned for all those sins.

Remind me about the comedian on TV: is the TV funny? *No, the man is funny!* Right, the TV is a medium, it transmits invisible stuff so we can laugh at the comedian in the studio. And when Moses hit the rock, the medium was...*the stick!* Yes, and when Isaac blessed Jacob? *His hands!* Yes, they transmitted the blessing. And when everyone atoned for their sins at the Meeting Tent, the medium to move the sins to the bulls was...*their hands!* Yes. And if the people didn't want to touch other people's heads, could they have removed their sins? *No!* And if the Levites didn't want to touch a smelly bull could they have removed their sins? *No!* Right. All that physical stuff matters, because we have a soul and...*a body!* Yes. God works through his creation.

From then on, Israelites had to come to the Levites to atone for their sins. They'd tell a Levite their sins, he'd give them a penance, tell them what to offer, say a calf, or a bird, or a lamb. He'd kill it and offer it. There was a different atonement for each type of sin, or seriousness of sin. It could get pretty complicated. The book of Leviticus in the Bible deals with all the details of sin, sacrifice, and atonement. It's named after the...*Levites*, yes. It's a kind of instruction manual. Here's an example, it's long and yucky: "[The priest] shall offer to the Lord for his sin a calf without blemish. And he shall bring it to the door of the testimony before the Lord: and shall put his hand upon the head thereof, and shall sacrifice it to the Lord. He shall take also of the blood of the calf: and carry it into the tabernacle of the testimony. And having dipped his finger in the blood, he shall sprinkle with it seven times before the Lord, before the veil of the sanctuary. And he shall put some of the same blood upon the horns of the altar of the sweet incense ... And he shall pour all the rest of the blood at the foot of the altar of holocaust in the entry of the tabernacle. And he shall take off the fat of the calf for the sin offering, as well that which covereth the entrails, as all the inwards: The two little kidneys...and the fat of the liver with the little kidneys. And he shall burn them upon the altar of holocaust. But the skin and all the flesh with the head and the feet and the bowels and the dung: And the rest of the body, he shall carry forth without the camp into a clean place where the ashes are wont to be poured out: and he shall burn them upon a pile of wood. They shall be burnt in the place where the ashes are poured out." (Leviticus 4, DR) How 'bout that, girls? *Ewww!* That's right. Boys? *Cool!* Uh-huh.

And this is what Leviticus says, over and over, sacrifice after sacrifice: "the priest shall make an atonement for him, and it shall be forgiven him." Trick question: if I was a good Israelite, and the priests made atonement for all my sins, and they were forgiven, when I died would I go to Heaven? *Yes...No!* Well, which is it? *No!* Why? *Cause Jesus hadn't died for our sins yet.* Yes. The problem was that God was perfect and sinless, but even the Levite priests were sinners like the rest of us. So even though sinful people and sinful priests, including the high priest, did their best to make up for their sins, they couldn't do a perfect job of it. To do that you'd need a high priest who was perfect, who had no sin.

Thank goodness though, people who faithfully followed God's laws as best they could didn't go to Hell. They went to a place called Sheol, neither pleasant nor painful. Greeks had a word for that abode of the dead, anyone know it? *Hades?* Yes, good. Yes, what? *Is that like Purgatory?* Good question daughter, it's like Purgatory in that it's not Heaven or Hell, and a temporary place; but being in Sheol is different from being in Purgatory. In fact, Jesus visited Sheol, we'll learn about that later this year.

Now so far all the purification and sacrificing involves spilling and sprinkling and slathering...*blood!* Yes, blood, because God's people believed life was in blood, which makes a certain amount of sense. They had so much respect for the life in blood that they wouldn't consume blood: wouldn't drink it or even eat meat unless all the blood had drained out of the animal first. But this next bit of Leviticus adds something to that sacrificial blood.

Who knows what a leper is, not a leopard...c'mon, what's leprosy? *A bad disease?* Yes, an awful disease: parts of your body die and fall off, like your fingers, ears, lips, nose. Eventually you die, but in the meantime you are ugly and people are afraid of touching you. Leviticus says, "Now whosoever shall be defiled with the leprosy, and is separated by the judgment of the priest: Shall have his clothes hanging loose, his head bare, his mouth covered with a cloth: and he shall cry out that he is defiled and unclean. All the time that he is a leper and unclean he shall dwell alone without the camp.." (Lev 13, DR) Poor people.

In Biblical times, lots of skin diseases were called leprosy, not just the worst type that we now call Hansen's Disease, where body parts fall off. Some infections might go away, might heal, but anyone whose skin ailment got better had to go to a priest to be declared clean, the way you'd need a doctor's note to return to school. There was a ritual for that. Leviticus says, "offer two living sparrows, which it is lawful to eat, and cedar wood, and scarlet, and hyssop. And he shall command one of the sparrows to be immolated in an earthen vessel over living waters. But the other that is alive, he shall dip, with the cedar wood, and the scarlet and the hyssop, in the blood of the sparrow that is immolated: Wherewith he shall sprinkle him that is to be cleansed seven times, that he may be rightly purified. And he shall let go the living sparrow, that it may fly into the field." (Lev 14, DR) Y'all know about blood being sprinkled with a hyssop brush, but in this case the blood is being mixed with what? *Water?* Yes, the blood is sprinkled for...making up for sin...A-T-O-Atonement! Yes, and the water is for...*cleaning?* Yes; we'd say 'cleansing' in this case. So water and blood together atone and cleanse. After this sprinkling the healed person offers lambs and some oil. The priest sacrifices the lambs and put some of the blood on the person. Then he pours a handful of the oil on the person's head, and declares the person is clean. Even the *house* of a leper had to be cleansed: "And he shall take to cleanse the house two birds, and cedar wood, and scarlet, and hyssop: And he shall kill the one of the birds in an earthen vessel over running waterhe shall take two sparrows, and cedar wood, and scarlet, and hyssop. And having immolated one sparrow in an earthen vessel, over living waters, he shall take the cedar wood, and the hyssop, and the scarlet, and the living sparrow, and shall dip all in the blood of the sparrow that is immolated, and in the living water: and he shall sprinkle the house seven times.." Blood and water go together. (Lev 14, DR) Yes? *What's immolate?* It means to sprinkle meal, like cornmeal, on an offering.

For centuries, the Levites sprinkled blood or water on people and things: marking them with the sacrificial blood, or by washing them clean with water. If you want to make something physically clean will sprinkling do a good job? *No, that won't do anything.* So why just sprinkle then? Why not really wash? *Well, it would take too long, and people have their clothes on.* That's right, and sprinkling's not about getting physically clean anyway, what's the point? *Spiritual cleaning?* Yes, and because we're made of a...*body'n'soul!* Yes, if we want our souls made clean, we...*sprinkle water on our bodies?* Yes, genius! But in Moses' day the sprinkling was symbolic. It showed that the people wished to be clean from sin... the water didn't do anything. But Jesus changes that in the New Testament.

And tell me the business about the Israelites starving the desert? *God gave them bread!* Yes, what's that bread called? *Manna!* Yes, Manna. For 40 years they ate it, what did it do for them? *Well, it kept them from starving?* Yes. For how long? *Umm...40 years?* Yes, and after that did they all get old and die? *Yes.* So that food miracle, the manna, worked for a while. Jesus talked about manna, as we'll discuss later on. And let's see...what is a human made of? *A body'n'soul!* Yes, and what part did the miracle bread help? *The body part?* Yes. Unfortunately it didn't do a thing for...*the soul part?* Right. But this is typical of food miracles in the Old Testament: they help bodies, but not...*souls.* Yes. Jesus is going to change this, too.

Now, has anyone ever seen any sprinkling happen in church? *I have!* Tell us about it. *Umm, the priest walks around with a bucket and a silver thing and slings holy water on everybody!* Yes. That thing is called an *aspergillum* [on the board]; it's the Latin word for 'little-sprinkler-thing.' Has anyone ever seen a priest use a bundle of sticks, instead of the silver aspergillum, to sprinkle the congregation? *I saw that at another church!* Yes, good. It's very interesting. The bundle of sticks looks like a little broom or brush, and it slings more Holy Water than the silver sprinkler, too. I like the sticks because they resemble the hyssop brushes the Hebrews used to put blood on their doorposts; and the Levites regularly used to sprinkle blood and water.

From now on in the Bible, we'll see the ritual use of water showing up in important ways. Sometimes by itself, sometimes together with blood. And we'll see people anointed with oil as well; watch for that.

Praised be Jesus Christ! *Now and forever!*

Class over!

Chapter Eight: Arks & Nazirites

(Judges, Samuel)

Exodus 35: handout of Meeting Tent plan and discussion. Numbers 9: setting up the Tabernacle: Aaron, Levites, presbyters, laying hands to bless, and also to transmit sin. Judges 13: Samson, Manoah and the angel [Mass] [miraculous conception]. Hannah and Samuel [miraculous conception].

Y'all remember from the last class that all the wandering Israelites lived in ...*tents!* Yes, and that God dwelled among them. So he *also* needed...*a tent!* Yes, it was called the Meeting Tent. It was a very expensive tent, which they took down and set up every time they moved. God told Moses, "..make me a sanctuary, that I may dwell in their midst...according to all that I show you concerning the pattern of the Tabernacle." God means that the Meeting Tent is patterned after his dwelling in heaven. *Tabernacle* is a Latin word which means "little house." Have y'all ever heard of a "tavern"? *Yes, people drink beer there.* Mmm, yes they do...well, a tavern is a kind of house; and a *tavern-acle*, or as we say, *tabernacle*, is a *little* house. Is there a little house, a tabernacle in church? *Yes!* Who dwells there? *God!* More specifically, please. *Jesus!* Yes. Churches have a lot in common with the Meeting Tent, as we'll see.

God gave Moses very particular instructions for making his Tent and the things that went in it. The Israelites provided "gold, silver, and bronze, blue and purple and scarlet stuff and fine twined linen, goats' hair, tanned rams' skins, goatskins, acacia wood, oil for the lamps, spices for the anointing oil and for the fragrant incense." Wow, that's quite a list! Let's look at a plan of this fancy Tent [full-size image in the Image appendix]:

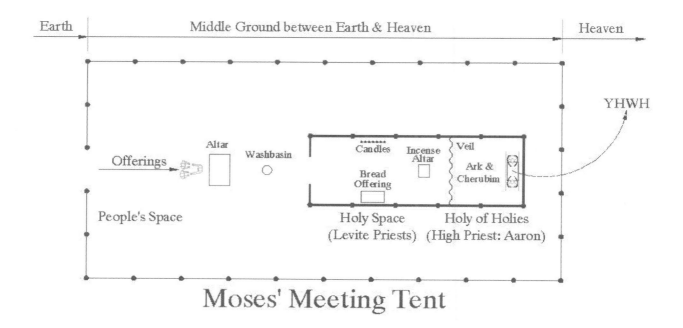

Moses' Meeting Tent

Do y'all know how to look at a plan? We're looking down at the Tent, but I took the roof off so we can see inside. Notice over to the left of the Altar, there are two people handing a sacrifice to a priest, we're looking at the tops of their heads....get it? *Yes!* OK. First, that line around the outside with the dots represents a big curtain that's held up by poles, which are the dots. That curtain separates God's dwelling, his holy place, from the people, who pitched their tents all around the outside. Let's imagine I've sinned, and seek atonement and forgiveness. I walk in the left side, which is the people's space. I have a lamb. When I come up to the front of altar, I stop. A Levite priest or an assistant comes around to the front, and takes my lamb. Now, what's that behind the altar? *A washbasin.* Yes, why do the priests wash their hands? *So they're clean when they make the sacrifice?* Yes, like at Mass.

Now most of the activity at the Meeting Tent is in this outdoor area. It's holy, but not so holy that regular sinners like me can't come in a bit. But the smaller area to the right is roofed over, and called what? *Holy Space.* Yes. Inside, the incense is burned, and bread is displayed; they are both continuous offerings. And of course being indoors, some light is needed...*the candles,* yes. Only priests, Aaron's sons get in here. No people, no assistants. See, the further in you go the more holy it gets, and the fewer people have access. Now the back half is even more holy, called...*Holy of Holies?* Yes. Only one person can go in here, the high priest. At first he was Aaron; later on he was a descendant of Aaron. This Holy of Holies is where God dwelled. What's a veil? *What a woman puts on her face so you can't see her.* Yes, good answer. When especially will a woman wear a veil? *At her wedding.* Yes, why? *So you can't see her!* Yes, so you can't see her *beauty*; but *why* aren't you supposed to see her beauty? OK, after the bride and groom take their vows, what does the groom do? *He kisses her!* Yes, does he kiss her through the veil? *No, he lifts the veil.* Yes, that symbolizes that only he has access to all of his wife's beauty. The veil on the plan does that, too. It limits access to God to the High Priest, just one person. People were too sinful to just stand around staring at

God's dwelling. What's in the Holy of Holies? *The ark and cherubim?* Yes. Remind me, what's an ark? *A container!* Yes, in this case, it's a box for which God gave specific instructions [I draw while I read]: "make an ark of acacia wood; two cubits and a half shall be its length, a cubit and a half its breadth, and a cubit and a half its height." A cubit is an Egyptian measure about from my elbow to my fingertips, so it's not all that big; about like a breakfast table. "And you shall overlay it with pure gold, within and without..." This is no ordinary box. "And you shall cast four rings of gold ...two rings on the one side of it, and two rings on the other side of it. You shall make poles of acacia wood, and overlay them with gold. And you shall put the poles into the rings on the sides of the ark, to carry the ark by them." See, this way men could carry the ark without touching it. "Then you shall make a mercy seat of pure gold..." The mercy seat goes on top of the ark like so... "And you shall make two cherubim of gold...one cherub on the one end, and one cherub on the other end... The cherubim shall spread out their wings above, overshadowing the mercy seat with their wings... toward the mercy seat shall the faces of the cherubim be." (Exodus 25) OK...there we go...isn't that a great picture? *Not really.* Hey, use your imaginations, pretend it's terrific.

So, where have we already seen a cherub in the Old Testament? Remember I called it a "kerub"...*it guarded Eden?* Yes, a kerub, a cherub, is one of God's bodyguards. If God's bodyguards both face inward like the picture, then what's between them? *God?* Yes, the LORD sits on the mercy seat, although not physically because God has no...*body!* Right! Exodus says, "There I will meet with you, and from above the mercy seat, from between the two cherubim that are upon the ark." Now, the ark is covered in...*gold!* Yes, because they put old magazines in it. *What?* Well, what would *you* put in a golden box? *Nice things.* Like pizza? *No, like diamonds or something.* Yes, precious, valuable things. The Israelites put Aaron's staff, a pot of manna, and the Commandments in what they called the Ark of the Covenant. They couldn't put God in the box, so they put his *stuff* in the box instead.

All this had to be moveable while the Chosen People wandered in the desert. But once they settled down in the Promised Land, the tent stayed in one place called Shiloh.

Y'all may remember when Abraham arrived in the Promised Land, it was already occupied by pagans who sacrificed... *their firstborn babies!* Yes, and Abraham fought them for the land. And now that the Israelites have returned, they have to fight again. Now in ancient times, who ran a country? Who was in charge? A golden monkey? *Ha, no a king!* Yes, all the pagan countries had kings. The Israelites wanted a king, too, but God said no, I'm your king, you don't need an earthly king. God gave them judges instead. A judge could make decisions and run things, but couldn't raise taxes to buy himself expensive presents like a king might do. For about 100 years there were judges; one of them, Deborah, was a woman. This Old Testament book about the judges is called...*umm, Judges?* Yes...that was a gimme.

Manoah and the Angel

In the book of Judges there's a married couple: a man named Manoah, and his wife. They were unhappy just like Abraham & Sarah...? *They didn't have any kids.* Right. Judges 13 (DR) says "And an angel of the Lord appeared to her, and said: Thou art barren and without children: but thou shalt conceive and bear a son." Where have you heard "you shall conceive and bear a son" before? *The angel said that to Mary?* Yes, good. "Now therefore beware, and drink no wine nor strong drink, and eat not any unclean thing. Because thou shalt conceive, and bear a son, and no razor shall touch his head: for he shall be a Nazirite of God, from his infancy, and from his mother's womb, and he shall begin to deliver Israel from the hands of the Philistine." (DR)

What's that mean: "No razor shall touch his head"? *Don't shave his head?* Yes, don't cut his hair. And he's going to be a *Nazirite* [on the board]. This doesn't mean he's from Nazareth, it's the Hebrew word for "separated." It means he will dedicate his life to God's service. His long hair will be a sign of that devotion. And he would be strong, and fight the Philistines who were pagan enemies of Israel. The Philistines lived in Philistia, what we call Palestine, although Palestinians aren't pagan anymore.

So she tells her husband the news. Later, the angel visits them both, still looking like a man. "Manoah said to the angel of the LORD, "Pray, let us detain you, and prepare a kid for you." *A kid?* C'mon, a young goat, you know better. And the angel of the LORD said to Manoah, "If you detain me, I will not eat of your food; but if you make ready a burnt offering, then offer it to the LORD." For Manoah did not know that he was the angel of the LORD." After all, whom should they thank for their son? *God?* Yes, the LORD. "So Manoah took the kid with the cereal offering, and offered it upon the rock to the LORD, to him who works wonders. And when the flame went up toward heaven from the altar, the angel of the LORD ascended in the flame of the altar while Manoah and his wife looked on; and they fell on their faces to the ground."

They didn't know he was an angel 'til he took off!

Tell me, what's the deal with the flame going up to heaven? *Huh?* Why does it matter which way the fire goes? *Well, it's going to heaven.* Yes...what's going to heaven, exactly...not the flame...*oh, the offering is going up!* Yes...all by itself I suppose, a burned-up goat... why is the angel going up? *He's going back to heaven, too.* Yes, so the angel and the offering are just going up separately, but at the same time to heaven, right? It's just a coincidence? *Well...maybe the angel is taking the offering up.* Yes, I think so. The angel takes the offering up. The angel connects earth and heaven. And where's the offering starting from? *Earth.* Yes, be more specific please, listen: "when the flame went up toward heaven from the altar." *Oh, from the altar!* Yes. So the angel carries the offering from the altar up to heaven. Something like that happens in church. At Mass, have you ever heard, "command that these gifts be borne by the hands of your holy Angel to your altar on high"? *Yeees...* OK, when? When you're sitting? *No, kneeling.* Yes. Remember Manoah's sacrifice when we discuss the Mass later this year.

So Manoah's son grew up to be one of Israel's judges, and a strong, long-haired warrior...what's his name? *Oh, Saul!* No, good guess! *Samuel!* No again, but y'all are right about starting with an 'S'....*Samson!* Yes, good. And part of being a Nazirite was being dedicated to God's service. Can you think of anyone today who's like that? *Huh?* Forget the hair for a second. Think of men today who are dedicated to God's service. *Oh...priests?* Yes, good. And who is someone in the New Testament who also lived apart like a hermit, had long hair, and wasn't married? *John the Baptist!* Wow honorary son, you nailed that one! Yes, John the Baptist!

Back to Samson, why was he so strong? *Cause his hair was long!* Yes, and the long hair meant...he... was....dedi...*dedicated to God!* Yes, his dedication made him strong, not so much his hair. But he got involved with a woman he wasn't married to named Delilah, somebody tell the story...yes, go ahead. *She tricked him into telling her how his hair made him strong, and she cut it off, and he was weak.* Yes, someone tell more. *Some bad people blinded him, but then he pushed their building down and killed them all.* Yes.

Now there's one more Nazirite to learn about tonight. By now I bet you can guess why his parents were unhappy. *No kids!* Yes! Y'all are fast learners! This couple was Hannah and her husband Elkanah. Poor Hannah wanted a baby so bad, partly because Elkanah had another wife who *did* have kids with him. If Hannah had been his only wife I think she wouldn't have felt so bad. Remind me how many ribs God took from Adam... two? *No, one!* And so? *One wife is enough!* Yes. Well, one day Hannah and Elkanah took a trip to offer a sacrifice to the LORD at the Meeting Tent...where was it? S-h-i...*Shiloh!* Yes, Shiloh. While they were there, Hannah prayed, "O LORD of hosts, if thou wilt indeed look on the affliction of thy maidservant, and remember me, and not forget thy maidservant, but wilt give to thy maidservant a son, then I will give him to the LORD all the days of his life, and no razor shall touch his head." So she's doing the same deal as Manoah and his wife: if you give me a son, then... *he'll be a N-naz...*look, it's right there on the board...*Nazirite!* Yes, dedicated and... *separated!* Yes. His name starts with an 'S' too, y'all already said it tonight. *Samuel?* Yes, good. This book I'm reading from is about Samuel...so...*the name of the book is Samuel!* Oh dear, another gimme. OK, let's stop there, we'll learn more about Samuel next week.

Praised be Jesus Christ! *Now and forever!*

Class over!

Chapter Nine: Mr. Slingshot

(1ˢᵗ & 2ⁿᵈ Samuel)

1 Samuel: Samuel, Eli, Shiloh, the Ark. Samuel and Saul. 1Sam 10: Samuel & Saul [Anointed, Christos, Mashiah]. 1Sam 16: Samuel & David; David & Goliath. Saul hates David; envy [Commandments 5 and 10], King David, Ark, Tent, Jerusalem.

Oral Contracts

Y'all remind me who we were talking about last week...*Samson*...after Samson, the other 'S' guy. *Samuel?* Yes. Samuel was dedicated to God by his mom Hannah before he was conceived. What's 'conceived'? *When you first have the baby?* Yes, when the mother becomes pregnant; and about 9 months later...*the baby is born.* Yes. Well, when Samuel was a little boy, his parents took him to the Meeting Tent at...*Shiloh,* yes, and he served God there, living with the judge and high priest Eli, and Eli's adult sons. Eli was old, and mostly sat around while his sons ran things. But his sons were corrupt, what's that mean? *They did bad things?* Yes, they abused their position as priests. They'd steal meat from the sacrifices, and even take advantage of women who helped out around the Meeting Tent. Eli knew there was evil right in God's house, but never did much about it.

One night, "Samuel was lying down within the temple of the LORD, where the ark of God was. Then the LORD called, "Samuel! Samuel!" and he said, "Here I am!" and ran to Eli, and said, "Here I am, for you called me." But he said, "I did not call; lie down again." So he went and lay down. And the LORD called again, "Samuel!" And Samuel arose and went to Eli, and said, "Here I am, for you called me." But he said, "I did not call, my son; lie down again." ...And the LORD called Samuel again the third time. And he arose and went to Eli, and said, "Here I am, for you called me." Then Eli perceived that the LORD was calling the boy. Therefore Eli said to Samuel, "Go, lie down; and if he calls you, you shall say, Speak, LORD, for thy servant hears." So Samuel went and lay down in his place. And the LORD came and stood forth, calling as at other times, "Samuel! Samuel!" And Samuel said, "Speak, for thy servant hears." (1Sam3) And God told Samuel he was going to punish Eli and his sons. From then on, God spoke to Samuel, "And the word of Samuel came to all Israel." People whom God speaks through like that are called prophets. Samuel *mediated* God's messages to Israel.

Now here's a story for you: just a few years ago there was a married man in Lebanon, near Israel. He didn't like his wife anymore, and met another woman online. They decided to meet at a cafe. The next morning the guy goes into the cafe...guess who is there to meet him? No guesses? An adult would get this: it was his wife!

They were both cheating on each other online! So the husband is furious at her, never mind his own sin, and yells, "Divorce, divorce, divorce!" and stomps out. In traditional Arab cultures a husband can divorce his wife by just saying it three times. Here's why: people got married and had contracts long before there were pens, pencils, paper or widespread literacy. What's literacy? *When you can read and write!* Yes. So most marriages and contracts were made by each person agreeing to the contract out loud three times. And to cancel a deal, you'd have to say so...*three times!* Yes, like that husband. When you *say* what a contract is instead of writing, it's an *oral* contract. It still counts even if it isn't written down on paper.

Tell me, how many times did God call Samuel? *Three times!* Yes...why three times? *'Cause he was making a contract with Samuel?* Yes, an oral contract. Remember oral contracts, we'll learn about an important one later on.

Back to Eli and his sons. At some point, Israel had just been defeated in battle by the Philistines. They decided to bring the Ark of the Covenant into the next day's fight. So Eli's corrupt sons brought the Ark to the army. The book of Samuel says, "When the ark of the covenant of the LORD came into the camp, all Israel gave a mighty shout, so that the earth resounded. And when the Philistines heard the noise of the shouting, they said, "What does this great shouting in the camp of the Hebrews mean?" And when they learned that the ark of the LORD had come to the camp, the Philistines were afraid; for they said, "A god has come into the camp." And they said, "Woe to us! For nothing like this has happened before. Woe to us! Who can deliver us from the power of these mighty gods? These are the gods who struck the Egyptians with every sort of plague in the wilderness." Help, the Israelites have brought their God Box, we're gonna lose! But the Philistines decide it's better to fight and die than be captured and become slaves. So Israel was defeated again, but much worse. The ark was captured, and Eli's sons were killed. Back at Shiloh, Eli was sitting by the Meeting Tent. A messenger ran up, told him the Ark was captured and his sons were dead. Eli is so shocked he falls backward, breaks his neck and dies. His pregnant daughter-in-law, who is married to one of the dead sons, is so shocked that she goes into labor, has the baby right there, and dies.

This is more bad news than anyone could have imagined! How could God allow the Ark to be captured? But God was making the point that Israel couldn't misbehave indefinitely and then expect God to cut them and the corrupt Levites tons of slack just because they were his Chosen People. Being Chosen is good, but then you have meet a high standard of behavior.

After God sent plagues on the Philistines like he did to Egypt, they eventually gave the Ark back to Israel, but it was never returned to Shiloh. God never dwelled in Shiloh again.

Now, after Eli died, Samuel became the last judge of Israel. But his sons were no good, just like Eli's; so the people pestered Samuel about getting a king. They didn't want his lousy sons to be in charge of anything. Finally God said OK, let them have an earthly king, but tell them what a bad deal it will be. So Samuel told Israel, "This will be the right of the king that shall reign over you: He will take your sons, and put them in his chariots, and will make them his horsemen, and his running footmen, to run before his chariots. And he will appoint of them to be his tribunes, and his centurions, and to plough his fields, and to reap his corn, and to make him arms and chariots. Your daughters also he will take to make him ointments, and to be his cooks, and bakers. And he will take your fields, and your vineyards, and your best oliveyards, and give them to his servants. Moreover he will take the tenth of your corn, and of the revenues of your vineyards, to give to his eunuchs and servants. Your servants also, and handmaids, and your goodliest young men, and your asses, he will take away, and put them to his work. Your flocks also he will tithe, and you shall be his servants. And you shall cry out in that day from the face of the king, whom you have chosen to yourselves: and the Lord will not hear you in that day, because you desired unto yourselves a king." (1Samuel 8, DR)

God sent Samuel out to find a king. He found "a handsome young man. There was not a man among the people of Israel more handsome than he; from his shoulders upward he was taller than any of the people." (1Sam 9:2) So he was tall and handsome...big deal, right? What was his name? *Saul!* Yes. And to show that Saul was king, does anyone want to guess what Samuel did? *Lay hands on him!* Great guess, but no: Samuel poured oil on his head, he *anointed* him. The Hebrew word for 'anointed' is *Mashiah* [on the board]; how do we say it? Jesus was Mashiah...*oh, Messiah?* Yes. The Hebrews got the word *Mashiah* from the Egyptians, who anointed the Pharaoh with crocodile oil. Their word for crocodile is *msha* [on the board]. What could be more interesting?

So Saul was Israel's first king. He was good in some ways, bad in others. For example, sometimes Saul wanted to offer his own sacrifices instead of letting the Levites do it...a big no-no. At least he was tall and handsome...must be a lesson in there somewhere. Anyway, God sent Samuel out to get a replacement for Saul. He said, "Fill your horn with oil, and go; I will send you to Jesse the Bethlehemite, for I have provided for myself a king among his sons." Why did Samuel need oil? *To anoint the new king!* Yes. And this Jesse the Bethlehemite...where'd he live? *Umm...in Bethlehem?* Yes. And if one of his sons would be king, then the king would be from...*Bethlehem too?* Yes; why do we care if the next king is from Bethlehem? *'Cause Jesus was born there?* Yes, much later.

So Samuel visits Jesse on the sly, has a look at his sons, Jesse has seven of them on display. God tells Samuel they won't do. "And Samuel said to Jesse, "Are all your sons here?" And he said, "There remains yet the youngest, but behold, he is keeping the sheep." And Samuel said to Jesse, "Send and fetch him; for we will not sit down till he comes here." And he sent, and brought him in. Now he was ruddy, and had beautiful eyes, and was handsome. And the LORD said, "Arise, anoint him; for this is he." (1 Samuel 16) Tell me, who is this next king...the shepherd boy...*David?* Yes, good. But this anointing is secret from Saul... why? *Saul might kill David?* Yes, Saul would not want to be replaced.

Now the book of Samuel says "...the Spirit of the LORD departed from Saul, and an evil spirit from the LORD tormented him." Some people think he may have suffered from depression and migraine headaches, which are awful. But maybe it was a demon, just like it says. "And Saul's servants said to him, "...seek out a man who is skillful in playing the lyre; and when the evil spirit from God is upon you, he will play it, and you will be well." What's a lyre? *Like a harp?* Yes, good. One of Saul's servants recommended David. "And David came to Saul, and entered his service. And Saul loved him greatly, and he became his armor-bearer. And Saul sent to Jesse, saying, "Let David remain in my service, for he has found favor in my sight." And whenever the evil spirit from God was upon Saul, David took the lyre and played it with his hand; so Saul was refreshed, and was well, and the evil spirit departed from him."

Now about this same time there was a giant Philistine soldier that all of Israel feared...yes? *Goliath!* Yes, tell the story. *Nobody would fight Goliath, but David said he would.* Yes, and he was too small to wear King Saul's armor; so what next? *He killed Goliath with a slingshot!* Yes, and used Goliath's sword to chop his head off! How about that, girls? *Ewww!* Boys? *Cool!* Uh-huh.

So David became very popular. Giant-killer, soldier, lyre-player, singer; an all-around great guy. As David grew into a young man, Saul became jealous of David and tried to kill him. David had to go away and hide until Saul and his sons were killed in battle; then David became king.

David was very close to God, enjoyed God's favor for most of his life. He even talked straight to God, and God would talk right back:

David inquired of the LORD, "Shall I go up into any of the cities of Judah?" And the LORD said to him, "Go up." David said, "To which shall I go up?" And he said, "To Hebron."

David inquired of the LORD, "Shall I go and attack these Philistines?" And the LORD said to David, "Go and attack the Philistines and save Keilah."

David asked, "Will Saul come down?" And the LORD said, "He will come down."

Then David said, "Will the men of Keilah surrender me and my men into the hand of Saul?" And the LORD said, "They will surrender you." (1Samuel 23)

Whether or not David heard God speaking out loud isn't the point, although he may have. What matters is that David had God's ear, so to speak. He went straight to God and heard right back: Old Testament Instant Messaging.

David won great victories over Israel's enemies, and captured Jerusalem, which became Israel's capital city. David built himself a palace of cedarwood there, which must have smelled terrific.

'Fess Up

David's life would seem pretty good at this point: a nice new palace, wives (he had a few), a new capital city. But one afternoon, David was on the roof of his palace, and saw a woman named Bathsheba taking a bath, and he wanted her for himself. He had an affair with her; unfortunately she was married to one of David's soldiers, named Uriah. So David arranged for Uriah to be killed in battle. Then David married Bathsheba. David clearly committed some serious sins, including conceiving a baby with Bathsheba while she was married to Uriah. (2Sam 11)

How did David do that? Do what? *You know...the baby.* I tell you what, ask your parents if you want to know the details- they conceived *you,* after all.

Now let's learn a bit about Samuel's successor, Nathan. Nathan was a prophet who had been authorized by God to be the King's advisor...to keep him out of trouble, and to scold him if necessary. Nathan knew David needed to repent of those serious sins in order to rule Israel well, but it's not smart to just tell a King, "hey King, you super sinner, everybody knows how bad you are, you'd better repent or else!" Kings have big egos. They think they're so great, a King would just get mad...king-scolding is how John the Baptist lost his head, by the way.

Instead of yelling at King David, Nathan tells him a sad story:

"O great King, let me tell you about a rich man and a poor man. The rich man had lots of sheep, more than he needed, but the poor man had only one little lamb. It grew up in his family along with his children; it was like another daughter to him. [I pretend to cradle a dear little lamb.] Then one day the rich man needed a sheep for a feast, but being a bigshot, instead of using one of his own, he took the poor man's lamb instead." (2 Samuel 12)

King David blew his top! He yelled, "that selfish jerk is gonna pay for that *big time*! That's outrageous! He treated that poor guy like dirt!" But Nathan said, "That rich man is *you*! God's given you so much, but you stole Uriah's wife Bathsheba, and then had him killed to try to cover up your sins!"

Now, here's where it gets interesting. Did God already know David's sins? *Yes.* In fact, did God know David's sins before David was even born? *Yes.* And David's a smart guy, he would have known that God was aware of his sins, right? *Right!* And of course, David knew he had sinned by having, umm, *married love* with a woman he wasn't married to, and getting her husband killed. So why hadn't David repented? *Well, he just put it off.* Yes. He could do what I like to do, just tell God he's sorry, what the heck, God knows all his sins anyway. He didn't have to admit it to anyone else, so he kept his pride. I like to keep my pride, too. Just like Adam and Eve.

But David acknowledged his terrible sins to Nathan, who was God's authorized advisor and scold. Instead of saying, "Interesting story Nathan, but I haven't killed any lambs, stop wasting Royal time," and later on going straight to God to apologize and seek forgiveness, he 'fesses up to Nathan, "I have sinned against the LORD." Now, tell me: did *God* know David's sins? *Yes!* And did *Nathan* know David's sins, at least the really big bad ones? *Yes!* And did *David* know David's sins? *Yes!* And could David go straight to God for all sorts of stuff, as we saw earlier? *Yes!*

So... why did David bother to confess to Nathan, "I have sinned against the LORD"? *Because God went through Nathan, David has to?* Yes, genius daughter! And think of it this way... have you ever been mean to your Mom? *Yeees....* And were you sorry right away? *Yes!* Did you 'fess up right away? *No, it's embarrassing!* Yes, you wanted to hang onto what Adam & Eve hung onto, your...*pride!* Yes, we all love our pride, our selves, instead of loving others. What's the opposite of being prideful? *Being humble!* Yes.

Back to your Mom- when you felt sorry, did she know you were sorry without you saying so? *Yes, she can tell.* So if you apologize, you're just telling her what she already knows. So why does she want you to say you're sorry out loud? *It makes her feel better.* Yes, but there's another reason. When you tell her you're sorry, what does she say back? *She says it's ok, she forgives me.* And how do you feel? *Better.* Yes, you humble yourself by saying that you did something wrong, and you're sorry; it's hard. But your apology allows your Mom to say she forgives you. It wouldn't be right for her to say it first, although she probably would want to because she loves you. You're humble; Mom's merciful. And after you say you're sorry and she says you're forgiven, how else might she show you're forgiven? *She'll hug me.* Yes, and how do you feel? *Happy.* Yes, often we're happiest after we've just repented and been forgiven, in spirit and....*physically!* And what 2 things make a person, by the way? *A body and a soul!* Yes, they go together, *bodysoul.* So if your soul is sorry, what else should be sorry? *Your body!* And one way your body shows it is? *By saying you're sorry.* Yes, out loud, just like King David. It's humbling.

Now back to King David. David didn't just privately confess to God. He confessed his sin to God *through Nathan,* who was God's physical representative. He physically humbled himself before another person, because being a *bodysoul* his spirit had to confess to a spirit, and his body had to confess to....? *another body!* Yes, and since Jesus wasn't around yet, God wasn't physically available... so what did David do? *He confessed to Nathan.* Yes. And what does your Mom do after you say you're sorry? *She forgives me!* Yes. So guess what Nathan did after David confessed? *Umm...he forgave David?* Yes! Plain as day, Nathan said, "The LORD has put away your sin..." Trick question: how do you know if your Mom forgives you for something you do? *Umm, she says I'm forgiven?* Yes, the words go right out of her mouth and into your ear. Next trick question: how did David know his sins were forgiven? *Nathan told him right in his ear!* Yes! But David didn't sin against Nathan...who said Nathan could speak for God? *Umm, God said so?* Yes, God appointed Nathan, and gave him that authority. We know this because the Bible says that God would tell Nathan what to tell David. So when David heard the words from Nathan, he could believe them. Nathan *mediated* God's forgiveness.

This story about David and Nathan should remind you of how Catholics confess our sins to God. Can we pray straight to God like David? *Yes!* But when we want to confess our serious sins, and be forgiven, what do we do? *Confess to a priest.* Yes, just as David confessed to Nathan. And how do we know we're forgiven? *The priest says so.* Yes, just like Nathan. And how do we know the priest can do that? *He speaks for God.* Yes...just like Nathan. He's got authority from Jesus' Church.

When I was a kid the priest would say: "May our Lord Jesus Christ absolve you; and by His authority I absolve you from your sins in the name of the Father, and of the Son, and of the Holy Ghost, Amen." The words are a bit different now, but the priest still speaks for Jesus so you can hear the words go right into your ear, just as Nathan spoke for God in the Old Testament. We and David are forgiven, body and...? *Bodysoul!* Yes, *bodysoul.*

By the way, after you are forgiven your sins, the priest usually wants you to do something......*oh, penance.* Yes. David had a penance too, but that's a story for next week.

Praised be Jesus Christ! *Now and forever!*

Class over!

Chapter Ten: Happy Days

(2nd Samuel, Psalms)

2Sam 10 & 11: David, Bathsheba, Uriah, Nathan. [Commandments 7 & 9] Chastity, fidelity; the little lamb, aural confession & absolution. Atonement vs. forgiveness. Psalms 51, 128, 78. 1Kings 2: Solomon, Bathsheba, Abishag, Adonijah. Queen Mother [intercession, Cana, Mary]. Compare Plan of the Temple to the Meeting Tent.

Y'all remind me, we were talking about...Mr. Slingshot...*David!* Yes. We were discussing his sins, which were? *He fooled around with the man's wife!* Yes, Uriah's wife, Bathsheba. And then? *David got him killed!* Yes. David broke some commandments, which are...*thou shalt not kill!* Yes, number 5, and...*thou shalt not commit adultery*, yes, number 7. Y'all wouldn't think about that at your age. That's a body sin, something you *do*: committing adultery. *What's adultery?* It's having married love with someone you aren't married to. And David also committed a soul sin, he coveted his neighbor's wife, commandment number 9. What's covet? *To want something real bad?* Yes, something that belongs to someone else.

But God forgave David; how was David sure about that? *Nathan told him.* Yes. But part of forgiveness is atonement and penance. David's sins were very serious and couldn't be fixed like a broken window. So David and Bathsheba's penance was that their baby died a few days after he was born. God took their firstborn as atonement.

Tell me some of David's talents. *He could sing and play the harp!* Yes. And he also wrote songs called Psalms [on the board]. Psalm is a Greek word for "play a harp, play a lyre" so we know they were meant for singing. By the way, words that start with "Ps" come from Greek. We sing Psalms at Mass: the choir sings one part, then we sing a response. We call them Responsorial Psalms.

Let's look at a few of my favorite Psalms.

First, the 51st Psalm, which David wrote right after his affair with Bathsheba. Here's a bit of that:

"A Psalm of David, when Nathan the prophet came to him, after he had gone in to Bathsheba. 1 Have mercy on me, O God, according to thy steadfast love; according to thy abundant mercy blot out my sins. 2 Wash me thoroughly from my iniquity, and cleanse me from my sin!" The washing bit is what the priest quietly says at Mass when he washes his hands. If you sit up front you can hear him quoting David.

"3 For I know my transgressions, and my sin is ever before me." This is how I feel before I go to confession: my sins hang over me all the time, I want to get rid of them. I imagine David felt the same way.

"7 Purge me with hyssop, and I shall be clean; wash me, and I shall be whiter than snow" What's *purge* [on the board] mean? *To throw up?* Oh, like people who binge and purge so they won't gain weight. Good guess, but not exactly: purge means to clean something inside out so thoroughly it hurts. So what happens in Purgatory? *Huh?* What happens in Purgatory? *Your sins get cleaned?* Yes, perfectly cleaned, purged, after which...*you go to heaven?* Yes. And David wants to be sprinkled with a hyssop brush as a symbol, an outward sign of God washing, purging his sins.

Then David says, *"10 Create in me a clean heart, O God, and put a new and right spirit within me. 12 Restore to me the joy of thy salvation, and uphold me with a willing spirit."* David wants to feel like I do when I get out of confession: brand new.

"16 For thou hast no delight in sacrifice; were I to give a burnt offering, thou wouldst not be pleased. 17 The sacrifice acceptable to God is a broken spirit; a broken and contrite heart." See, David knows killing and burning animals doesn't mean much to God. What God really wants is for us to sacrifice our pride, to be humble and contrite. What's contrite? *Sorry?* Yes, like when we pray an Act of...*Contrition!* Yes.

And here's a bit from Psalm 78, it's just like teaching catechism class:

"1 Give ear, O my people, to my teaching; incline your ears to the words of my mouth! 2 I will open my mouth in a parable; I will utter ...sayings from of old, 3 things that we have heard and known, that our fathers have told us. 4 We will not hide them from their children, but tell to the coming generation the glorious deeds of the LORD, and his might, and the wonders which he has wrought. 5... he commanded our fathers to teach to their children; 6 that the next generation might know them, the children yet unborn, and arise and tell them to their children, 7 so that they should set their hope in God, and not forget the works of God, but keep his commandments..."

That's my job: to teach y'all. And what's your job? *To learn?* Yes, but more, listen again and tell me: "[he] commanded our fathers to teach to their children; 6 that the next generation might know them, the children yet unborn, and arise and tell them to *their* children..." Well? *We have to learn so we can tell our kids.* Yes. You don't learn about God just for yourself.

I like this next Psalm, number 128 because it's about family:

"1 Blessed is every one who fears the LORD, who walks in his ways! 2 You shall eat the fruit of the labor of your hands; you shall be happy, and it shall be well with you. 3 Your wife will be like a fruitful vine within your house; your children will be like olive shoots around your table." This is exactly like my house, when my beautiful wife is at the other end of the table, and my beautiful children are at the sides. They're beautiful, both boys and girls, and even though the youngest one is 20.

" 4 Lo, thus shall the man be blessed who fears the LORD. 5 The LORD bless you from Zion! May you see the prosperity of Jerusalem all the days of your life! 6 May you see your children's children! Peace be upon Israel!" And here again, it's like my life, when I play with my grandchildren!

Thanksgiving dinner always makes me think of this Psalm. As y'all get older you should pay attention to the Psalms and see if there are some you especially like.

So David dwelled in...*a palace!* Yes, and God dwelled in....a *tent!* Yes. David felt bad for God: "Now when the king dwelt in his house, and the LORD had given him rest from all his enemies round about, the king said to Nathan the prophet, "See now, I dwell in a house of cedar, but the ark of God dwells in a tent." David wanted God to have a big house, too, a temple. But "the LORD came to Nathan, "Go and tell my servant David, 'Thus says the LORD: When your days are fulfilled and you lie down with your fathers, I will raise up your offspring after you, who shall come forth from your body, and I will establish his kingdom. He shall build a house for my name." So we see God expects David to have another son, who will build God's big house, not David. And did God just tell David all this directly? *No, he told Nathan.* Yes, Nathan was the intermediary, the medium between God and David. Remind me please, Nathan spoke with God's... *authority!* Yes.

And after their first baby died, David and Bathsheba did have another son who became King after David; who? *Solomon!* Yes, good. Solomon became King after David died...who sat beside Solomon in the palace? *His wife!* Ha! Trick question! No! His momma sat next to him. She was called the Queen Mother; who was...*Bathsheba!* Yes! What commandment would Solomon be obeying by having his mother sit at his right hand? *Honor you father and mother?* Yes, what number is that? *The fourth?* Yes, good.

Sometimes people would want a favor from Solomon, and would ask his mom to ask the King for them. Why is that? *'Cause his mom is nicer?* Maybe...another reason? *He has to do what she says?* Well, let's say he would want to honor her wishes. You could still ask Solomon directly for something, but still, if his mom asks for you that can't hurt. This reminds me...someone tell us about the wedding Jesus went to. *They were at the wedding and they ran out of wine.* Yes, who was there? *Jesus and Mary.* Yes. And when the wedding party ran out of wine, did they bug Jesus? *No they got Mary to do it.* Yes, so the same way that people might talk to Solomon's mom, people would talk to Jesus' mom that same way, even now by praying to her. And let's see...is Jesus a King? *Yes.* Of...*heaven?* Yes, so in heaven we have God the Father sitting on a throne, and to his right is...*Jesus,* yes, and to *his* right is...*Mary!* Yes, who is...*Queen Mother.* Yes, good.

What was Solomon famous for? *Being smart?* Yes, wisdom; somebody tell the wisdom story. *Two women were arguing about a baby.* Arguing what about the baby? *Who it belonged to, they both told Solomon it was their baby.* And? *Solomon said to cut in half and give each of them a part. Then the real mom said to give it to the other lady instead.* What did Solomon do then? *Give it to the real mom.* Yes, he figured out who the real mother was; she loved the baby more than she loved herself.

Well, as Nathan prophesied, Solomon built God a permanent house, a temple, which was much bigger and more spectacular than that old Meeting Tent. But even so, the plan was still like the Meeting Tent, just bigger and sturdier. Look at this plan. It doesn't show all the many washbasins, tables, candles and lampstands a big Temple would have because it still works like the Meeting Tent:

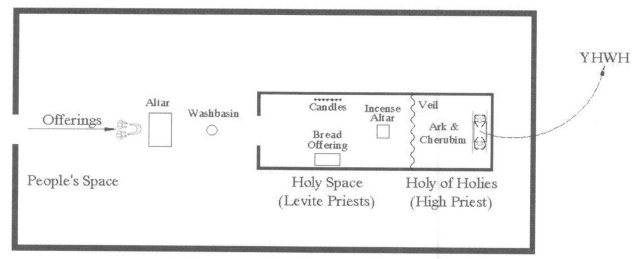

Solomon's Temple

See, it's still the same: people come up to the altar with offerings, Levites receive them, priests wash their hands and offer the sacrifices, incense burns, and in the Holy of Holies where only the High Priest goes, God dwells in his Ark, the tabernacle, the...*little house!* Yes, which is guarded by...*cherubs!* Yes. Just like in church. Yes, what? *Are there cherubs in church?* Excellent question, yes indeed there are, but you have to look carefully to see them. Later on this year we'll talk about it, but I don't want to give it away right now.

Israel's happiest days were when the Temple was new and Solomon was King. Israel was rich, and had beaten all her enemies. But things were never so good again. After Solomon died, his son Rehoboam was a terrible king, and Israel split into two parts, Israel in the North, and Judea in the South. The people who lived in the South, around Jerusalem, are called Jews. We won't talk about Israelites anymore. And after the split, both kingdoms were conquered by a series of much bigger enemies, including Persia (which is Iran today), Assyria (Syria), Babylon (Iraq), Greece, and Rome. Who was running things when Jesus was alive? *Romans!* Yes. It was a thousand years from David to Jesus, and almost two thousand more years after Jesus until Israel became independent again after World War 2. And the Jews are still fighting for the land with Philistines, the Palestinians.

During the thousand years leading up to Jesus, God spoke to his Chosen People through a series of prophets, just as he spoke to Saul through...*Nathan?* No, guess again. *Samuel?* Yes. And who did Nathan advise? *David!* Yes. Sometimes the prophets scold the Jews for worshiping false gods and generally ignoring the LORD; other times they say things about the future. They even work miracles. We'll look at some of them for the next class or two, starting with Elijah.

Praised be Jesus Christ! *Now and forever!*

Class over!

Chapter Eleven: Dry Ground

(1ˢᵗ and 2ⁿᵈ Kings)

1 Kings 17: Elijah in Zarephath: food miracle, Gentile non-believer saved through works. 1Kings 19: Elijah cloaking Elisha (using my jacket as a prop), authority physically handed down. [Church hierarchy]. 2Kings 2: Crossing the Jordan (using my jacket again as a prop), physical media of divine power [Sacraments]. Oral contracts. Elijah bodily taken up to heaven in the fiery chariot: body & soul not separated [Ascension/Assumption]. 2Kings 5: Elisha and Naaman, healing through physical media [Sacraments, Baptism]; non-believer healed; action counts for more than status. 2Kings 13: Elisha's bones (using a chicken bone as a prop), physical media of divine power [Relics, Saints, Sacraments]

Elijah lived shortly after Solomon died and his kingdom was split in two. Elijah wore animal skins for clothes and lived alone in the desert, slept under trees or in caves, that sort of thing. Tell me who was like Elijah in Jesus' day. *John the Baptist?* Yes, good. Elijah and John both may have been Nazirites like...*Samuel*, yes, and... *Samson.* Yes, good.

In Elijah's day the king of Israel was named Ahab. He had a pagan wife named Jezebel, and let the people worship Baal, the baby-eating false god that his pagan wife worshiped. We think we're too smart for that nowadays, but people still kill their babies. What's that called, killing babies before they are born? *Abortion?* Yes. So the LORD sent Elijah to speak to the king. What are you if God speaks through you? *A prophet.* Yes. Elijah said to Ahab, "As the LORD the God of Israel lives, before whom I stand, there shall be neither dew nor rain these years, except by my word." If there would be no rain until the king and people got right with God, then there'd be...*no food?* Right, a famine. Naturally everyone from the king on down would want to wring Elijah's neck like a chicken, so God told him, "Depart from here and turn eastward, and hide yourself." That is, get out of Israel! By the way, this book I'm reading from is all about Israel's Kings, so its name...might...be...*Kings!* Yes. 1st Kings; there's a 2nd Kings too.

Elijah fled Israel and went to a pagan city called Zarephath. People there were starving too. Kings chapter 17 says: "...and when he came to the gate of the city, behold, a widow was there gathering sticks; and he called to her and said, "Bring me a little water in a vessel, that I may drink." And as she was going to bring it, he called to her and said, "Bring me a morsel of bread in your hand." And she said, "As the LORD your God lives, I have nothing baked, only a handful of flour in a jar, and a little oil in a jug; and now, I am gathering a couple of sticks, that I may go in and prepare it for myself and my son, that we may eat it, and die."

"And Elijah said to her, "Fear not; go and do as you have said; but first make me a little cake of it and bring it to me, and afterward make for yourself and your son." Now I'd've told Elijah to get lost, my child & I would eat first, but "...she went and did as Elijah said; and she, and he, and her household ate for many days. The jar of flour was not spent, neither did the jug of oil fail, according to the word of the LORD which he spoke by Elijah." Because the pagan widow was generous, Elijah worked a miracle for her: they were able to eat for the next 3 years of drought.

Later on, the widow's son got very sick, "and his illness was so severe that there was no breath left in him." What's that mean? *He died.* Yes, he ex-spired. And Elijah said to her, "Give me your son." And he took him from her bosom, and carried him up into the upper chamber, where he lodged, and laid him upon his own bed. (Elijah was staying with them) And he cried... "O LORD my God, let this child's soul come into him again." And...the soul of the child came into him again, and he revived." These miracles are extra special because they were done for pagans, when Chosen People were still starving. Why did Elijah work these miracles? *'cause she was good to him?* Yes, being charitable outweighed being pagan.

Tell me about the first miracle. *Umm...he made a lot of food?* Yes. Who else miraculously made a lot of food? *Oh, Jesus!* Yes, he made pizza...*ha, bread and fish!* Oh yeah, you're right. And the next miracle, raising the widow's son from the dead? *Jesus did that too!* Who'd he raise...y'all know this [on the board]...L-a-z...*Lazarus!* Yes. Because of Jesus' miracles, some people wondered if he was...*Elijah?* Yes.

After 3 years God sent Elijah back to Samaria, Ahab's capital. What would you call someone who lived in Samaria? *Umm...a Samarian?* Close, a *Samaritan*, like in Jesus' parable...*the Good Samaritan!* Yes, good. In Samaria, the pagan priests didn't like seeing Elijah back in town, so they challenged him to a contest to see whose god was stronger. Elijah & the Ba'al-worshiping priests built wood altars with sacrificed bulls on them, and prayed to their gods to set the altars on fire. God set Elijah's altar on fire, and the pagan priests who worshiped baby-eating Ba'al lost. Elijah slit all their throats in a creek. The people returned to the LORD, and the drought ended.

Now as Elijah grew old, God directed him to anoint as his successor a young man named Elisha. Elijah "found Elisha the son of Shaphat, who was plowing, with twelve yoke of oxen before him, and he was with the twelfth." The 12 oxen represent the 12 tribes, who descended from Israel's....*12 sons.* Yes. When you see 12 of anything in the Bible it refers to the nation of Israel united, not separated. So, how do you think Elijah showed that Elisha would be in charge? *He laid hands on him!* Like Isaac and Jacob, great guess, but no! Another guess? *Put oil on him?* Yes, but something more. Let's see, I need an Elisha volunteer, get up, you're the volunteer. OK Elisha, what are you doing? *Umm...farming?* Oh, like planting little peas? You're *plowing*, bossing around a dozen huge oxen, show us that, grab some reins, *be in charge*, yeah, that's it. Now, "Elijah passed by him and threw his coat upon him." Come on Elisha, pass me by. [as he does, I take off my coat and put it on Elisha's shoulders] Elijah shows that he's picking Elisha and also protecting him a bit, since Elisha's young and isn't a prophet yet. Elisha is Elijah's *protégé*, that's a French word for "protected one."

"And he left the oxen, and ran after Elijah, and said, "Let me kiss my father and my mother, and then I will follow you." I'm impressed. I would have made excuses, but Elisha drops his old life right there, and follows

Elijah. Who was it that dropped everything and followed Jesus? *Peter?* Yes. I bet Peter knew this story about Elisha and thought to himself, "Wow, I'm just like Elisha." And when Elijah left Earth, who'd he put in charge? *Elisha.* And when Jesus left? *He put Peter in charge!* Yes!

After Elisha learned the prophet business, it was time for him to take over from old Elijah. On the day that Elijah would leave Earth, they had to cross a famous river we haven't mentioned yet, where Jesus would later be baptized...*the Jordan river?* Yes, good! As they traveled to the Jordan, Elijah told Elisha 3 times that he didn't have to make the journey. And 3 times Elisha said, "As the LORD lives, and as you yourself live, I will not leave you." Tell me about the 3 times. *It's a covenant!* Yes, an oral contract- for what? *For Elisha to be the next prophet?* Yes.

Back when the Israelites were wandering in the desert, they had to cross the Jordan to enter Canaan, the Promised Land. But before that, what water did they cross to leave Egypt? *The Red Sea?* Yes, good; did they swim? *No, Moses split the water so they could walk.* Yes, Exodus says "the people of Israel walked on dry ground." And 40 years later when they got to the Jordan, they carried the Ark of the Covenant in front. When the Ark got to the river's edge, guess what happened. *The water split?* Yes, "And while all Israel were passing over on dry ground, the priests who bore the ark of the covenant of the LORD stood on dry ground in the midst of the Jordan..." (Joshua 3:17)

When Elijah and Elisha arrived at the Jordan, "Elijah took his mantle, and rolled it up, and struck the water" like so [I do this with my coat] and...*the water split!* Yes: "the water was parted to the one side and to the other, till the two of them could go over on dry ground". Notice how each event is described in the same way, "crossing on...*dry ground!"* Yes. This is how the Bible writers show events are related, by using the same words or similar phrasing. We'll see more of that this year.

Once they were on the far side, "behold, a chariot of fire and horses of fire separated the two of them. And Elijah went up by a whirlwind into heaven." Wow....did Elijah die? *No, God took him to heaven.* Yes. Quick now, remember Enoch for me. *He went up to heaven, too.* Yes, so here are at least two people who went straight to heaven without dying. Their body'n'souls...*didn't separate!* Right!

But when Elijah whooshed up to heaven, his cloak came off. Elisha "took up the cloak of Elijah that had fallen from him, and went back and stood on the bank of the Jordan [I do so]. "Then he took the cloak of Elijah that had fallen from him, and...*hit the water!* [I do so] And...*the water split and he walked over!* On...*dry ground!* Yes. "Now when the sons of the prophets who were on the other side at Jericho saw him, they said, "The spirit of Elijah rests on Elisha." How did they know that? *Elisha had the coat.* Yes. Remember Moses' stick: was it magic? *No.* Right. It was just a physical medium of God's power, like Isaac's hands, or the Ark, or Elijah's...*coat.* Yes, which still worked on the water even after Elijah was gone, because Elisha had faith. If some pagan had come by and whacked the water all day with the cloak, he'd just get worn out from slinging a wet coat.

Miracle Water

Y'all remind me about leprosy. *It's a disease that eats up your body.* Yes, your nose dies and falls off, your fingers & toes fall off, eventually you die. The Bible's full of lepers that no-one wants to be around. Everyone was scared to death of touching a leper. Well, when Elisha was older, he healed an important pagan leper. The story starts off like this: "Now Naaman, captain of the host of the king of Syria, was...a mighty man, but he was a leper." Naaman is a general in Syria, a country that still exists next to Israel. He's got money, power, camels, iPods. But he's caught leprosy, his lips and ears are falling off, and his wife won't kiss him anymore. How about that, girls? *Ewww!* Uh-huh...y'all never disappoint me.

"But Naaman's wife had a slavegirl from Israel, who said the prophet Elisha could cure Naaman's leprosy." With nothing to lose, Naaman took a pile of money with him and traveled to Israel. "So Naaman came with his horses and with his chariot, and stood at the door of the house of Elisha." Hey, old man in the shack, get out here! Don't make me wait! But "Elisha sent a messenger to him, saying, Go and wash in the Jordan River seven times.....and you will be clean." Naaman has a fit! He says, "I thought that he would surely come out to me, and wave his hand over the place, and cure me." Naaman wants some respect! Elisha should come out of his little hut and take care of business instead of handing out instructions to a general! Seven times!? And Naaman objects to having to bathe in that brown Jordan water: "The rivers of Damascus are better than all the waters of Israel. Could I not wash in them, and be clean?" So he turned and went away in a rage." This trip isn't working out....who does this Elisha think he is? Naaman's puffed up like a frog; he ain't takin' no bath in dirty water! I guess he'd rather be a leper. "But his servants said, "My father, if the prophet had commanded you to do some great thing, would you not have done it? How much rather, then, when he says to you, 'Wash, and be clean'?" Alright! Alright already! "So Naaman went down and dipped himself into the Jordan seven times."

"So what do you think happened? *He wasn't a leper anymore!* That's right! "his flesh was restored like the flesh of a little child, and he was clean." So Naaman got himself some humility, did as he was told (everyone hates to do as they're told) and his disease was miraculously washed away by the water. So what does this remind you of? *Baptism?* Yes, it foreshadows Baptism. Baptism is the Greek word for "immerse" in the sense of washing.

Trick question #1: Suppose Naaman decided the water was just a symbol, and instead of getting in the muddy water, he just stood beside the river and went through the motions of washing [I do so], would that have worked? *Ha! No!* Why not? *He had to use the water!* Yes. The water was part of the miracle. The water wasn't just a symbol. God worked through the water. It was the medium.

Trick question #2: Naaman's leprosy was washed away; were Naaman's *sins* washed away? *Ummm, no?* No, they weren't. Jesus hadn't been born yet, so there were no Sacraments. No spiritual cleansing for Naaman. By the way, what river did Naaman immerse, or baptize, himself in? *The Jordan.* Yeah. Remember the guy named John who baptized people, what's he called? *Ha, John the Baptist!* Yes, what river did he baptize in?

The same one, the Jordan! Yes...imagine that. Also remember that Naaman was a pagan, but he was still healed because he believed enough to obey Elisha. How do we know Naaman had at least a little bit of faith? *'Cause he got in the water!* Yes. We see his faith through his actions; what the the Bible would call his "works."

Miracle Bones

Years passed, and Elisha worked other miracles we aren't going to cover in class. "So Elisha died, and they buried him. Now bands of Moabites used to invade the land in the spring of the year." Moabites are just another bunch of pagan troublemakers. "And as a man was being buried, lo, a marauding band was seen and the man was cast into the grave of Elisha." I imagine the men who were burying him panicked and just threw him into the grave. "...and as soon as the man touched the bones of Elisha, he revived, and stood on his feet." (2Kings 13) Now look at this bone; [I have a chicken's thighbone] pretend it's one of Elisha's bones. Is it magic? *No.* What is it? *A thing like Moses' stick.* Yes and...*the coat?* Yes, Elijah's coat. A medium. Trick question: if Elisha's dead, why do his bones still work miracles? *'Cause God makes the miracle, not Elisha?* Yes. God worked through Elisha both alive and dead. Have y'all ever heard of relics [on the board]? No? They're bones or bodies or clothes of saints that Catholics honor. Where are the saints? *In heaven?* Yes, their souls are; but their *bodies* are...*buried?* Yes, they're still on Earth, and we have reverence for their bodies or clothes the way we would have reverence for Elisha's miracle-working bones or Elijah's cloak.

OK, that's it for Elisha; next week we'll cover Isaiah, who had a lot to say about Christmas.

Class over!

Chapter Twelve: The Christmas Prophet

(Isaiah)

Isaiah 6: Isaiah's unclean lips, sin purged by fire [Purgatory]. Is 25: the feast for all nations, Chosen people vs. Gentiles [Wedding Feast of the Lamb]. Is 1 & 60, Isaiah's Nativity prophecies: virgin, dromedaries, kings, gifts, star, news; ox, ass & manger. Is 40 & 49: Isaiah and John the Baptist, make straight, etc.

Isaiah is our next prophet. He lived in the Southern Kingdom, which was called Judah; its capital was Jerusalem. Judah was named after one of the tribes of Israel, which...would...be...*Judah?* Yes, that was a gimme! Y'all may remember that the Northern Kingdom, where Elijah lived, was called Israel, and its capital was Samaria [I draw a quick map]; what do we call people who live in Samaria? *Samaritans!* Yes. Judah's, or Judea's, main enemy at this time was Assyria. But even when they weren't fighting Assyria, the Judeans, or Jews, could never relax, because they were a small country surrounded by bigger ones. Just like today.

Anyway, like many other people in the Bible, Isaiah was minding his own business when out of the blue God spoke to him. In Isaiah's case he was at the Temple- in what city? *Jerusalem?* Yes. Isaiah says, "...I saw the Lord sitting upon a throne, high and lifted up in the temple." (Isaiah 6) Isaiah's having this vision in Solomon's Temple, but he's also seeing the Heavenly Temple, which Solomon's Temple is patterned on, like the Meeting Tent. "Above him stood the seraphim; each had six wings: with two he covered his face, and with two he covered his feet, and with two he flew." Seraph is Hebrew for "burning one"; remember *Kerub, Cherub,* is Hebrew for... *bodyguard!* yes, "near one." Cherubim & Seraphim serve the LORD in Heaven. Look at this painting of a Seraph with his six wings:

[I use a printout of Viktor Vasnetsov's Seraph from the Cathedral of St. Vladimir in Kiev, Ukraine.]

Isn't that cool? *He's not on fire.* No...but don't get picky. Seraphs are spirits, they don't have bodies anyway. "And one called to another and said: "Holy, holy, holy is the LORD of hosts; the whole earth is full of his glory." Where have you heard that? *In Mass!* Yes, the Mass quotes Isaiah. "And the foundations of the thresholds shook at the voice of him who called, and the house was filled with smoke. And I said: "Woe is me! For I am lost; for I am a man of unclean lips, and I dwell in the midst of a people of unclean lips; for my eyes have seen the King, the LORD of hosts!" What's all this "unclean lips" business? *He says bad things?* Yes, Isaiah's a sinner, and isn't worthy of seeing the LORD, much less speaking for him out of a sinful mouth. "Then flew one of the seraphim to me, having in his hand a burning coal which he had taken with tongs from the altar." How hot would a burning coal be that you had to pick it up with tongs? *Too hot to touch!* Yes! "And he touched my mouth, and said: "Behold, this has touched your lips; your guilt is taken away, and your sin is purged." Remind me, what "purge" mean? *To clean something.* Yes, usually it means to burn bad stuff away until only good stuff is left. The Bible talks about using fire to purge the impurities out of gold, for example. Imagine our souls are gold, what impurities would we want burned off? *Sins?* Yes, our sins. So Isaiah's sins are purged, burned away by this coal. That's why we think of Purgatory as being a swimming pool, right? *Ha, it's fire, it burns!* Oh, yeah, fire: it cleans away our sins, but it may hurt some.

Then Isaiah says, "And I heard the voice of the Lord saying, "Whom shall I send, and who will go for us?" Then I said, "Here I am! Send me." Isaiah is ready to be God's prophet...what other prophet said "Here I am" to God? *Samson!* No, the other Sam...*Samuel!* There you go. What I'm reading comes from a book mostly written by Isaiah; its name- *Isaiah!* would be Isaiah, yes.

Isaiah is my favorite prophet, and Jesus' favorite, too. In the Gospels we'll see Jesus say things that Isaiah said; I always imagine his listeners thinking, "Oooh, Jesus is quotin' Isaiah...I wonder what he means." Isaiah prophesied about lots of things, including Christmas, so let's get started.

Ever since the Happy Days of King David and King Solomon, the Judeans wanted peace and security; that is, they wanted a new King to *provide* them peace and security. They wanted an Anointed One, a...*Messiah,* yes, a Messiah, to save them. And Isaiah had a lot to say about a Messiah, as we'll see.

First, Isaiah announces not that a Messiah is coming, but that the LORD is coming: "Comfort, comfort my people, says your God. Speak tenderly to Jerusalem, and cry to her that her warfare is ended, that her iniquity is pardoned, that she has received from the LORD's hand double for all her sins. A voice cries: "In the wilderness prepare the way of the LORD, make straight in the desert a highway for our God. Every valley shall be lifted up, and every mountain and hill be made low; the uneven ground shall become level, and the rough places a plain. And the glory of the LORD shall be revealed, and all flesh shall see it together, for the mouth of the LORD has spoken."(Isaiah 40) How is the mouth of the LORD speaking? *Through Isaiah!* Right. So Isaiah speaks with God's...*authority?* Yes. People can't just tell Isaiah to keep his opinions to himself.

So Isaiah's telling the Judeans get ready for the coming of the LORD, although they're really interested in getting a...*King?* Yes, an...anointed one...*a Messiah!* That's it. But if God's coming too, well, it can't hurt, right?

Remember that ever since God first spoke to Abraham he wasn't God to everybody. God chose Abraham's descendants to be his people; that's why they called themselves the Chosen People, the Chosen Ones. Like being married to one wife, not a dozen. So the people in Isaiah's day were expecting the prophet to tell them how God was looking out just for them; but that wasn't Isaiah's message. For example, many Judeans were worshiping baby-eating gods again, Ba'al and Moloch, so you'd expect Isaiah to say they should stop. He does say that, but says more (Isaiah 56):

"Blessed is the man who...keeps the Sabbath, not profaning it, and keeps his hand from doing any evil." That's obvious, just be good. "Let not the foreigner who has joined himself to the LORD say, "The LORD will surely separate me from his people" What's a foreigner? *Someone from another country.* Yes, someone who isn't a Jew; we call these people *Gentiles* in English. "For thus says the LORD: "To [those] who choose the things that please me and hold fast to my covenant, I will give in my house and within my walls a monument and a name better than sons and daughters; I will give them an everlasting name which shall not be cut off." Who are God's sons and daughters? *The Jews?* Yes. But Isaiah says that if Gentiles, foreigners, hold on to the covenant God made with Moses, God will give them a name "*better* than sons and daughters." How would you feel if your parents told you that? *That they didn't love me!* Yes. But God isn't telling the Jews that he doesn't love them, but that they have to do the right thing to be counted as his children. If they worship false gods, that's like you calling other adults Mom and Dad and ignoring your parents. How would your parents feel? *Like I didn't love them.* Right, so it goes both ways. And if there are Gentiles who weren't lucky enough to be born into God's family, but treat God like their Father, why shouldn't he give them "a name better than sons and daughters"? They had to make a special effort to be included in the family. What's that called when someone becomes the son or daughter of parents who didn't conceive them? *Adoption?* Yes. God is saying he will adopt other children into his family.

Isaiah continues: "And the foreigners who join themselves to the LORD...these I will bring to my holy mountain, and make them joyful in my house of prayer; their burnt offerings and their sacrifices will be accepted on my altar; for my house shall be called a house of prayer for all peoples."

What would this "house of prayer" on a "holy mountain" be? *The Temple?* Yes. So God will treat the foreigners just like his own children, and the Temple will be not just for Jews, but "all peoples." Just to make the point about everyone being able to be God's children, his Chosen, Isaiah says, "Thus says the Lord GOD, who gathers the outcasts of Israel, I will gather yet others to him besides those already gathered." And remember, the Temple isn't only on Earth, it's also...*in Heaven.* Yes.

And there will be a feast on the holy mountain: "On this mountain the LORD Almighty will prepare a feast of rich food for all peoples, a banquet of the best of meats and the finest of wines." I know y'all would prefer pizza and pop, but they hadn't been invented yet. Have we had this fabulous feast yet? *No.* Right, but *we will,* you'll see. And it's not just for the Chosen people, but for...*all people!* Yes! Then Isaiah says, "On this mountain he will destroy the veil that veils all peoples, the web that is woven over all nations. He will destroy death forever. The Lord GOD will wipe away the tears from all faces." What veil is Isaiah talking about? *The one in the holy space?* In the Holy of Holies? Maybe...what does that veil do? *Keep people from seeing God.* Yes, but they'd like to see Him. So when God destroys the veil...*people can see Him.* Yes, we won't be separated from Him. And when we can see God, and death is destroyed, and tears are wiped away, where is that? Heaven! Yes; *more* than Heaven as we'll see. *How can you have more than Heaven?* I don't want to give it away...we'll see later on.

Back to the Messiah: Isaiah gives a hint of where this Anointed One will come from:

"There shall come forth a shoot from the stump of Jesse, and a branch shall grow out of his roots. And the Spirit of the LORD shall rest upon him..." Who was Jesse? *David's father.* Yes. He's the forefather of Israel's kings. Jesse fathered David, who- *Solomon!* ya too fast, yes, and so on. Isaiah is treating Jesse like the root of a tree that should grow to be big and healthy, but it's been cut down through the worship of baby-eating false gods, a divided kingdom, weak kings, big enemies, you name it. But a shoot, a branch, will grow out of the stump; that is, someone related to Jesse and David and Solomon.

Being a King, this Messiah should be tough like David, a good...*soldier?* Yes. But Isaiah says, "he shall smite (strike) the earth with the rod (you know, a stick, whack!) of his *mouth*, and with the *breath of his lips* he shall slay the wicked." The breath of his lips? That sounds more like a *talker* than a *doer*...not a tough guy at all!

And "The wolf shall dwell with the lamb...and the calf and the lion...and a little child shall lead them. ... In that day the root of Jesse shall stand as an ensign (a sign) to the peoples; him shall the nations seek, and his dwellings shall be glorious." (Isaiah 11) Now if lions and wolves don't eat lambs and calves, what's that sound like? *Eden!* Yes, so Isaiah prophesies: God is coming, and a Messiah is coming, but he's not a typical tough guy. And somehow things will be more like Eden than like slaughtering your enemies.

OK, on to Isaiah and Christmas. Class, what's 'Christmas' mean? *It's when Jesus was born.* Yes, good, that's what Christmas *is*...but what does 'Christmas' literally mean? *Oh, Christ's Mass.* Yes again. And you're right, it celebrates Jesus' birth. ¿Quién aquí habla Español? Who speaks Spanish? *Me!* ¿Cómo se llama Christmas en Español? How do you say Christmas in Spanish? *Navidad.* Yes [Navidad goes up on the board]. Does 'Navidad' mean 'Christ's Mass'? *No, it means the baby is born.* Right. In English we say *Nativity* [on the board]. Somebody tell me, what's a Nativity scene? *It's the little statues of baby Jesus and the 3 Kings and all.* Yes...one reason I like the word *Navidad* is that it reminds me of Jesus being born in that little humble stable.

OK, here's the deal. I'm going to read Isaiah's Christmas prophecies one at a time. You tell me what part of the Nativity scene is prophesied and I'll draw it in. We're going to create a New Testament picture by using Old Testament prophecies. Here we go.

"Hear ye therefore, O house of David... Therefore the Lord himself shall give you a sign. Behold a virgin shall conceive, and bear a son and his name shall be called Emmanuel. (Is 7:13-14, DR) *Mary and Jesus!* Yes; they aren't all this easy, I'm just being nice to start. [Mary (and Joseph) are drawn, but not baby Jesus, for reasons that will become apparent later....maybe you can guess.]

Next: "Get thee up upon a high mountain, thou that bringest good tidings to Sion: lift up thy voice with strength, thou that bringest good tidings to Jerusalem: Behold your God:" (40:9, DR) Ha! I *told* you the first one was easy. What are good tidings? *Good news?* Yes. In Luke's Christmas Gospel, who borrowed from Isaiah and said, "...be not afraid...behold, I bring you good tidings of great joy"? No guesses yet? Look at this Greek word, *evangelousios* [on the board]; it means good news, glad tidings. In Isaiah's day how did the king get his news? From TV? *Ha, no, from messengers!* Yes, messengers. So let's think of *evangelousios* as meaning "good message" instead of "good news." Tell me again, who brings the message? *The messenger!* Yes. Please observe the magic finger [I erase from *evangelousios* until I have *angel*]. If *evangelousios* means "good message," what does "angel" mean? *Umm, messenger?* Yes, genius! So at Christmas, who said, "..behold, I bring you a good message of great joy"? *Oh, the angel!* Yes, God's messenger. And since the message comes from heaven, the messenger should have...*wings!* Yes. [On the board goes a winged messenger.] *Make a halo!* OK...there ya go.

Next: "Behold, the Lord GOD..... He shall feed his flock like a shepherd: he shall gather together the lambs with his arm, and shall take them up in his bosom. (40:10-11, DR) All the flocks of Cedar shall be gathered together unto thee. (60:7, DR) *Shepherds and sheep!* Yes. [I draw them.] *That one looks like a dog instead of a sheep!* Stop whining...pretend it's the best sheep you've ever seen.

And: "Arise, be enlightened, O Jerusalem: for thy light is come, and the glory of the Lord is risen upon thee. For behold darkness shall cover the earth, and a mist the people: but the Lord shall arise upon thee, and his glory shall be seen upon thee. And the Gentiles shall walk in thy light, and kings in the brightness of thy rising." (60:1-2, DR) No guesses...here's more: "And the Gentiles shall come to thy light, and kings to the brightness of thy rising." *The star!* Thank you [up it goes], and what else...? Listen again: "And the Gentiles shall walk in thy light, and kings in the brightness of thy rising." (60:3, DR) *The kings!* Yes, both of them! *There were three!* Well, Luke doesn't say how many. For now I'm showing two.

"The multitude of camels shall cover thee...(60:6, DR)" *The camels!* Yes...see if you can tell me how many humps. *Two! One!* Y'all wait a second and listen to it all, don't just guess like monkeys: "The multitude of camels shall cover thee, the dromedaries of Madian and Epha." So? *Two?* You're just guessing again. Does anyone know the main difference between the Dromedary camels in this passage, and Bactrian camels? *One of them has two humps!* Yes, the Bactrian, so I'm drawing one-hump Dromedaries.

"...all they from Saba shall come, bringing gold and frankincense: and [showing] forth praise to the Lord..." (DR) *The three kings brought gold and incense!* Yes, *two* gifts...so I'm drawing only *two* kings, see? *But there were three gifts!* Well, if y'all can name the third gift that Isaiah left out I'll draw it and a third king. So? *Umm...myrrh?* Yes genius, myrrh! [3 kings and 3 gifts on the board] We'll look at the gifts again later on this year.

Then: "I have brought up children, and exalted them: but they have despised me." Just like teenagers! "The ox knoweth his owner, and the ass his master's [manger]: but Israel hath not known me, and my people hath not understood." (Is 1:3-3, DR) Tell me...*the ox?* Yes, and? *the...the donkey?* [on the board] Yes, and what's a manger? *Baby Jesus' crib.* Yeah, sort of..."manger" is the French word that means "to eat," so...*it's what the animals eat out of.* Yes, the name tells us. [on the board] Listen again: "The ox knows its owner; and the ass its master's manger." Whose manger is it? *The master's?* Yes, and who is the master? *Jesus?* Yes. [He goes in the manger] "But Israel hath not known me, and my people hath not understood." This line doesn't give us anything to draw, but something to think about.

Notice that Isaiah says Israel doesn't know the master, but the dumb animals, the ox and ass do; maybe they aren't so 'dumb' after all. And as we see from the picture, the humble, uneducated shepherds know who Jesus is, and so do the Gentile Kings, who aren't even Jewish. So we see that Jesus will come for the Jews, for non-Jews (that's us), the rich and the poor. Jesus will come for everyone, "all peoples," as Isaiah prophesied.

OK, that's all the time we have tonight; next week we'll have an Isaiah story, which is about keys, before we move on to Jeremiah.

Praised be Jesus Christ! *Now and forever!*

Class over!

Chapter Thirteen: Who's in Charge?

(Isaiah, Jeremiah, Ezekiel, Daniel)

Isaiah 22, Shebna & Eliakim: authority of office (using my car keys as a prop) [Jesus & Peter]. Jeremiah 7, Den of thieves. Jer 31, New Covenant. Ezekiel 36, I will sprinkle you, etc. [Baptism, sprinkling vs. immersion]; change of heart, sprinkling water vs. sprinkling blood [Leviticus]. Daniel 7 , Son of Man prophecy.

Y'all remember last class we talked about the Christmas Prophet...*Isaiah!* Yes. We have a couple more of his prophecies to look at.

In this one Isaiah is telling the Jews to cheer up, God is going to make things better. I like this passage, because it shows that although God is masculine, and is our father, that he loves his children like a mother as well:

"Sing for joy...For the LORD has comforted his people... But Zion said, "The LORD has forsaken me, my Lord has forgotten me." Can a mother forget her infant, be without tenderness for the child of her womb? Even should she forget, I will never forget you. See, upon the palms of my hands I have written your name." Isn't that sweet? It reminds me of how my wife loves our children, even though they are mostly adults now. Then Isaiah says, "All [your enemies] come to you. As I live, says the LORD, you shall be arrayed with them all as adornments, like a bride you shall fasten them on you." (Is 49) I like that part because it reminds me of how beautiful my wife was at our wedding. [I pull out a photo from our wedding] Just look at this picture, isn't that great, boys? *No!* Girls? *I think y'all look cute!* Thank you! Boys, I'm tellin' ya, wise up: this is the future...*your* future.

So whenever God talks about his people being his children or his bride, I know just what he means.

Now, y'all may remember from last week Isaiah prophesied that God was coming; a Messiah, an Anointed One, a king was coming; but he was a talking, persuading king, not a fighting king; and his kingdom would be made of all nations, all peoples, not just the Chosen People. God also describes this Messiah as his servant:

"Behold my servant, ...in whom I am pleased; I have put my Spirit upon him, he will bring forth justice to the nations....Behold, the old things have come to pass, and new things I now declare...Behold, my servant shall prosper, he shall be exalted and lifted up, and shall be very high." That all sounds pleasant; but then Isaiah says, "...many were astonished at him-- his appearance was so marred, beyond human semblance, and his form beyond that of the sons of men..." What's that mean, marred? *Like...dented?* Yes, let's say damaged, beat-up. Again: "..his appearance was so marred, beyond human [re]semblance" What's that mean? *He's so beat up he doesn't look like a person?* Yes, people were mean to the servant; that seems odd. "[And] he shall sprinkle many nations." (Is 42) Who sprinkles people? *Priests!* Yes, with...*Blood!* and...*Water!* Yes, so if God's servant will sprinkle many nations, then he must be a...*priest?* Yes. And when a priest sprinkles you what does it show? *You got your sins forgiven.* Yes, you were cleansed of your sins. And this servant will sprinkle "many nations," not just the Chosen Ones...which is also odd.

Isaiah says so much about this "suffering servant" that we can only look at a few things...please, don't thank me. All this is from Chapter 53: "He was...avoided by men, a man of suffering...One of those from whom men hide their faces...and we held him in no esteem. Yet it was...our sufferings that he endured, while we thought of him as stricken, as one smitten by God and afflicted." Smitten means hit, like with a fist or a weapon. "But he was pierced for our offenses, crushed for our sins, upon him was the chastisement that makes us whole, by his stripes we were healed." If someone has been "smitten" why would he have "stripes"? *'Cause he was whipped?* Yes, good. "We had all gone astray like sheep, each following his own way; But the LORD laid upon him the guilt of us all." That seems unfair. "...he was harshly treated...Like a lamb led to the slaughter...he was silent and opened not his mouth. Oppressed and condemned, he was taken away...he was cut off from the land of the living and smitten for the sin of his people...though he had done no wrong nor spoken any falsehood." Poor servant, why should he suffer for other people's sins? But here's the good part: "Through his suffering, my servant shall justify many, and their guilt he shall bear. Because he surrendered himself to death...he shall take away the sins of many, and win pardon for their offenses." So, who was unjustly put to death and took away other people's sins? *Jesus?* Yes. All this prophecy is about Jesus. We'll come back to Isaiah as we discuss the Gospels, and see how Jesus fulfilled so many prophecies.

Well, we've covered a lot of Isaiah's prophecies; now let's hear a story from Isaiah before we move on to Jeremiah. It's not a parable, though, it's real. Hmm...I already need a volunteer! Get up here & stand by me! Your name is Shebna, Shebna. OK class, my name is Hezekiah. I'm the king of Judah, and he isn't, so I have *all* the power, and he...*doesn't have any!* That's right. But being the king, do I want to run around the kingdom all day collecting taxes and taking care of business, or do I want to lounge around the palace and eat pizza? *You want to lounge around the palace and eat pizza!* That's right! Boy, y'all are smart. And even if liked running the kingdom I might have to leave town to visit other kings, or lead the army, or maybe I'd get sick sometimes...I'm just not going to be available 24/7...[I put my arm around my powerless volunteer] dear me, what shall I do? *Make him your helper!* Now, there's an idea...does that suit you, Shebna? *Yes!* OK, Shebna, you're going be my *prime minister*...anyone know what a prime minister is? *Like the president?* Umm...sort of. More like the vice-president. Who's the head of England? *The Queen?* Yes, Queen...*Elizabeth.* Yes. Queen Elizabeth has a whole lot of ministers, each one's in charge of something: the army, the navy, the treasury, stuff like that. She lets them use her authority to do all the things she doesn't have time to do. They don't have any power of their own, just however much of the Queen's power that she lends them. And she has one minister who is in charge of all the rest: the *prime* minister. If she's traveling the world he is in charge while she's gone.

Shebna, I won't be here very often and I'm leaving you in charge [I take out my key wallet & show the contents]. Here's my palace key, my chariot key, my castle key, my credit card, my bank card, and my library card. Take care of everything for me [I put the wallet on his shoulder]. Class, have I put someone in charge? *Yes, Shebna!* How do you know? *You put your wallet on his shoulder.* Yes...why didn't I just slip it in his pocket? *So we could see.* That's one reason. Now I won't give my wallet just to anyone...only to...*someone you trust!* Yes!

As it turns out, Shebna started using his position to make himself rich. Isaiah says, "Thus says the Lord GOD of hosts, "Come, go to this steward, to Shebna, who is over the household, and say to him: What have you to do here and whom have you here, that you have built here a tomb for yourself, you who make a tomb on the height, and carve a habitation for yourself in the rock?" See, Shebna has bought him himself a very fancy tomb to be buried in; God only knows what else he's done. He...can't...be...*trusted!* Yes!

[I address Shebna] "Behold, the LORD will hurl you away violently, O you strong man. He will seize firm hold on you, and whirl you round and round, and throw you like a ball into a wide land; there you shall die, and there shall be your splendid chariots, you shame of your master's house. I will thrust you from your office, and you will be cast down from your station." Shebna, you're fired [I take back my wallet]! Dear me, if I fire Shebna how will stuff get tended to? *Get another prime minister!* Can I do that? *Yes!* You're right, the prime minister-ship is an *office*; he's an *official*. I'll just get a new one. OK, I need another volunteer. Get up here, your name is Eliakim.

The Key Business

"...I will call my servant Eliakim the son of Hilkiah, and I will clothe him with your robe," hand it over Shebna; "and will bind your belt on him (hand it over as well), and will commit your authority to his hand; and he shall be a father to the inhabitants of Jerusalem and to the house of Judah." [I act these things out on Eliakim] Go sit down, Shebna. Class, how should I show you Eliakim's in charge now? *Put your wallet on his shoulder!* Yes! Isaiah says, "And I will place on his shoulder the key of the house of David; he shall open, and none shall shut; and he shall shut, and none shall open." [I put the wallet on Eliakim's shoulder] So when someone in the Bible or even today gives someone else a key...*he's putting them in charge!* Yes, geniuses! Go sit down, Eliakim, and give me back my wallet!

"Somebody remind me, why didn't I just hand Eliakim my keys like a regular person? *So everybody could see.* Yes, but why did I put them on his *shoulder?* *Cause he's shorter than you!* Oh my, you are the clever one, but no. Listen to this bit of prophecy from Isaiah Chapter 9 and see if you can figure it out.

"For to us a child is born, to us a son is given; and the government will be upon his shoulder, and his name will be called "Wonderful Counselor, Mighty God, Everlasting Father, Prince of Peace."

Who's this prophecy about? *Jesus?* Yes, why? *Because he's the Prince of Peace?* Yes, good. Why will the government be upon his shoulder? *'Cause he's the Prince?* Well, yes, but why is it on his *shoulder?* No guesses...ok, look, when I carry my keys I can do it like so (I take the keys from Eliakim's shoulder and hold them between two fingers). Can I carry my 20-lb. grandson like this? *No, he's too heavy.* Right, I carry him more like so (I pretend to carry him slung in the crook of my arm). Now if I'm a fireman carrying another grown man out of a burning building, can I tote him like my grandson? *No he's too big!* So what do I do? *You have to put him over your shoulders!* Yes. When someone carries something on his shoulders, what do you know? *That he's carrying a lot of weight!* Yes, if you're carrying all you can bear, the load is on your shoulders. OK Eliakim, I'm going to put my keys back on your shoulder...how do those little keys feel now? *Heavy!* Yes, that responsibility is a great burden. C'mon, show us how heavy all that responsibility is...that's it. But isn't it also a great honor to be trusted with the king's keys? *Yes.* OK class, tell me: who bears responsibility for Hezekiah's kingdom? *Hezekiah! No...Eliakim!* Yes, Eliakim...how do you know? *He got the keys!* Yes, and why are they on his shoulder...because keys are heavy? *No, 'cause the kingdom is heavy!* Yes...is it *literally* heavy? *No...but to do it is hard.* Yes, as we said before it's a heavy responsibility.

That's all for Isaiah, let's learn about our next prophet, Jeremiah. I will be reading from... *Jeremiah!* Yes, the book of Jeremiah. Jeremiah was born about 650 years before Jesus. By comparison, the Pilgrims came to America about 400 years ago. In Jeremiah's day, Judah had been conquered by a new, bigger enemy, Babylon, which had beaten the old enemy, Assyria. The king and the Jewish people had returned to their old bad habits, worshiping the baby-eating false god Baal, and taking the LORD for granted. Jeremiah tries to warn Judah that even worse may happen:

The LORD tells Jeremiah, "Stand in the gate of the LORD's house, and proclaim there this word...Amend your ways and your doings, and I will let you dwell in this place." What's the house of the LORD? *The temple?* Yes, built by...*Solomon?* Yes. In what city? *Jerusalem!* Yes. And remember, the seraph, the burning one, purged Isaiah's lips where? *In the Temple?* Yes. Jeremiah goes on to say, " Do not trust in these deceptive words: 'This is the temple of the LORD, the temple of the LORD, the temple of the LORD.' Of course it's obvious that Jeremiah is standing at "the temple of the LORD," so what's his point? No guesses, that's OK. He means that if the Jews keep misbehaving, the temple won't save them, won't make any difference. And worse, he won't let them "dwell in this place." "For if you truly amend your ways and your doings, if you truly execute justice one with another, if you do not shed innocent blood in this place...then I will let you dwell in this place, in the land that I gave of old to your fathers for ever." How would the Judeans "shed innocent blood in this place"? *Umm, by sacrificing babies?* Yes, I think so. How awful. "Will you steal, murder, commit adultery, lie, burn incense to Baal, and go after other gods that you have not known, and then come and stand before me in this house...only to go on doing all these abominations? Has this house, which is called by my name, become a den of thieves in your eyes?" Imagine if your house, or our church, was turned into den of thieves; why should God put up with that? *He shouldn't!* Right; Jeremiah says: "Go now to my place that was in Shiloh, where I made my name dwell at first, and see what I did to it for the wickedness of my people Israel. And now, because you have done all these things, says the LORD, and when I spoke to you persistently you did not listen, and when I called you, you did not answer, therefore I will do to this house...as I did to Shiloh." What happened at Shiloh? *Everybody got killed!* Yes, more or less: Eli, the high priest died; his bad sons died, and his daughter-in-law died. Even worse, what was captured? *The Ark!* Yes. God abandoned Shiloh and never dwelled there again, due to all the sinful behavior.

So, did the Judeans listen to Jeremiah? *No!* Of course not. Jerusalem was a huge, fortified city with a spectacular Temple, not some bump-in-the-road like Shiloh. Wise up, Jeremiah. But within a few years Judea rebelled against Babylon, and was crushed. The people were hauled off as captives to Babylon, the Temple was demolished, and Jerusalem was left desolate, just...like...*Shiloh!* Yes, *worse* than Shiloh.

But the Judeans were humbled by their defeat, and inclined to repent. Jeremiah offered them hope: "Behold, the days are coming, says the LORD, when I will make a new covenant with the house of Israel and the house of Judah, not like the covenant which I made with their fathers when I took them by the hand to bring them out of the land of Egypt, my covenant which they broke, though I was their husband, says the LORD." Remind me please, what covenant do the Judeans have with God? No guesses...it's the one they made when "I took them by the hand to bring them out of the land of Egypt" *The one with Moses?* Yes, we call it the *Mosaic* Covenant. And God is Israel's husband, that makes Israel his bride, and I can imagine how he loves her and how his heart breaks when she isn't faithful. "But this is the covenant which I will make with the house of Israel after those days, says the LORD: I will put my law within them, and I will write it upon their hearts; and I will be their God, and they shall be my people..." Where did God write the Law he gave the Israelites? *On the tablets?* Yes, on stone tablets. And now "I will write it upon their hearts." Which is the better place to write laws, stone or hearts? *Hearts.* Why? *Because then you believe it?* Umm, sort of; if someone's name is "written on my heart" then...*you love them!* Yes. So law written on one's heart is based on...*love?* Yes. That's how parents are with kids. Parents don't want to make up a bunch of rules; they want you to obey them because...*we love them.* Yes. And because they love you- just like God. Finally Jeremiah says, "I will forgive their iniquity, and I will remember their sin no more." That's like parents, too. I forget most of the bad things my kids have done, just as my parents have forgotten the bad stuff I did. Parents and God are alike: they both want to forgive the children they love, but the kids...have...to...*be sorry!* Yes. They have to repent.

Our next prophet is Ezekiel. *Is the book called Ezekiel?* Yes. *How many more prophets are there?* Well in our class, after Ezekiel there are only two more, Daniel and Malachi, but none of them take as long as Isaiah. We're only going to look at one thing Ezekiel said...but first, tell me about Naaman and the Jordan river. *He had leprosy and washed it off in the river.* Yes, and did his sins get washed away, too? *No, just the leprosy.* Yes, physical healing, but not spiritual. Now listen to Ezekiel's prophecy, he was in Babylon, and wanted the Judeans to feel better about going home someday: "For I will take you from the nations, and gather you from all the countries, and bring you into your own land." That would make me feel better; but he goes on: "I will sprinkle clean water upon you, and you shall be clean from all your uncleannesses, and from all your idols I will cleanse you. A new heart I will give you, and a new spirit I will put within you; and I will take out of your flesh the heart of stone and give you a heart of flesh." Being sprinkled clean from idol worship isn't physical, it's... *spiritual,* yes, getting cleaned from...*sin.* Yes. Do people ever have their sins washed away by water in church? *Yes, at baptism.* Yes. And when that happens it's like getting a new spirit and a heart of flesh. Y'all may not know that on the night before Easter there's a Mass called the Easter Vigil. Lots of adults get baptized at that Mass, it's pretty interesting. When you're older and can stay awake, get your parents to take you. Seeing them get baptized always reminds me of Ezekiel's prophecy: sprinkling water to take away spiritual uncleanness, also known as... *sin!* Yes.

On to Daniel. *The book is Daniel!* Yes, good. Daniel lived in Babylon with the captive Judeans; who knows the story about Daniel and the Lions' Den? *The king put him in there with the lions but they didn't eat him.* Right, that was the Babylonian king, Nebuchadnezzar. Well, one day Daniel had a vision of God judging all the earthly kingdoms that had oppressed Israel at one time or another; they appeared as fantastic beasts. "And as I looked, the beast was slain, and its body destroyed and given over to be burned with fire. As for the rest of the beasts, their dominion was taken away... I saw in the night visions, and behold, with the clouds of heaven there came one like a Son of Man, and he came to the Ancient of Days (that's God) and was presented before him. And to him was given dominion and glory and kingdom, that all peoples, nations, and languages should serve him; his dominion is an everlasting dominion, which shall not pass away..." So after all the earthly kingdoms are swept away, a "Son of Man" comes on heavenly clouds, and is given a never-ending kingdom that includes "all peoples," as Isaiah would say. Who does that sound like? *Jesus!* Yes. Not only is that prophecy about Jesus, but when Jesus is arrested after the Last Supper, he quotes Daniel's prophecy. But all that comes later on.

At long last we're down to our last prophet. Don't cry, but class is over for tonight, so we'll pick up next week with Malachi.

Praised be Jesus Christ! *Now and forever!*

Class over!

Unit 2

The New Testament

Chapter Fourteen: Miraculous Mothers (Malachi, Gospels part 1)

Malachi 1 purifying fire, [Purgatory] sacrifices around the world. Mal 3, sending Elijah to "prepare the way." Luke 1, Elizabeth, another miraculous conception. Gabriel, the Annunciation: free will, another miraculous conception. Mary the new Eve. Recall Isaiah. Hail Mary prayer, line-by-line analysis. Visitation: miraculous conception, recall Sarah, Rebekah, Manoah's wife and Hannah. Elizabeth and Mary, leaping John (using the plastic fetus as a prop) [Abortion, Contraception]. John 6 months older than Jesus.

Y'all remember from last week we almost finished with the prophets; the next book that we're going to look at is the last book of the Old Testament. It's called Malachi; but the prophet's name...*Malachi!*... isn't Malachi! Ha! I tricked you! *No fair!* Yes fair, you jumped the gun! Malachi is the Hebrew word for "messenger." Why would a prophet call himself "messenger"? *'Cause he brings God's messages.* Yes. We don't know his name...do you think it might have been Herman? *No!* Oh.

In Malachi's day, the Judeans were slacking off in keeping the covenant: divorcing their wives; marrying pagan women; and offering stolen, blind, lame, sick or otherwise second-rate animals to God. Instead of acting like Abel, and offering the best...*they acted like Cain!* Yes, giving God, oh, whatever was on sale. Junk animals. And the priests at the Temple go along with this slack attitude; they don't care either.

Malachi the messenger scolds them: "I have no pleasure in you, says the LORD of hosts, and I will not accept any sacrifices from your hand." Oh, dear. As usual God isn't fooled. But if God's children don't want to do the right thing, there are other people who do. Malachi prophesies: "For from the rising of the sun to its setting my name is great among the nations, and everywhere incense is offered to my name, and a pure offering." Now, what is the *only* place God accepts sacrifices? It's a building...*oh the temple!* Yes, in...*Jerusalem!* Yes. But Malachi prophesies that God will accept offerings and incense *everywhere* among the nations, and not just a *good* offering, but a *pure* offering. How's all that going to happen? We'll see.

Y'all may remember that Isaiah said that God was coming, and that the people should prepare the way of the LORD. God now has more to say on that subject. Through Malachi, God tells the Levite priests: "Behold, I send my messenger to prepare the way before me, and the Lord whom you seek will suddenly come to his temple..." So not only is the LORD coming to his temple, but a messenger will come *before* him to prepare the way. "But who can endure the day of his coming, and who can stand when he appears? For he is like a refiner's fire...he will purify the sons of Levi and refine them like gold and silver, till they present right offerings to the LORD." Uh-oh...what's the word for purifying gold by burning away its impurities? *Purging!* Yes, which..*hurts!* Yes! So when the LORD comes, it probably won't be pleasant for those with, umm, *impurities.* And God tells us who the messenger will be: "Behold, I will send you Elijah the prophet before the great and terrible day of the LORD comes." Remind me, did Elijah die? *No, he went to heaven in a chariot.* Yes...we'll have to see how this prophecy works out.

That was the last line of the last book of the Old Testament.

Somebody tell me what an iceberg is. *It's a big piece of ice that floats in the ocean.* Yes, is most of it above the water, or below? *Below.* Yes. Most of the ice is below the water, and holds up the ice that sticks out. The Bible's like that: the Old Testament is bigger, and holds up the New, which is easier to see. Now that we've learned about the big part, we can move on to the smaller part that sits on top.

So tell me, the New Testament is about...*Jesus!* Yes, mostly. So I suppose we should start with, oh, the apostles? *No, Jesus comes first.* So we should start with Jesus? *Yes.* But Malachi said a messenger would come before the LORD; so let's start with the messenger. I'll be reading from Luke's gospel.

About a year before Jesus was born, there was a priest named Zechariah who had a wife named Elizabeth. *Priests could get married?* Yes, but remember they were priests in Moses' Covenant, not New Covenant priests like we have now. *Was Jesus married? No.* Right. New Covenant priests imitate Jesus: they don't get married. Now, Zechariah and Elizabeth were old...and...sad...*they didn't have any children!* Yes! Like who? *Abraham and Sarah!* Yes, and like Samson's parents, and Samuel's parents, and so on. Well, one day Zechariah was offering incense in the Temple Holy Space, like the priest does around the altar at Mass, "And there appeared to him an angel of the Lord standing on the right side of the altar of incense"...guess who? *Gabriel?* Yes! "I am Gabriel, who stands in the presence of God; and I was sent to speak to you, and to bring you this good news." What good news? *That his wife would have a baby!* Yes! "Your wife Elizabeth will bear you a son, and you shall call his name John...he will be great before the Lord, and he shall drink no wine nor strong drink..." That's like Samson and Samuel, who also weren't supposed to cut their hair or get married, or have any alcohol. They were "separated ones", you know this [on the board] N-a-z-i-r *Nazirites!* Yes. "...and he will be filled with the Holy Spirit, even from his mother's womb. And he will turn many of the sons of Israel to the Lord their God, and he will go before him in the spirit and power of Elijah, to prepare a people fit for the Lord." And who did Malachi say God would send as his messenger? *Uhh...Elijah?* Yes. So Zechariah understood that his son would do important things for God, just like Samuel, Samson, and Elijah did, and prepare the way for the Lord in some way. And of course Elizabeth got pregnant just as Gabriel had said.

How long does a baby grow before it can be born? *Nine months!* Yes. In Luke's Gospel, which I'm reading from, it says, "And in the sixth month," that's when Elizabeth was 6 months pregnant with John [I draw & talk] here she is, she's happy...and here's John upside down in her tummy...

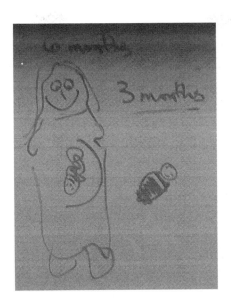

...*another* woman gets visited by...*Gabriel.* Yes. "...the angel was sent from God unto a city of Galilee, named...*Bethlehem!* no, try again...*Jerusalem! Babylon!*...no, no, NO! Stop guessing like monkeys and think: where did Jesus grow up? *umm, Nazareth?* Yes, "to a virgin espoused to a man whose name was Joseph, of the house of David; and the virgin's name was...*Mary.*" Yes, y'all know all this already. What's this mean: "of the house of David"...that Joseph lives in David's house? *He's part of David's family.* Yes. Joseph and Mary are descendants of King David. Remember the Jesse Tree...who's at the bottom? *Jesse.* And next is his son...*David,* then his son...*Solomon,* yes. And at the top is...*Jesus!* yes, and under Jesus is his mother...*Mary!* Yes. Here's a famous stained-glass Jesse Tree in Chartres Cathedral in France:

The kings run up the middle from Jesse to Mary, and the prophets are on the sides.

Back to Mary. Luke writes: "And the angel came in unto her" that's me, I'm Gabriel. [I see a girl daydreaming in the back] I have huge rainbow-colored wings and my face shines like the sun. [I walk back to the daydreamer, get down on one knee, throw my hands out toward her and proclaim] "Hail, full of grace, the Lord is with thee: blessed art thou among women!" Where have y'all heard that before? *In the Hail Mary!* Yes, the prayer quotes Gabriel. And how does our volunteer Mary feel about this? *She thinks it's weird!* Ha! I bet! Genuflecting and saying "hail" is not how you'd greet a girl, but a queen, someone who was superior to you. Luke says, "But she was greatly troubled at the saying, and considered in her mind what sort of greeting this might be. [And I say to my volunteer] "Do not be afraid, Mary, for you have found favor with God. And behold, you will conceive in your womb and bear a son, and you shall call his name Jesus." Wow...Gabriel sounds like Isaiah, when he prophesied, "Behold, a virgin shall conceive and bear a son, and shall call his name Immanuel." Now Mary was a good Jewish girl, and she probably knew that prophecy, and recognized that Gabriel was quoting from it. How do you feel about having a baby, Mary? *I don't know!* Right! Mary said to the angel, "How shall this be, since I have no husband?" That's a good, practical question, isn't it, Mary. "And the angel said to her, "The Holy Spirit will come upon you, and the power of the Most High will overshadow you; therefore the child to be born will be called holy, the Son of God."

Y'all tell me, if it's a hot summer day, and a cloud overshadows you, how do you feel? *Good!* Why? *'Cause I'm in the shade.* Yes, the cloud protects you from the hot sun, and it protects only who is under it. Y'all remember the God Box that the Israelites carried on the poles with the angels on top [I draw and talk], what's it called? *The Ark!* Yes, the Ark of the Covenant. When they wandered in the desert, a cloud would *overshadow* the Ark in the Meeting Tent; [draw & talk] we call it the Glory Cloud. The Hebrew word is *Shekhinah*, which is *not* the name of a hip-hop star as far as I know...it's the cloud. You don't have to remember the word *Shekhinah*; I just like to say it. *Shekhinah.*

In the Bible, Hebrew says "cover" for "overshadow," so when the Shekhinah *overshadowed* the Ark, it *covered* it, sort of like the way Elijah covered Elisha with his cloak to show Elisha was chosen and protected. So when Gabriel tells Mary, "The Holy Spirit will *come upon* you, and the power of the Most High will *overshadow* you," he's reminding her of how the cloud overshadowed the Ark. So here's Mary [draw & talk], that dot is Jesus...here's the Holy Spirit.

OK tell me: here's the Ark with the God stuff in it, overshadowed by the...*Shekhinah!*, yes, the Glory Cloud. Over here we have Mary overshadowed by the Holy Spirit. What's she got in her? *Jesus?* Yes, Mary's got not just God's *stuff* in her, but God Himself. She's got more God in her than the Ark does. Now if the God Box is the Ark of the *Old* Covenant, what might we call Mary? *Umm...the Ark of the* New *Covenant?* Yes, genius! Mary's the New Ark.

Then Gabriel said, "And behold, your kinswoman Elizabeth in her old age has also conceived a son (that sounds like Isaiah, too)...For with God nothing will be impossible." And Mary said, "Behold, I am the handmaid of the Lord; let it be done to me according to your word." Y'all may remember this Latin phrase: [on the board] 'Fiat lux' from Genesis...no? OK, what's 'light' in Spanish? *Luz!* Yes, and *luz* comes from the Latin word *lux*, so *lux* means...*light.* Yes. And in Genesis the creation line about light is...*let there be light!* Yes, so 'fiat lux' means...*let there be light!* Yes, more like 'let light be done.' In Latin Bibles when Mary says 'let it be done to me' she says, 'Fiat mihi.' [on the board] Mary uses the same word 'fiat' that God spoke to create light and everything else. Why's that? *'Cause Jesus is like light?* Yes, sort of. Sometimes we call Jesus the 'Light of the World.' When Mary says 'fiat' like God did, it reminds me that what she's agreed to, having this baby, will be as significant as God making light, creating the world.

What's this whole story called, when Gabriel announces to Mary she'll be having a miracle baby? *The Immaculate Conception?* No, that's when Mary was conceived. Think: an announcement...*the Annunciation!* Yes. What a gimme that was.

Let's remember all those women we've learned about from Sarah and Hannah right up to Elizabeth. Their babies were miraculous because they were all unable to conceive. And now Mary is also going to have a miracle baby, not because she's too old, but because...*she's too young?* Well, sort of. She isn't married yet. But she stands at the head of a long line of miraculous mothers, and her baby will be the most miraculous of all.

Now Mary's baby is Jesus who's going to grow in her, live in her for 9 months. Baby John has a 6-month head start on Baby Jesus, and Mary decides to visit her cousin Elizabeth. This visit is called...the...*Visitation?* Yes. John's getting to be a load, and Jesus is just a dot, so Elizabeth can't get around like young Mary, who can help her out. Luke says, "When Elizabeth heard the greeting of Mary, the babe leaped in her womb; and Elizabeth was filled with the Holy Spirit." Have y'all ever looked at a pregnant woman's stomach and seen the baby moving inside? *Eww, gross.* That's not gross, it's great! You can see the baby poking its elbows and knees out, it's very cool. People put videos on YouTube of babies kicking their moms from the inside. I bet y'all were all momma-kickers before y'all were born. Your moms know just what Elizabeth felt when John jumped around in her. Time for the rubber babies! [out they come] Just imagine John and Jesus being in their moms and about this size. Look, John's jumping around like a little monkey in Elizabeth's tummy! Then Elizabeth said to Mary, "Blessed art thou among women, and blessed is the fruit of thy womb!" Where've you heard that? *In the Hail Mary!* That's right. The prayer first quotes Gabriel, now it quotes Elizabeth. "And why is this granted me, that the mother of my Lord should come to me?" Now who is Elizabeth's Lord? *God?* Yes, and so Mary is the mother of...*God?* Yes, that's why we say "Holy Mary, Mother of God, pray for us." But some people say Mary wasn't God's mom, that she was only the mother of Jesus' human parts. But you can't divide Jesus into pieces: Mary is the mother of Jesus' whole person even though that person was God, who created her. We can't understand it: it's...a...*mystery!* Yes! By the way, is it ok to ask people to pray for us? *Yes.* So is it ok to ask Mary to pray for us? *Yes!* Sure, just like the prayer says. If I pray to Mary, and ask her to pray for me, am I worshiping her? *I don't think so.* What am I doing? *Just asking for a favor?* Yes. Not all prayer is worship: some is just communication, or saying thanks, or asking for a favor, as you said.

About 3 months after Mary visited her older cousin, Elizabeth had her baby, John. [draw] He's swaddled, see? When she and Zechariah took him to the Temple to be circumcised, Zechariah made a little prophecy about John. *What's circumcise?* It was a ritual for baby boys before there was Baptism. *Well, what ritual?* Ask your parents. Zechariah said, "you, child, will be called the prophet of the Most High; for you will go before the Lord to prepare his ways, to give knowledge of salvation to his people in the forgiveness of their sins... And the child grew and became strong in spirit, and he was in the wilderness till the day of his manifestation to Israel." We'll see how John fulfilled this prophecy in a couple of weeks, this is a good stopping point.

See you back here in two weeks! *Are we going to have a Christmas party?* You mean during classtime? No indeed, but let's all bring fun stuff to eat, we'll have an un-party. And *of course* I'll see y'all at Mass next Wednesday for the Immaculate Conception. Come tell me hello afterwards and I'll say nice things about you to your parents.

Praised be Jesus Christ! *Now and forever!*

Class over!

Chapter Fifteen: The Sinless Tummy

(Gospels 2)

We do not have games or crafts or movies or parties of any kind in Wednesday Sunday School. All class time is...class time. Whatta concept. These children will be graduating from high school in 6 more years; babydays are slap out the window. But during the Christmas class the kids can eat snacks and drink pop; that's called an unparty. I lose about 20 minutes of productive time to unparty inefficiency, but even Scrooge let Bob Cratchit take the afternoon off on Christmas Day. And most of the class material is Christmas-related, and they are good kids, and well...I'm weak.

"Hey, it's almost Christmas; what season is it? *Winter?* Not yet. *Fall?* No, I mean what *Church* season? *Advent.* Yes, which means *Arrival*. I was thinking this week about the first Advent, when Mary was waddling around [I do so] with a huge stomach, saying, "Joseph, I am *so* ready to have this baby." Advent is a time of expectation, like "O come, O come, Em-ma-a-an-u-el," but I never really thought about Mary being *tired of waiting* and wanting to get it done. That's how my wife and daughter-in-law are; I think all mothers have their own personal Advent season every time they are pregnant.

Ark of the New Covenant

Y'all remember last class we were talking about Mary, and the Immaculate Conception came up? *Yes.* It's related to Baby Jesus and Christmas. Which reminds me I didn't see any of you at Mass last Wednesday, but I know you young'uns can't drive yourselves to church. Anyway, let's think a bit about the Immaculate Conception. Who was immaculately conceived? *Jesus!* Well, yes, he was. Let me ask it this way: who is honored by the feast of the Immaculate Conception? *Mary.* Yes. It's not about when *Jesus* was conceived without sin, but about...*when Mary was conceived without sin.* Yes. It's about Mary growing in *her* momma, not Jesus growing in Mary. OK, let's review some [on the board goes the Ark of the Covenant & pregnant Mary to the right]: here's the Ark of the Old Covenant and ...*the Ark of the New Covenant.* Yes. The old Ark contains God's *stuff*; the New Ark contains...*God!* Yes. What's more precious and holy: God's stuff, or God Himself? *God Himself.* Yes. Now let's look at the Old Ark for a second. It wasn't just some old box the Israelites kept pots in. It was made of expensive wood and the inside was lined with gold. It was the finest, purest, most precious container they could make. And how did they move the Ark around? *They carried it on poles.* Yes, so they wouldn't touch it. Why would they not want to touch the Ark? *Cause it was important?* Yeah, sort of. People felt unworthy to touch the Ark because of their sins; the Ark was set apart from sinful things. Y'all know the nuns we have in our parish? *Yes.* Well, suppose some young man thought one of them was cute, and asked her to go on a date, go out dancing. *That'd be weird!* Yes, but why...nuns aren't married. *Nuns don't do that after they're nuns!* Right, they are set apart, like the Ark, or Samuel. They're reserved for God by their own choice. And Mary freely chose to be set apart, too, and be the Mother of God.

Now, the Ark never contained anything but the jar of manna, Aaron's staff, and the Commandments. Can you imagine if the Ark was empty, and I came along and wanted to keep my shoes in it? *That'd be wrong!* Suppose they were brand-new shoes? *No!* Suppose they were *golden* shoes? *Umm...no!* Why not? *Cause it's for God's stuff, not regular stuff.* Right. The Ark is permanently set apart for God's stuff, *even if it's empty.* Now here's Mary, the...*New Ark!* Yes. What's in her? *Jesus.* Yes, who is...*God.* Yes. Now we know that God is more valuable than his Stuff. And we know how much respect the Israelites had for the Ark. So how much respect might we have for Mary? *More!* Yes, way more. Now was that stuff in the Ark perfect? *Perfect?* Yeah...would you expect anyone to worship the pot of manna? *I don't think so.* Me neither...even if it's God's Stuff it's still just stuff. Was the stuff in Mary perfect? *It wasn't stuff, it was Jesus!* Right, who is perfect. So do we worship what was in the New Ark? *Yes.* So which Ark should get more respect? *The New one!* Yes.

Now tell me, are we born in sin? *Yes.* Why? *'Cause Adam and Eve sinned!* Yes, we inherit that original sin from our parents...what's it called? *Umm...Original Sin?* Yes. I thought I'd trick you on that, y'all're too smart. Do our parents create us? *Yes?* Yes, with God's help. We inherit sin though our parents because we're made from them. Tell me, who was Jesus' Father? *God the Father?* Yes. Does he have a body? *No.* Is God a sinner? *Well, isn't God perfect?* Yes, just checking. And Jesus' mom was? *Mary!* Who had...a...*body'n'soul!* Yes. So if she was sinful...*Jesus would get it from her?* That would make sense.

Jesus Had a Belly Button

OK what's this? [I pull up my shirt enough to show my belly button] *Ha, that's your belly button!* Uh-huh...what's it for? *Nothing.* Well, what was it for before I was born? *It was the thing... the umbilical cord!* Yes, like so. [I draw a fetal Jesus and connect it to Mary's tummy with an umbilical cord]

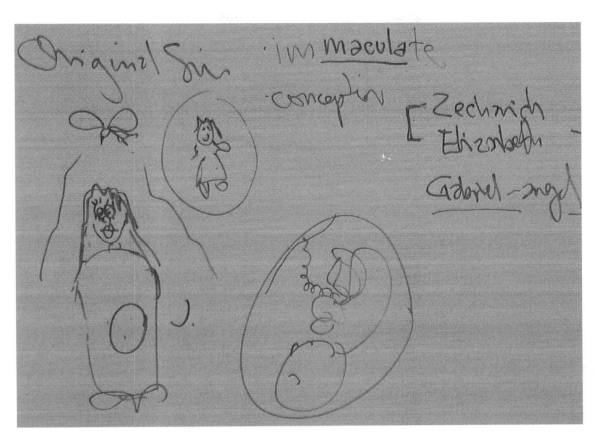

Let's imagine I'm baby Jesus. Do I breathe while I'm in Mary? *No.* Do I eat? *No.* Drink? *No.* Right. Everything I get comes from Mary. We are as close to being one thing as you can get. Mary breathes, eats, & drinks for both of us, and she shares all that with me while I'm growing inside her, just like all mothers do. Now imagine perfect baby Jesus so completely joined to his mom...how could that work if she were a sinner like me? *That'd be weird.* Yes; and we're made of a... *body'n'soul!* Yes, so if our souls are messed up by sin... *our bodies are too.* Yes. And if Mary's soul were stained by sin...*her body was too.* Yes. And she would not have been a very good Ark for Jesus. Imagine I'm a good Israelite back when they were making that beautiful Ark. I come up with a nice box. I say, hey y'all don't need to make a special box, my new washing machine came in this one, it's very sturdy. *They didn't have washing machines!* Pretend they did! What would they say? *They'd say no!* Right, a regular container won't do for holding something special. And remember, Jesus floating in Mary's tummy was much closer to her than the jar of manna was to the Old Ark, just sitting there for centuries. If Mary were sinful, body'n'soul, how would Jesus get oxygen and nutrition from her without also getting sin? *He couldn't.* Right. So the Church teaches that Mary was conceived in *her* mom without sin, and never sinned, so she'd be a good Ark for God to live in for 9 months. And look, one last thing. [I put a dot on Mary's tummy] This is Mary's egg, the one that's going to become Jesus. If she were a sinner, body'n'soul, then...*the egg has sin in it?* Yes, it's part of her body. So how are you gonna get that sin out before Jesus is conceived? *Well, God can do whatever He wants.* Yes, you are right: God could make Jesus be conceived without sin any way He wanted to. God never *has* to do something in a particular way. But what's better: to take a sinful egg and clean it off right before Jesus' conception, or just have it always have been clean from the get-go? *From the get-go!* Right. So those are the two main ways I think about Mary being sinless from the first moment she existed in her momma: Mary's sinless tummy for God to grow in, and a sinless bit of her to make Jesus from.

Now, not only was Mary conceived without sin, but the Church teaches that she *never* sinned. Somebody tell me why Adam and Eve could die. *They sinned!* Yes. St. Paul said the wages of sin is death. But if Mary never sinned, how could she die? *I don't think she died.* So what happened instead? *She just went to heaven.* Yes, did she launch herself up there? *Didn't God bring her there?* Yes. We say she was *assumed* into heaven; the feastday for that is called...*the Assumption.* Yes. She didn't *ascend* under her own power like Jesus did. The Greek-speaking churches call the Assumption the *Dormition* [on the board]. Somebody digame what *dormir* means in English. *Sleep?* Yes, so the Dormition suggests that Mary didn't *die* to go to heaven, she... *went to sleep?* Yes.

Old and New Eves

Now, we know Mary's the New Ark. But There's Something Else About Mary...do y'all get that? *Get what?* Never mind. [I draw a sad Eve beside Mary] Who is this sad woman? She's in the Bible. *Elizabeth?* Ooh, good guess, but no. *Mary?* No... she's maybe the saddest woman in the whole universe...look, she's wearing some kind of animal skin...*Eve!* Yes, it's Eve. Eve feels terrible because when the devil tempted her with the fruit, she could've said no, right? *Yes!* 'Cause she had...*free will!* Yes. But she said yeah, sure, ok I guess; ate the fruit and then her dimwit husband had a bite, too. So now we're all miserable living in a sinful world and suffering on Wednesday nights. Anyway, I saw a terrific picture a couple of days ago... I need a Mary! No, I used you last week! You daughter, get up here. And an Eve, yes, c'mon. Y'all face each other. OK, Mary you are *way* pregnant...put your left hand in your hoodie pocket, poke it out so we can see that baby...good. Now Eve, you look sad because...*I ate the apple.* Yes, and wouldn't you love to be able to fix that? *Yes.* Now Mary, take Eve's hand...and put it on your tummy so Eve can feel your baby...who...is...*Jesus!* Yes. Class, would this make Eve feel better, to know Jesus is going to be born? *Yes.* Why? *'Cause Jesus will fix our sins?* Umm, sort of. Jesus will undo the damage of that first sin in the Garden. Eve, are you feeling better? *Yes.* OK, remember Mary is the New Ark; we also call her...? No guesses. Who's this? *Eve.* What Testament is she in? *The Old Testament.* Yes, and Mary is in...*theNewTestamentMaryistheNewEve!* Mega-genius, yes! Mary is called the New Eve. Eve, what bad thing did you freely agree to do? *Eat the apple!* Yes; and Mary, what *good* thing did you freely agree to do? *Have Jesus?* Yes. Mary & Eve, sit down. Through Eve we got a mess; through Mary...*the mess got fixed!* Yes. Trick question: could Mary have chosen not to have Jesus? *No, she had to.* Why? *So He could die and all.* So Mary didn't have any free will? God forced her? *No, but if she said no then Jesus wouldn't have been born.* Right. That's scary to imagine. But God *did* leave it up to Mary, just like he left it up to Eve. This shows how much God loves us: he leaves us free to make incredibly important choices that don't just affect us, but the whole world, the whole universe, even.

Now y'all have a look at this handout, it's what the girls were acting out:

Eve and Mary by Sr. Grace Remington O.C.S.O. Used with permission.

Y'all take that home and explain it to your parents.

Well, it looks like we're covering less material tonight because y'all insisted on wasting valuable class time eating junk food and drinking sugar water. Is that right? *Ha! Yes!* Philistines. *Huh?* Never mind.

Praised be Jesus Christ! *Now and Forever!*

Class over, see y'all after Christmas!

Chapter Sixteen: Bug Eater

(Gospels 3)

Matthew 1 & 2, Luke 2: Nativity, Isaiah prophecies, Magi, Christmas, Herod. Chosen people vs. Gentiles (Magi); refuge in Egypt. Jesus as a child in the Temple, 4th Commandment. Matthew 3, Mark 1, Luke 3, John 1: John the Baptist and the baptism of repentance, but not forgiveness. Drowning and cleansing.

Y'all remember from our last class before Christmas we had stopped at the birth of...*John the Baptist!* Yes, and now we're going to cover...*when Jesus was born!* Yes.Y'all know the story already so it won't take long. Tell me please, where did Jesus grow up? Oh, *do* come along: N-a-z- *Nazareth!* Yes. And where was he born? *Bethlehem.* Yes. Why were Joseph & Mary in Bethlehem? *Because that was where David was born?* Yes, genius, Micah's prophecy said the Messiah would be born in Bethlehem just like David. But why did *Joseph* have to go there? *Because the King said so.* Yes, the Roman emperor Caesar Augustus wanted a census taken, and Joseph was descended from David so he had to go there for the census. Tell me about Joseph & Mary in Bethlehem. *They had to stay in a stable 'cause there were no rooms.* Yes, and? *Mary had Jesus in the stable and put him in a manger.* Yes, and remember Isaiah's Christmas prophecies included an ox, an ass, and a manger, so it makes sense that they'd stay in a stable. What was Jesus wearing? *Huh?* Was he wearing a tuxedo? *No...something like...*he was swaddled, do y'all know what that is? *No.* It's when you wrap a baby up tight so he can't move. Do y'all know why parents do that? *So the baby won't hurt himself?* Yes, more please. *So his bones grow straight?* Mmm, maybe. It's to calm him down. When a baby is close to being born it's all very tight inside the mother and it's used to that cozy world where there's no room to stretch out. So when babies get upset, if you swaddle them so they can't move it calms them down. It's like being in their mommas again. When one of my children used to get upset, we'd swaddle him tight and put him in a dark room. He'd shut right up and look like an angel; and we could eat dinner in peace. Y'all remember that when you have babies.

So who came to see Jesus first? *Shepherds?* Yes, who were poor and smelled like sheep. Who told them to come? *Angels!* Yes. The poorest people came to see Jesus first. And who came later? *The Magi?* Yes, which means...*wise men.* Yes. Magi is where we get the word *magician.* But back then it meant they had special knowledge; they studied the stars and so...*they followed the Star.* Yes. They were foreigners, not Jews, but they came to see Jesus anyway. Before they went to Bethlehem, they stopped in Jerusalem to see...*umm, the King?* Yes, a mean king named...*Pericles?* Hey, interesting guess, but Pericles was Greek and not mean...y'all know this, H-e-r *Herod! King Herod!* Yes. The Magi told Herod they had come to see the new King...what did he think about that? *He didn't like it.* Because...*he was already the King.* Right. But Herod knew what had been foretold about Bethlehem by a prophet named Micah. Micah had said "But you, O Bethlehem

Ephrathah, who are too little to be among the clans of Judah, from you shall come forth for me one who is to be ruler in Israel." So he told the Magi, "Yes, I think he'll be born in Bethlehem. Go check it out, come back & tell me where he is so I can pay him homage too." So they followed the star and found Jesus. Tell me about it. *They brought him gifts.* Yes, what was first? *Gold.* Yes. What sort of person would get a gift of gold? *A King?* Yes. Next gift? *Umm...incense?* Yes, *frankincense,* which is crazy expensive...who'd that be for? No guesses? Who burns incense at Mass? *The priest?* Yes, just like in Solomon's Temple...so? *It's for a priest?* Yes. *Jesus is a priest?* Yes he is, good question. We'll see why later on. Last gift? *Myrrh?* Yes, do ya'll know what that's for? It's for preparing dead people for burial; it's as expensive as gold too. Why do they bring myrrh? *Because Jesus will die?* Yes.

Before they leave Bethlehem, the Magi dream that they shouldn't go back to Herod, so they go home without seeing him. Tell me the story. *Herod is mad and he wants to kill Jesus!* Why? *'Cause he wants to stay King!* Right, but he doesn't know who Jesus is, so? *He kills all the babies!* Yes, he "killed all the male children in Bethlehem and in all that region who were two years old or under, according to the time which he had ascertained from the wise men." These babies are the first martyrs; we call them the Holy Innocents. Had they been baptized? *No...was there baptism yet?* No, John the Baptist and Jesus were just babies themselves. So could they go to heaven? *No?* Good answer, but the Church teaches that unbaptized people who are martyrs are baptized by their *own blood.* Remember when a priest would sacrifice a bull in Leviticus, what did he do with the blood? *Sprinkle it on the people!* Yes, but martyred people's Original Sin is washed away by their own blood, not an animal's blood, or the water of Baptism. Yes? *But they couldn't go to heaven 'til Jesus died.* Yes, that's right.

And how did Jesus escape Herod? *An angel told Joseph to leave!* Yes, he took his family to Egypt until Herod died. Then they returned to live in...*Bethlehem?* No...*Nazareth!* Yes.

We don't know much about Jesus' childhood. There's just one story about the time he and his family went to Jerusalem for Passover, tell it please. *They were going back home and Jesus wasn't with them?* Yes, and? *They went back and found Jesus in the Temple.* Doing what? *Teaching the grownups!* Yes, discussing the Old Testament with the teachers, the rabbis. That's very unusual for a 12-year-old, as you 12-year-olds would know. I bet that years later when Jesus came back to Jerusalem as an adult, some of those rabbis at the Temple remembered him from when he was a smart kid. By the way, why weren't they discussing the *New* Testament? *It wasn't written yet!* Right!

When she found Jesus at the Temple, Mary said, "Son, why have you treated us so? Behold, your father and I have been looking for you anxiously." And he said to them, "How is it that you sought me? Did you not know that I must be in my Father's house?" What's the 4th Commandment? *Honor your Father & Mother!* Yes...why didn't Jesus do that? *He had to honor God first.* Yes, and who was Jesus' father? *God the Father!* Yes. God comes first, then our parents.

More Washing in the Jordan

Now we jump ahead to when John and Jesus are grown men. John lives in the desert, wears animal skins, doesn't cut his hair, doesn't drink alcohol, and eats bugs. Girls, how about it? *Eww, gross!* Boys? *Gross!* I think so, too, but there's no pizza in the desert. Who is John like? *Samson?* Yes, and...*Samuel?* Yes, Nazirites; and also like Elijah. So Jewish people would know John wasn't a nut, but a... *prophet.* Yes. John preached in the wilderness, "Repent, for the kingdom of heaven is at hand. Now John wore a garment of camel's hair, and a leather girdle around his waist; and his food was locusts and wild honey. Then went out to him Jerusalem and all Judea and all the region about the Jordan, and they were baptized by him in the river Jordan, confessing their sins." Remind me, the Old Testament was written in...*Hebrew!* Yes, and the New Testament was written in...*Latin?* No...*Greek!* Yes. Baptize is the Greek word for "immerse." So why was John baptizing in the river? *So they could go under the water!* Yes. It's a bit like drowning: the old sinful self dies and comes up reborn and clean. Y'all watch out, we'll learn a lot more Greek words the rest of this year. And remind me, who had been miraculously cleansed in the Jordan centuries before? *Umm... the guy with leprosy!* Yes, Naaman. All the people John baptized knew that story, and knew the Jordan was special.

Tell me please, what was King David's big sin? *He had an affair with the other man's wife and killed him!* Yes, he had an affair with Bathsheba, Uriah's wife. And did he just confess to God he was sorry? *No, he had to tell, ummm...*C'mon, N-a-t-h *Nathan!* Yes. Why did he have to confess out loud and not just pray? *'Cause he's a body'n'soul!* Yes, so he had to confess both in spirit and in flesh as the Bible might say. And why would people come from all over Judea and Jerusalem to confess their sins to John? Why didn't they stay home & confess to God? *'Cause they had to confess out loud to somebody!* Yes! And it's humbling to hike out of town, let everyone see you acknowledge your sins to this wild man of the desert, and get dunked in the river.

John was getting a lot of attention from everyone, so "priests and Levites from Jerusalem" came to see him. Because they made their living at the Temple dealing with peoples' sins, John was cutting in on their business, and aggravating them. The priests wondered if John might be the Messiah, or at least might *think* he was the Messiah. They asked John, "Who are you?" He confessed, "I am not the Christ." By the way, *Christ* isn't Jesus' last name. 'Christ' comes from the Greek word *Christos,* [on the board] which means 'Anointed One,' or 'Messiah.' So when you see the word *Christ,* think Messiah. "But he said no. And they asked him, "What then? Are you Elijah?" He said, "I am not." "Are you the prophet?" And he answered, "No." They said to him then, "Who are you? Let us have an answer for those who sent us. What do you say about yourself?" He said, "I am the voice of one crying in the wilderness, 'Make straight the way of the Lord,' as the prophet Isaiah said." John is starting to aggravate them: they want simple answers, but John won't give them any. He just quotes Isaiah, and expects them to figure it out on their own. This is very typical behavior for prophets like John and Jesus, who was also a prophet. Prophets give partial answers so their listeners have to do some work to understand what they say. Because if you have to figure out an answer...*you know it better?* Yes, and you remember it better. Y'all have to figure stuff out in class too, it's good for you.

Then John pulls out his flamethrower: "You brood of vipers! Who warned you to flee from the wrath to come? ...do not begin to say to yourselves, 'We have Abraham as our father'; for I tell you, God is able from these stones to raise up children to Abraham." Like other prophets, John is telling the priests & Levites, the special men who work in God's House, that being Chosen People, Sons of Abraham, won't save them from God's wrath. What's 'wrath'? *God's mad at them!* Yes. They need to repent like everyone else, but they're too proud to be baptized by John. And they sure feel insulted that John called them nothing but a mess of snakes. Then John says, "Even now the axe is laid to the root of the trees; every tree therefore that does not bear good fruit is cut down and thrown into the fire." What fire is that? *Hell?* Yes, and the trees? *People.* Yes. And the good fruit? *Doing good things!* Yes. So God isn't too concerned with who you are, but...*what you do!* Yes. And the axe will be cutting down the bad trees shortly. No doubt the priests & Levites leave in a huff.

The next day John was baptizing as usual [we act out this section] I'm John, you be Jesus, you're being baptized, and the rest of y'all are the crowd by the Jordan. Daughter, are you a sinner? *Yes.* Are you sorry for your sins? *Yes.* Are you repentant? *Yes.* OK down you go...and up. All done. Crowd, are her sins forgiven? *Yes!... No!* Uh-oh, that was a trick question! Who can forgive sin? *God.* Yes. Not John. John's job is to call people to *repentance*, he can't take their sins away...who can? *Jesus!* Yes. So what's the baptism for? *To show you are sorry?* Yes, John's baptism is symbolic. Baptism doesn't wash away sin yet. John said "I baptize you with water for repentance, but he who is coming after me is mightier...he will baptize you with the Holy Spirit and with fire." But I bet the people wanted to experience a miracle like Naaman, but have the water wash away not *physical* sickness, but... *spiritual sickness?* Yes, which is... *sin!* Yes. Daughter, you can join the crowd.

Then John saw his cousin Jesus coming toward him, and said, "Behold, the Lamb of God, who takes away the sin of the world!" Tell me crowd, what do Jews use lambs for? *Eating?* I mean, why do they *need* lambs? *For sacrificing!* Yes. Why do they need to sacrifice? *'Cause they're sinners!* Yes. Does God sin? *Ha, no!* So why does God need a lamb? *Well, he doesn't.* So who's this Lamb of God for? *For us?* Yes. And this one lamb will "take away the sins of the world." What kind of lamb could do that? *A perfect one!* Yes. So God's lamb is a perfect gift. Why does he give it to us? *Because he loves us?* Yes. We know all this now, but that day by the Jordan people probably went home telling their families that John had made a very odd prophecy about his cousin.

Jesus, come on into the water...why are you here? *To be baptized.* Crowd, is Jesus a sinner? *Ha, no!* In fact, "John would have prevented him, saying, "I need to be baptized by you, and do you come to me?" But Jesus answered him, "Let it be so now; for thus it is fitting for us to fulfill all righteousness." Then he consented." Jesus isn't being humble for *his* sins...*but for ours!* Yes. OK cousin, down you go....and up. "And when Jesus was baptized, he went up immediately from the water, and behold, the heavens were opened and he saw the Spirit of God descending like a dove, and alighting on him; and lo, a voice from heaven, saying, "This is my beloved Son, with whom I am well pleased." Who's the voice? *God the Father!* Yes, now tell me whom God is quoting here. *What?* Who said "this is my servant in whom I am well-pleased"? *Jeremiah?* Close, it was Isaiah. So God is borrowing from Isaiah so the people will connect Isaiah's prophecy to Jesus. Who's the dove? *The Holy Spirit!* And my cousin? *God the Son!* Who all make? *The Trinity!* Yes. And John says, "I have seen and have borne witness that this is the Son of God." And the people thought, "ooh, the Bug Eater just called his cousin the Son of God! I wonder what he means?"

After all this baptism excitement, where does Jesus go? *To the desert!* Yes, for how long? *40 days!* Yes which is a time of… *preparation!* Yes. Preparation for Jesus to do what? *To go around and do miracles!* Umm…yes!

Debutantes' Ball

Digame por favor, cual es un quinceañera? What's a quinceañera? *It's when a girl has a big party when she's fifteen.* Yes, it shows she's a young woman on her way to be her own person, not just a girl under her parents' wings. In English we'd say it's a coming-out party. Between Thanksgiving and New Year's there are balls where young women called *debutantes* are presented to society in a similar way. Well, Jesus' baptism is like that: he's a grown man about 30 years old, but he's led a quiet, private life until now. But John has said prophetic things about Jesus in front of crowds of people, who will all be talking about Jesus to their families and neighbors. When he returns from his 40 days of fasting and preparation for what we call his public ministry, his life will never be quiet or private again.

That's it for tonight; next week Jesus begins his public ministry. Yes, honorary son? *Why don't boys get parties like that?* Like debutantes, with photos in the paper? *Yeah!* Because women have the babies, and we don't. So we treat them special. Right, daughters? *Right!*

Praised be Jesus Christ! *Now and forever!*

Class over!

Chapter Seventeen: Right Through the Roof (Gospels 4)

John 2: Cana, wedding feast, Mother's intercession (Bathsheba), no rebuke, 4th commandment. Food miracle, best for last, abundance, alcohol. John 4: Jesus' disciples baptize, but not Jesus: delegating authority to ministers. Luke 4: Jesus reads in synagogue, everyone goes nuts, Zarephath, Naaman, salvation not limited to Chosen People who have no guarantees. Matthew 9, Mark 2, Luke 5: Healing the paralytic: action required, not just faith. Sickness & sin, body & soul. Intercession. Authority and power to forgive sin.

Last week we saw John announce that Jesus was the Lamb of God who would take away the sins of the world; not that anyone understood exactly what that meant. I don't think even John understood it all that well, but prophecies usually aren't so obvious that we, and even the prophets, don't have to think about them, figure them out.

Tell me please, if the President were going to visit Greenville, would he just drive down from DC, park on Main Street, get out and start to shake hands with people? *Huh?* C'mon, new topic. Answer the question. *No, there'd be a lot of people around him.* Yeah, like who? *Secret Service guys!* OK, so they would all show up in a bus together? *No, the bodyguards come first and check things out.* Yes. When an important person comes to visit, other people come ahead of him to get things ready, to "prepare the way" as John the Baptist said. That's what John did, get people ready for Jesus. In the Eastern churches they call him John the Forerunner; I like that. But now Jesus has started his public ministry, and John's job is done. In fact, two of Jesus' first followers, his first two apostles Andrew & John (not the Baptist) came to him from John the Baptist. A bit later, "Jesus and his disciples went into the land of Judea; there he remained with them and baptized. John also was baptizing at Aenon near Salim, because there was much water there; and people came and were baptized." So both Jesus and John were baptizing at the same time; and people said to John, "he who was with you beyond the Jordan, to whom you bore witness, here he is, baptizing, and all are going to him." John answered, "I am not the Christ, but I have been sent before him (the Forerunner, see?)...He must increase, but I must decrease." (John 3) So John's ministry is winding down and he is content. Notice that Jesus is baptizing along with his disciples; they are sharing that responsibility.

But later on, "when the Lord knew that the Pharisees had heard that Jesus was making and baptizing more disciples than John (although Jesus himself did not baptize, but only his disciples), he left Judea and departed again to Galilee." (John 4). The Pharisees were starting to worry more about Jesus than John. Notice that Jesus isn't doing the baptizing now...who does it? *The disciples?* Yes. I suppose he's trained them well enough to take care of business. So if you went to Jesus to get baptized, what would he say? *Go get them to baptize you?* Yes. What does that tell you about the disciples? *Jesus put them in charge?* Yes. Jesus authorized them to do this work for him. You can't go straight to Jesus anymore to get baptized...you have to...*go to his guys!* Ummm, yes, the men that Jesus *authorized.* Later on we'll see other examples of how Jesus put the apostles in charge of his new Church.

Intercession at Cana

Can anyone tell me Jesus' first miracle? *He turned the water into wine.* Yes, at a funeral? *No, a wedding!* Yes, at the reception; where'd this happen...y'all may know this...*Cana!* Yes. Were they drinking Cokes at the party? *No, wine, but they ran out!* And? *They told Mary.* Yes, and Mary said to Jesus "I'm your mom and I'm telling you, make this right." *Huh? I don't think she told him what to do.* No, she didn't. She just said, "They have no wine." But then Jesus says, "Woman, how does your concern affect me? My hour is not yet come." Jesus isn't fussing, he's just giving Mary a chance to set a good example for the rest of us. What does she say to the wine stewards? *Do what Jesus says.* Yes, "do whatever he tells you;" that would be good advice for anyone, to do what Jesus tells you. So then? *They fill up big jugs with water.* Yes, and? *Then they taste it, and it's wine.* Yes, the best wine they've ever had; and there were 6 jugs, each one could hold about 20 gallons of water. So Jesus made way more wine than they started with, and better wine, too. That's how God blesses people: with more than they imagined. My life is like that: I've been blessed better than I could have imagined for myself. And did the hosts go ask Jesus for this big fat favor? *No, Mary did.* Yes. That's called *intercession*, like when Moses asked God not to wipe out the Israelites for worshiping the Golden Calf. God the Father and Jesus both did favors for people who didn't even ask for the favor, because another faithful person asked *for* them. And that still happens today as we'll see.

Now, when Jesus changed water into wine, he was hinting at something he'd do later. What did he do with wine at the Last Supper? *Changed it into his blood?* Yes. I bet the apostles thought, "Well, if he turned water into wine at that wedding a few years ago, he can turn this wine into his blood." Jesus first works miracles that people *can* see, so they'll believe it when he works miracles later that...*they can't see?* Yes. Physical miracles prepare people for spiritual miracles. Let's look at a great example.

Visible & Invisible Miracles

Hey, I need two sturdy volunteers, you and you get up here, I volunteered you...no whining. OK, now daughter, you volunteer next. Lie down over there on the floor. *What?* Lie down, it's carpet, it's clean. Don't be fastidious. *What's fastidious?* It means fussy. Lie down. *Why?* You're paralyzed, all you can do is lie down, stop arguing with Jesus. *You aren't Jesus!* That's right, but I'm playing Jesus right now. Hey y'all, what is this story we're about to do? *When Jesus heals the paralyzed man!* That's right! So you're the paralyzed man, lie down. *But I'm a girl!* Yes I know...you're light so these two friends of yours can pick you up. C'mon y'all, why do they pick him up? *To put him through the roof!* Yes. OK you two, get ready to pick up your friend...don't pick him up yet! You're still outside the house where Jesus is. Paralyzed man, is Jesus a miracle worker? *Yes.* Why don't your friends just stand out here and pray for Jesus to fix you? *Umm...I don't know.* That's OK...friends, why do you think you have to go through the roof? *Cause it's crowded?* Yes. Let me ask it this way: why do y'all have to get your friend right in front of Jesus? If Jesus is the son of God, he must already know you're out here, right? *Yes.* In fact, why didn't you just stay home and pray instead of toting your poor friend across town in the hot sun? Anybody in the crowd? No guesses...it's a tough question. Let's move on. The Bible says: "And they came, bringing to him a paralytic. And when they could not get near him because of the crowd, they removed the roof above him, and when they had made an opening, they let down the bed on which the paralytic lay. OK two friends, go through the roof and put Mr. Paralysis in front of Jesus...hey, you're interrupting my teaching, I'm busy! *We're sorry!* That's ok, maybe I can turn this into a teachable moment. Mr. Paralysis, what do you want? *I want to be healed!* Yeah? From what exactly? *Well, I'm paralyzed, fix that.* Two friends, what do you want? *Well, the same thing, heal him please.* Crowd, whatcha want? *Heal him!* Let's see what happens: "...they let down the bed on which the paralytic lay. And Jesus saw their faith..." Crowd, look at these two friends: do they have faith in Jesus? *Yes!* How do you know...can you see their souls? *No we saw them make a hole in the roof and put their friend through.* Yes, you know they have faith because of...*what they did!* Yes. That's how Jesus *and everyone else* could see their faith. Body'n'Soul go together. Crowd, can you imagine the paralyzed man's friends thinking, "Let's lower our paralyzed friend through the roof so Jesus will forgive his sins?" *That sounds weird.* Yes. Everyone expects Jesus to heal the man's *body;* that's why they put him through the roof.

So Jesus looks down at the paralyzed man and says what? *Get up and walk!* No! Trick question! I win again! Jesus said, "Son, your sins are forgiven." Mr. Paralysis, is that what you want, forgiven sins? Are you happy now? *Well, I guess so...but I'm still paralyzed.* Oh. I'm sorry, I must've fixed the wrong thing! Friends, crowd, how about it: good news? *I guess so.*

But "...some of the scribes said to themselves, "Why does this man speak thus? It is blasphemy! Who can forgive sins but God alone?" And they are right! Could John the Baptist forgive sins? *No!* Elijah? *No!* Isaiah? *No!* Right. And we know that Jesus came to free us from.....*sin?* Yes, Jesus could forgive sins, take away sins. But like the scribes said, only God can forgive sin. So Jesus...*must be God?* Yes, or at least acting with God's *authority.* But watch me now: "Your sins are forgiven, Mr. Paralytic!"...see any difference? *No.* Mr. Paralytic, do you *feel* any different? *No.* So can any of you tell if Jesus *really* forgave his sins or not? *No.* Right. It's an invisible miracle, forgiving sins. Why would it be hard for the crowd, or any human being, to believe in an invisible miracle? *'Cause we can't tell it really happened.* Yes, we want some physical evidence, because we're made of a... *BodynSoul!* Yes. But sins are invisible...it's a problem.

So now Jesus asks a question. That's what Rabbis and teachers do. They don't just *answer* questions; they *ask* them, and make people think. It's just like being in Wednesday Sunday School. Jesus says, "Which is easier, to say to the paralytic, 'Your sins are forgiven,' or to say, "Rise, take up your pallet and walk?" Well? *Your sins are forgiven.* Why? *Because nobody can tell if you did anything or not.* Yes. And so the harder thing to say is...*get up and walk!* Yes, because...*if he doesn't walk people know Jesus was just saying stuff!* Yes! "But that you may know that the Son of Man has *authority on earth* to forgive sins, I say to you, rise, take up your pallet and go home." And? *He gets up and goes home!* Yes! Go on home, Mr. Used-to-be-Paralyzed; well, back to your desk. Do you feel any different? *Yes!* Show us your new jumping skills...that's it! I bet you believe in Jesus now even if you didn't know who he was 15 minutes ago. So Jesus has worked a physical miracle, cured a paralyzed man; crowd, do you think maybe Jesus can forgive sins too? *Yes!* Because...*we saw him jump!* Uh-huh. Jesus works these *visible* miracles to help us believe in the...*invisible ones!* Yes, and this won't be the only time.

Tell me again, why do people die, get sick, have zits, all that bad stuff? *Because of sin.* Yes, back in...*Eden.* Yes. Now, how exactly did Jesus make this man's arms & legs start working all of a sudden? *I don't know, it's just a miracle.* Yes, but let's think a bit. Did Jesus first say, "I heal you from your paralysis"? *What?* Did Jesus first heal him physically? That's what people were expecting, right? *Yes.* But what did Jesus heal first? *Well, he forgave his sins.* Yes, what kind of healing is that? *Huh?* Is that physical healing, to have your sins forgiven? *No, it's spiritual, your soul.* Right. Jesus was making a point: the man's *physical* sickness was related to...*his umm, spiritual sickness?* Yes, genius, and spiritual sickness is called....*sin!* Yes. But even if the paralytic got his sins fixed and also his body fixed, would he still die? *Yes.* Would he still sin again? *Yes!* Creation is still messed up by sin. Now, one thing is for sure: everyone in the crowd is glad they aren't...*paralyzed!* Yes. Y'all felt sorry for him and you're happy that being paralyzed isn't your problem, thank ya God! But Jesus wasn't too concerned with the man's sick *body*; he was concerned about his...*sick soul!* Yes. That's why Jesus forgave his sins and didn't make a peep about his paralysis until the scribes complained. But crowd, even if your *bodies* weren't sick...*our souls are sick!* From...*sin!* Yes, so actually all of us sinners are as spiritually sick as the paralyzed man...maybe even *more* sick, it's hard to tell with sin, you can't see it. So instead of us just being glad the man was healed, we'd also be excited that Jesus could forgive our sins: "When the crowds saw it, they were afraid, and they glorified God, who had given such authority to men." What men today have authority to forgive sin? *Priests!* Yes, and the authority comes from...*Jesus!* Yes.

But what sort of sins could a paralyzed man have? *Suicide?* Yes, good guess. He might've been so miserable for so long he'd wish he were dead. Maybe he was angry with God, hated God because he was paralyzed, that'd be a serious sin, too. We can be sure he had sins that needed to be forgiven.

Body'n'Soul

OK, now let's go back to question y'all haven't answered yet...why didn't the paralyzed man's friends just stay home and pray? No guesses. Listen to this about Jesus: "...he had healed many, so that all who had diseases pressed upon him to touch him." Over and over in the Gospels we'll see people try to touch Jesus or his clothes to get healed. Are they superstitious? *No.* OK...so? Remind me why Moses had to hit the rock with a stick instead of just pray for water. *'Cause the power went through the stick!* Yes, *God's* power; and Isaac laid his hands on Jacob because...*his blessing went through his hands.* Yes, and so sick people would touch Jesus because...*Jesus' power went through his body?* Yes. So in the Gospels, God's power still goes through something physical, but it's not a stick, or manna, it's...*Jesus' body?* Yes. So why did the paralyzed man's friends go to all that trouble to plop him down through the roof instead of staying home and praying real hard? *To get him close to enough to touch Jesus!* Yes. The Gospels don't say if Jesus touched the man or not, but the man still heard Jesus through his ears and saw him with his eyes; maybe even smelled him with his nose. We call that having a physical encounter with Jesus. Jesus has a body and a soul, and we have...*a body and a soul, too!* Yes. So people who want to know, or *encounter*, Jesus completely want to do it in spirit and...*with your body?* Yes, physically. Now I need a genius to tell me how *we* can have a physical encounter with Jesus. *Well, God's in all of us?* Yes, but be more specific...it's at Mass...*oh, Communion!* Yes, why? *Because it's Jesus' Body and Blood!* Right. Just having a *spiritual* encounter is only half of the deal, as the paralytic's friends perfectly understood, *as well as everyone else in the Gospels who wanted a miracle.* Praying wasn't enough.

Another question: did the paralytic man have faith? Did he believe in Jesus? *Yes?... No?* Let me ask it this way: who do we *know* had faith? *His friends!* Yes. And Jesus healed the man because "he saw their faith;" he saw what they *did*, just like the crowd could see. Tell me again how the wedding party at Cana got new wine. *Jesus made it out of water.* Well, yes, but *why* did he work that little miracle? *Mary told him they didn't have any more wine!* Yes, Mary *interceded.* So what did the paralytic's friends do? *They interceded too!* Yes. We don't know if the Paralytic or the wedding party had faith in Jesus or not. But Mary and the paralytic's friends did, and that was enough. The Gospels are full of intercession stories, you'll see. And we still intercede for each other both in daily life, like "Honey, don't be too hard on Junior about not taking out the trash; he's feeling bad because he was teased at school today about his third nostril;" and in our faith life. Y'all remember my daughter almost died in a bad fall recently, and sustained serious brain damage; well, we ask people we know on earth to pray for her, and people in heaven too. I especially ask my grandmother in heaven to pray for Francie's complete healing. I ask Mary and my buddy saints to pray to Jesus for her healing too. Yes? *How do you know your grandma is in heaven?* Good question...I don't. But if she isn't, I believe Jesus lets another saint hear my prayers for intercession. We're all part of the same family. And if I pray to my grandma, do I worship her? *No, you're just talking I think.* Yes. Praying is communicating; it's not always worship. Whom do we worship? *God.* Yes. Not Mary or saints or grandmas. That reminds me, y'all know Pope John Paul 2, JP2? *Yes.* He died a few years ago from Parkinson's disease, which slowly destroys your nervous system so that your brain can't control your body. There's no cure. People just get worse & worse until they die. Many people think JP2's a saint, that is, he's...in...*heaven!* Yes. One way the Church figures out if someone is a saint is to see if the person in heaven intercedes for someone on Earth. In JP2's case, a French nun had Parkinson's disease just like the Pope; she prayed to JP2 for his intercession, and she was miraculously healed. So the Church concludes that he is indeed in heaven and interceded for her. *How do they know it was a miracle?* Good question. The Church does an investigation, doctors testify; it's a long process. Because of this miracle, JP2 is called *Blessed* John Paul 2. If one more miracle is attributed to him, the Church will declare him Saint John Paul 2. So intercession works; the paralytic's friends believed in it, and we can too.

Finally, this whole paralytic business aggravated the scribes. What's a scribe? *Someone who can write!* And...*read!* Yes. They were religious authorities, they worked at the temple along with the priests. And like the Pharisees, they knew the Scribe-tures, the Scriptures, very well, and made their living from it. So when Jesus shows he has more authority than they do, that's a problem for them. We'll see Jesus aggravate them even more on other occasions, but that's it for tonight.

Praised be Jesus Christ! *Now and forever!*

Class is over 15 seconds early!

Chapter Eighteen: Mr. Aggravation (Gospels 5)

Luke 4, Jesus reads in synagogue, everyone goes nuts. Zarephath, Naaman, salvation not limited to Chosen People, who have no guarantees. John 5, Matthew 12: Heal on Sabbath/ Rub grain on Sabbath/ Pharisees: cui bono Sabbath? [Commandment 3]. Matthew 8, Luke 9: Jesus heals leper, centurion's servant, Jairus' daughter, and demon-possessed son. Healing through intercession, action required, not just faith. Chosen people vs. Gentiles. Faith of the servant, daughter and son? Woman w/ hemorrhage: healing through physical media, action required, not just faith. Who touched me? Jesus working in the physical world.

- Y'all remember last week we covered a couple of Jesus' first miracles, such as...*making wine from the water*, yes, and...*healing the paralyzed man*. Yes. You may remember, in that story Jesus aggravated the scribes...why? *Because they said he couldn't forgive sins.* Yes; and by working the *physical miracle*, Jesus showed he had authority to work the...*spiritual miracle*, yes, which was...*forgiving sins!* Yes.

Jesus aggravated a lot of people over the 3 years of his public ministry, but they were aggravated because Jesus told the truth. But even average people could get angry with Jesus, not just scribes and Pharisees; let's look at an example.

After John baptized Jesus, Jesus spent 40 days in the desert fasting and preparing for his mission. While he was out of the public eye, people would have talked about John the Baptist fussing over Jesus at the Jordan: all that Lamb of God business, and the dove. So in Luke's Gospel, after Jesus leaves the desert he pays a visit to his hometown...*Beth...Nazareth!* Yes, and he goes to the synagogue on the Sabbath. Everyone is pleased to see the famous local boy, and he is invited to read from the Torah, like the way lectors read from the Bible at Mass. (Luke 4) Jesus reads a bit from his favorite prophet, Isaiah: "The Spirit of the Lord is upon me, because he has *anointed* me to preach good news to the poor. He has sent me to proclaim recovering of sight to the blind, to set at liberty those who are oppressed, to proclaim the year of the Lord." And he closed the book...and he began to say to them, "Today this scripture has been fulfilled in your hearing." And all spoke well of him, and they said, "Is not this Joseph's son?" The scripture reading sounds like good news: healing the blind, maybe some prophesying, Jesus saying he's anointed, the scripture is fulfilled...this ain't no ordinary Saturday! Now tell me, what's the Hebrew word for anointed? *Messiah?* Yes. Who gets anointed? *Kings...*yes, and...people like Elisha...*prophets?* Yes. So Jesus must be...*a king or a prophet?* Yes...or both. And in those days who was in charge of Judea? *Caesar?* Yes, who was...a banana...ha, the Roman emperor! Yes, and did the Jews enjoy being subjects of the emperor? *No!*

Because? *He took their money and stuff!* Yes, the Jews were oppressed, but they remembered when Israel was independent, and they were waiting for a...*Messiah*, yes, an Anointed One; in Greek, a Christos; a King like...*David!* Yes, or...*Solomon!* Yes, to "set at liberty those who are oppressed." When Jesus said that, who did the people at the synagogue think were the oppressed people who would be set at liberty? *Themselves!* Yes, that'd be nice news! No more Caesar and his taxes and soldiers. Everybody's feelin' alright.

But then Jesus says, "I tell you, there were many widows in Israel in the days of Elijah, when the heaven was shut up three years and six months, when there came a great famine over all the land; and Elijah was sent to none of them but only to Zarephath, in the land of Sidon, to a woman who was a widow." Tell me that story, we've had it in class. *She was starving but let him have some of her food so he made a miracle and she never ran out.* Yes. God had Elijah miraculously help a pagan woman, not one of the starving Chosen People in Israel.

And Jesus went on: "And there were many lepers in Israel in the time of the prophet Elisha; and none of them was cleansed, but only Naaman the Syrian." Tell it please. *He washed in the river 7 times and he wasn't a leper anymore.* Yes, so even though "there were many lepers in Israel," God saw fit to have Elisha miraculously heal a pagan.

"When they heard this, all in the synagogue were filled with wrath. And they rose up and put him out of the city, and led him to the brow of the hill on which their city was built, that they might throw him down headlong. But passing through the midst of them he went away." (all from Luke 4) One minute Jesus is the hometown boy, the next minute they're gonna throw him off a cliff! Why's that? No guesses? That's ok, even grownups don't always figure this out. Jesus is telling them that the good news he's proclaiming about liberation from oppression and so forth may not apply to them even though they're "Sons of Abraham," as John the Baptist would say. Jesus is saying that in the past, sometimes God gave miracles to pagans instead of Jews. Jesus is reminding everyone that God rewards people not because of *who they are*, their status, but by...*what they do!* Yes. Isaiah used to say this same thing; he aggravated people, too. And both Jesus and John would tell people a tree is judged good or bad by the fruits it produces: "for the tree is known by its fruit." Of course they're talking about...*people,* and the fruits are...*what you do.* Yes. We're made of a...*body'n'soul,* uh-huh, and if we do good things, then...*our souls are good.* Yes. Unless you're being deceitful, which of course is a sin.

What's the 3rd Commandment? *Huh?* Topic change, tell me please. *Don't use the Lord's name in vain?* Close, that's #2. *Keep holy the Lord's Day?* That's it! Let's see...for the first 6 days what did God do? *Make everything!* Yes, and then? *He rested!* Yes. The Hebrew word for 'rest' or 'cease' [from working] is *Shabbat.* What's a word we have for the Day of Rest? It's like Shabbat. *Umm...Sabbath?* Yes! On the 7th day, God *shabbated,* he...*rested.* Yes, because he was tired? *No, so we would rest.* Yes, he set the example, just like Jesus. Well, if I'm shabbating, resting on the Sabbath, can I cut the grass? *Yes.* Can I wash the car? *Yes.* Can I fix a bicycle? *I think so.* Suppose I hate to fix bikes or do yard work? *I don't know.* Go to the office? *I don't think so.* See, deciding what work is can be tricky; and the Jews had 39 rules for the Sabbath so they could be absolutely positive they were resting and not doing *any* work. And the Pharisees took all these rules very seriously. They'd busybody other people and say, "hey darlin' you can't be patching those pants on the Sabbath" or "don't sharpen that knife on the Sabbath." The Pharisees were obsessed with the rules. I can't imagine feeling restful by checking 39 rules. Anyway, one Sabbath day Jesus and the apostles were walking, and were hungry (Matthew 12). So they picked some wheat, and as they walked they were rubbing the grains hard between their hands like this to get the chaff off; chaff's the hard outside that people usually don't eat. "But when the Pharisees saw it, they said to him, "Look, your disciples are doing what is not lawful to do on the Sabbath." They meant that rubbing the wheat was preparing a meal, which is work. "He said to them, "Have you not read what David did, when he was hungry, and those who were with him: how he entered the house of God and ate the bread of the Presence, which it was not lawful for him to eat nor for those who were with him, but only for the priests?" When David was on the run from King Saul, he and his men were allowed to eat bread that had been saved for God in the Temple. Jesus is telling the Pharisees that he has as much authority as David. Then he says, "I tell you, something greater than the temple is here." And the only thing more important than God's temple would be...*God?* Yes, so Jesus is hinting in a roundabout way that he is God. And he ices the cake by saying, "For the Son of man is lord of the Sabbath." (all Matthew 12) Uh-oh, Jesus means his judgment about what counts for work on the Sabbath is more authoritative than the 39 rules and the Pharisees. So they are...*aggravated!* Yes! But they could've listened to Jesus and thought about what the point is of a day of rest, and whether so many rules really help or are just a burden that keeps people from resting. But their pride prevented them.

And "he went on from there, and entered their synagogue. And behold, there was a man with a withered hand. And they asked him, "Is it lawful to heal on the Sabbath?" so that they might accuse him." If a doctor heals someone on the Sabbath he's working, and the Pharisees want to trip Jesus up. They ask him a simple, direct question, "but He said to them, "What man of you, if he has one sheep and it falls into a pit on the Sabbath, will not lay hold of it and lift it out? Of how much more value is a man than a sheep! So it is lawful to do good on the Sabbath." Then he said to the man, "Stretch out your hand." And the man stretched it out, and it was restored, whole like the other. But the Pharisees went out and [discussed] how to destroy him."

This time Jesus aggravates the Pharisees by not answering their picky question about the 39 rules; instead he says there is a higher law, "to do good on the Sabbath," and heals the man. Jesus is teaching a lesson about God and excessive rules, but they don't want to listen. And like those people at the Nazareth synagogue, they are angry enough to kill him.

A couple more aggravation stories and we'll move on. Jesus was in Jerusalem, and healed a man who was sick and lying on a pallet. A pallet is a thin little mattress you can carry. "Jesus said to him, "Rise, take up your pallet, and walk." And at once the man was healed, and he took up his pallet and walked. Now that day was the Sabbath. So the [Pharisees] said to the man who was cured, "It is the Sabbath, it is not lawful for you to carry your pallet." Afterward, Jesus found him in the temple, and said to him, "See, you are well! Sin no more, that nothing worse befall you." I like this line, because the man was sick for 38 years; but what does Jesus think is worse than that? *Sinning?* Yes. Jesus is reminding the man that spiritual sickness, sin, is worse than physical sickness. Then "The man went away and told the Jews that it was Jesus who had healed him. And this was why the Jews persecuted Jesus, because he did this on the Sabbath. But Jesus answered them, "My Father is working still, and I am working." Now let's think a bit: in Genesis, God worked for...*6 days*...then...*rested!* Yes, and did he just *Shabbat,* relax, for all eternity after those 6 days? Well? *That sounds weird.* Yes, it does, and Jesus said his father is still working, so he must be. Tell me, how did God make light? Did he make a fire? *No, he just said let there be light.* And... *then there was light.* Yes, so if God *thinks* about something existing then...*it exists!* Yes. For God, to think of something is to create it. Jesus said once that we are each so precious to God that he knows every hair on our heads; but how does the hair exist in the first place? *God thinks about it?* Yes, God knows every hair because he is thinking about each one all the time. Suppose he just forgot about my hair one day...what would happen to my hair? *It... it'd disappear!* Yes. Actually there's a place on the back of my head where I think he's forgetting...oh well. So what is the work that God is still doing? *Thinking about everything!* So that...*it keeps existing?* Yes. One way I think about Jesus saying his Father is still working is that the Universe is made of the energy of God thinking about how much he loves his Creation, and us in particular. So if God still does good work all the time, even on the Sabbath, it's ok for us "to do good on the Sabbath" without checking 39 rules.

"This was why the [Pharisees] sought all the more to kill him, because he not only broke the Sabbath but also called God his Father, making himself equal with God." Once again, Jesus' critics want to protect their positions of authority, and would rather get rid of him than listen to him.

Now in addition to healing the man with the withered hand, Jesus healed lots of other people. For example there was a man named Jairus, whose daughter was deathly sick. Do you suppose he stayed home and prayed? *No he went and got Jesus!* Yes! "Now when Jesus returned, the crowd welcomed him, for they were all waiting for him. And there came a man named Jairus, who was a ruler of the synagogue; and falling at Jesus' feet he besought him to come to his house, for he had an only daughter, about twelve years of age, and she was dying." So what did Jesus do? *He went to their house!* Yes.

"As he went, the people pressed round him. And a woman who had had a hemorrhage for twelve years and had spent all her money upon physicians, and could not be healed by anyone came up behind him, and touched the tassel of his garment; and immediately her flow of blood ceased." (Mark 5, Luke 8) Do y'all know the word 'hemorrhage'? No? It's a Greek word that means 'blood-flow' in the sense of uncontrolled bleeding that's hard to stop. So...did the woman stay home and pray? *No she went to find Jesus and touch him.* Yes genius, and she didn't actually touch him, but touched what? *His clothes?* Yes, the tassel of his cloak. "...Jesus said, "Who was it that touched me?" When all denied it, Peter said, "Master, the multitudes surround you and press upon you!" So there's a crowd pressing against Jesus, but Jesus means he *particularly* felt someone touch him; that is, he felt a single person touch the tassel on the hem of his cloak. But how could he feel such a tiny touch amidst all these people? "Jesus said, "Someone touched me; for I know that power has gone out of me." [I pull out my chicken bone relic.} What's this? *Elijah's bone!* Close, *Elisha's* bone. Tell it to me. *The dead man fell on his bones and he came back to life.* Yes, so God's life-giving power went through...*the bones!* Yes. So it would be reasonable that God's healing power could go through Jesus, who wasn't even dead like Elisha. But I like how the power in this case went from God, through Jesus' body, through the cloak, down to the little tassel, into the woman's hand, and then healed her. The power went through *stuff, not just a holy person.* And nowadays even though Jesus is in Heaven, God's power still goes through stuff, like... well, you tell me. Tell me about the stuff that we have in Sacraments. *Water?* Yes, for...*Baptism?* Yes. Another, please. *Bread and wine.* Yes, which become...*Jesus' body'n'blood.* Yes. And we have oil at Confirmation and at Ordinations. How about Confession? *There's no stuff in Confession.* Oh yes there is! *Umm... the priest?* Yes, good. People are God's stuff, too; we're part of Creation.

"And when the woman saw that she was not hidden, she came trembling, and falling down before him declared in the presence of all the people why she had touched him, and how she had been immediately healed. And he said to her, "Daughter, your faith has made you well; go in peace." But her faith wasn't only what she believed, but...*what she did.* Yes, she *acted in faith* because body and soul...*go together.*

Back to Jairus' sick daughter: "While he was still speaking, a man from the ruler's house came and said, "Your daughter is dead; do not trouble the Teacher any more." But Jesus on hearing this answered him, "Do not fear; only believe, and she shall be well." Jesus doesn't want Jairus' faith to fade even if his daughter has died. "And when he came to the house...all were weeping and bewailing her; but he said, "Do not weep; for she is not dead but sleeping." And they laughed at him, knowing that she was dead. But taking her by the hand he called, saying, "Child, arise." And her spirit returned, and she got up at once; and he directed that something should be given her to eat." So Jesus touched her, and she came back to life. (Luke 9)

Now Jairus had faith, but he was like most people, who wanted Jesus to go with them to heal the sick child, or the possessed person, or the leper. They believed in Jesus, but still, it helped their faith to be able to see Jesus have a physical encounter with the afflicted person. We might say, "Hey Jairus, don'tcha have any faith? Jesus doesn't have to grab your daughter to heal her." And he'd say, "Sure, I have faith...but I'm afraid to go home without him...what if I get home by myself and she isn't better?" Our faith isn't as strong as we'd like it to be.

One more healing and we're done for tonight.

"As [Jesus] entered Capernaum, a centurion came forward to him, beseeching him and saying, "Lord, my servant is lying paralyzed at home, in terrible distress." What's a centurion? *A soldier.* Yes, from China? *No, a Roman soldier.* Yes. [*Centurion* goes on the board] How many men does he command? *100!* How do you know? *'Cause c-e-n-t means a hundred!* Yes, in what language? *Latin.* Yes, so how many cents are in a dollar? *100!* Years in a century? *100!* ¿Cómo se llama *hundred* in Español? *Cien!* [on the board] Yes, and in Italian, it's cento [on the board] ("chento"). So this officer is important, he orders 100 soldiers around all day long. And being in the occupying army, he can order Jesus around too if he feels like it. But instead of saying "Hey you Jewish healer, go fix my sick servant," he calls Jesus *Lord.* So what does that tell you? *That he thinks Jesus is important.* Yes. The Roman officer knows Jesus has more power than he does; maybe more than even Caesar. "And [Jesus] said to him, "I will come and heal him." Jesus knows people want to see him do the healing with their own eyes. "But the centurion answered him, "Lord, I am not worthy to have you come under my roof; but only say the word, and my servant will be healed." Where've you heard that before? *At...at Mass!* Yes, and when we get to the Mass later this year, y'all remember this story. Why doesn't the centurion feel like Jesus needs to hike over to his house? *'Cause he has faith?* Yes, lots of faith. The centurion says, "For I am a man under authority, with soldiers under me; and I say to one, 'Go,' and he goes, and to another, 'Come,' and he comes, and to my slave, 'Do this,' and he does it." What does he mean? *That he knows you don't have to see everything to know it will happen?* Yes. He knows how authority works, and that Jesus has authority. "When Jesus heard him, he marveled, and said to those who followed him, "Truly, I say to you, not even in Israel have I found such faith." Jesus means that this pagan soldier, who just takes Jesus at his word, has more faith than the Jews, who ought to know better than a Roman. Then he aggravates everyone, just like he did at the synagogue: "I tell you, many will come from East and West and sit at table with Abraham, Isaac, and Jacob in the kingdom of heaven, while the sons of the kingdom will be thrown into the outer darkness; there men will weep and gnash their teeth." People who come from East and West are foreigners, like the Roman. Who are the "the sons of the kingdom"? *The Jews?* Yes, the Chosen People. Like Isaiah, Jesus is reminding them that God may choose people who aren't Sons of Abraham to dine at the heavenly feast; while those who counted on getting in just because they were Chosen may be thrown out.

"And to the centurion Jesus said, "Go; be it done for you as you have believed." And the servant was healed at that very moment." (all Matthew 8) I love that story. I'd like to have the centurion's faith; but I'm more like Jairus.

Hey we still have a couple of minutes, we could get started on the Loaves and the Fishes miracle...ehhh, it'll be better to cover it all in one class next week. I guess y'all get out a couple of minutes early. I'm sorry! *That's OK!*

Praised be Jesus Christ! *Now and forever!*

Class over!

Chapter Nineteen: Pizza Buffet

(Gospels 6)

Matthew 14 & 15, Mark 6 & 8, John 6: Loaves & Fishes through Bread of Life discourse. Food miracle, delegated authority of apostles, eating flesh & blood, Mass, Apostles' faith vs. understanding. Jesus is already setting up the Church.

As I said last week, tonight we're doing the Loaves and Fishes; but first, who can tell me a story about Jesus and little kids? *There was a boy in the story about the Loaves and Fishes!* Yes, don't give it away yet! I mean *another* story with child*ren,* not just one kid. *When the children wanted to visit Jesus?* Yes, that's the one, tell it. *There were some kids who wanted to be with Jesus but they said no.* Who's "they"? *The apostles?* Yes, the *disciples,* which may include the apostles and other close followers of Jesus. Matthew's gospel says, "...children were brought to him that he might lay his hands on them and pray. The disciples rebuked the people..." Who brought the kids? *Umm, their parents?* Yes, because...*they wanted Jesus to bless them.* How? *By laying hands on them!* Yes! "But the disciples rebuked the parents": Hey, getcha little monkeys offa Jesus; the big man's busy with important stuff, and we are too. So beat it. But what did Jesus say? *He said they could come to him.* Yes, Jesus said, "Let the children come to me, and do not hinder them; for to such belongs the kingdom of heaven. And he laid his hands on them and went away." (Matthew 19)

I just want y'all to see that Jesus likes kids.

Miracle Bread

So, Loaves & Fishes. (Matthew 14 & 15; Mark 6; Luke 9; John 6) "...a multitude followed [Jesus], because they saw the signs which he did on those who were diseased." Everybody likes to witness a healing, 'cause seeing is believing. Jesus "had compassion on them, because they were like sheep without a shepherd; and he began to teach them many things." How is it, to be sheep without a shepherd? *Lost?* Yes, and? *Not safe?* Yes. So Jesus is preaching to a few thousand people in the countryside, and it's getting late...and...so...*they're hungry 'cause they didn't eat all day!* Yes. And when sheep are hungry do they go hunt rabbits? *No somebody feeds them.* Oh...somebody like a fireman? *No, a shepherd!* Oh, OK. "Now the Passover, the feast of the Jews, was at hand." Y'all tell me about the first Passover. *They had to splash the blood on the door so the Angel of Death wouldn't kill their kids.* Not *all* the kids, just...*the firstborn.* Yes. But they also had to eat something...*the lamb and the bread!* Yes; it was a kind of food miracle: eat this, splash that, and your firstborn will be spared. So Jesus will be doing another food miracle on a food miracle anniversary.

OK, time for a picture [I draw]...here's Jesus, he's in a good mood 'cause he's about to dump one of his problems on the apostles; way over here are 5,000 hungry people with sad faces. *That's not 5,000 people.* So use your imagination. And in the middle are the apostles...well, *some* apostles, I'm not drawing 12 of them.

"When it was evening, the disciples came to him and said, "This is a lonely place, and the day is now over; send the crowds away to go into the villages and buy food for themselves." The apostles are expecting Jesus to take care of business, but Jesus said, "They need not go away; you give them something to eat." Jesus is telling the apostles that this is *their* problem! The apostles don't want Jesus to dump this on them. And they said to him, "Shall we go and buy two hundred denarii worth of bread, and give it to them to eat?" A denarius is a piece of money, 200 denarii would be several thousand dollars nowadays. "And he said to them, "How many loaves have you? Go and see." Jesus isn't being a lot of help, is he? He wants the apostles to take charge. The apostles need to look stressed-out...there we go.

"One of his disciples, Andrew, Simon Peter's brother, said to him, "There is a lad here who has five barley loaves and two fish; but what are they among so many?" Here's the boy, with all this food...he's happy to help. Jesus likes kids...so... *the boy brings the food to Jesus!* Great guess, but no! Another answer? *The apostles bring it!* Yes. "Jesus said, Bring them to me." Now isn't this odd: Jesus has the *apostles* bring him the food, not the child who was willing to share it. [I draw an arrow from the boy to the apostles; and an arrow from the apostles to Jesus]

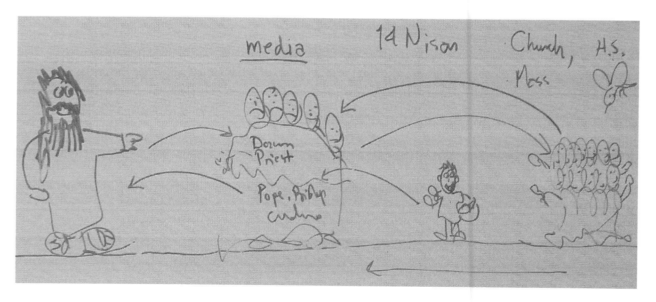

"And Jesus said, Make the men sit down." [arrow from Jesus to the apostles] So who made 'em sit down...Jesus? *No, the apostles.* [arrow from apostles to the crowd] Yes. "Now there was much grass in the place. So the men sat down, in number about five thousand. And taking the five loaves and the two fish he looked up to heaven, and blessed, and broke the loaves..." Then did everyone come up and grab some bread & fish from Jesus? *No, Jesus gave them to the apostles.* Yes; [Jesus-to-apostles arrow] he "gave them to the disciples to set before the people." So the crowd took what they wanted from the apostles? *No, the apostles give it to them.* [apostles-to-Jesus arrow] And when the crowd was full did they take the leftovers home? *Umm, did the apostles get the leftovers?* Yes. "When they were filled, he said to his disciples, Gather up the fragments that remain, that nothing be lost." The apostles cleaned up and kept the extra food, the people didn't take it with them. "Therefore they gathered them together, and filled twelve baskets with the fragments of the five barley loaves, which remained over and above what they had eaten." Remember how much wine was left over at the wedding at Cana? *A whole lot!* Yes, an abundance; and how much leftover bread is there now? *A whole lot!* Yes, in both cases more than there was to start. This is how God blesses, not with a little dab, but...*a whole lot!* Yes. Now, I know getting bread and fish isn't real exciting to y'all. If I were hungry and you handed me a fish, I'd just look at you like you'd lost your mind. So I like to imagine something like a miraculous pizza buffet, all-you-can-eat with soft drinks for you kids and beer for the grownups. In a meadow. And let me put smiles and bulging stomachs on the crowd now that they've had dinner. *They look pregnant!* Well, maybe some of them are women...who can say?

Now look at the picture; there isn't a single arrow going from Jesus to the crowd or from the crowd to Jesus. The crowd didn't even speak to Jesus, and he never spoke to the crowd. In fact, what's the only thing Jesus did? *Multiply the bread?* Yes. He did the God-part, the miracle-part. Who did all the rest of the work? *The apostles!* Yes...why? No guesses, that's ok. Recall that Jesus thought the people were like sheep without...*a shepherd.* Yes, so Jesus might want to provide them with...*a shepherd*...yes, who would be...*well, wouldn't Jesus be the shepherd?* Yes. Jesus is the shepherd of his flock, as he says later on. Tell me, what did Jesus do 40 days after Easter? *He rose from the dead!* Well, on Easter he did that...what did he do 40 days later? *Oh, he went up to heaven.* Yes. Is he still the shepherd in heaven? *Yes.* And a king? *Yes.* And if a shepherd, or a king like Hezekiah go away for a while what do they do? *Leave somebody in charge!* Yes. Now when he fed the multitudes, did Jesus know he'd be going to heaven soon? *Yes.* So by having the apostles do everything but the God-work, he was training them to...*be in charge.* Yes, and what was he was showing the crowd about the apostles? *That they were in charge?* Yes, Jesus showed the people that they couldn't always go straight to him for everything. For some things they might need to go through his authorized agents, like when Jesus wasn't baptizing anymore. Jesus was only going to be around for two more years; so he needed to train the apostles to manage without him physically being there.

And even today every parish has its local shepherd. [Shepherd goes on the board] Dígame, por favor, cómo se llama "shepherd" en Español? How do you say 'shepherd' in Spanish? *Is it 'pastor'?* Yes [on the board]. So what do we call the shepherd of a parish? *Pastor!* Yes. That wasn't too tough was it...yes? *Why do we use a Spanish word?* Good question: both English and Spanish get the word from Latin. In a Latin Bible you see 'pastor' all the time (e.g. John 10:11: ego sum pastor bonus/ I am [the] pastor good).

This miracle of the loaves and fishes is a model for the Church. Look, over here is Jesus; over there are the people; and in the middle are...*the apostles?* Well, yeah, but I mean *today* who are they, the people Jesus left in charge. *Oh..priests?* Yes, and the bishops, and the pope. And the story is also a model for the Mass. People are hungry, not so much for *physical* nutrition, but...*spiritual nutrition?* Yes, so they come to church, where Jesus is. Who provides the bread and wine? *We do?* Yes, and do we bring the bread and wine to Jesus? *No, to the priest.* Yes, and whose power makes the food miracle happen at Mass? *Jesus'?* Yes. And do we all grab what we want? *No the priest gives it to us.* Yes, and do we take home the leftovers? *No.* Right...who cleans up and put away the leftovers? *The priest.* Yes. All like that food miracle 2,000 years ago.

And this miracle food the people ate...did it cure their diseases? *No.* Keep them from getting old and dying? *No.* Take away their sins? *No!* Right. There were no long term benefits.

After this food miracle, the crowd is fired up! "When the people saw the sign which he had done, they said, "This is indeed the prophet who is to come into the world!" Perceiving then that they were about to come and take him by force to make him king, Jesus withdrew again to the mountain by himself." Oh dear, the people have the wrong idea about Jesus; they expect him to be a Messiah, a king like...*David!* Yes. But Jesus goes away to pray, and sends the apostles back across the Sea of Galilee, where they came from earlier that day. Tell me about their trip across the water. *There was a storm and they were afraid, but they saw Jesus walking on the water.* Yes. "he spoke to them, saying, "Take heart, it is I; have no fear." And Peter answered him, "Lord, if it is you, bid me come to you on the water." He said, "Come." So Peter got out of the boat and walked on the water and came to Jesus." I like Peter: he's always out in front of the other apostles, either the most fearless or the most chicken. Now remember all those people that got healed last week: they didn't just pray, they...*acted!* Yes. They *acted in faith* because they were made of a...*body'n'soul!* Yes, so like them, Peter acts in faith. He doesn't just have faith and stay in the boat, he...*gets out on the water!* Yes! "But when he saw the wind, he was afraid..." what then? *He started to sink!* Yes, he's still acting, walking, but his faith is wavering, and down he goes! See, ya gotta have both faith *and* action, they work together in your body'n'soul. Peter cried out, "Lord, save me." Jesus immediately reached out his hand and caught him, saying to him, "O man of little faith, why did you doubt?" Faith isn't always easy. Thank goodness Jesus saves people like Peter even when their faith is flimsy, like mine. So then what happens? *Jesus makes the storm stop.* Yes.

(Class typically continues into the next chapter.)

Chapter Twenty: Cannibals

(Gospels 7)

John 6, Bread of Life discourse: food miracle, delegated authority of apostles, eating flesh & blood, Mass, Apostles' faith vs. understanding. Jesus is already setting up the Church. Matthew 16: Peter's confession of Christ. Jesus renames Simon "rock," founds Church, and quotes Isaiah (keys that open & shut, using my car keys as a prop).

The day after Jesus and the apostles crossed over the Sea of Galilee, the crowd couldn't figure out where Jesus was, since the apostles had taken the only boat. John's gospel says they had to walk along the shore to find some more boats, and "they themselves got into the boats and went to Capernaum, seeking Jesus. When they found him on the other side of the sea, they said to him, "Rabbi, when did you come here?" Jesus answered them, "Truly, truly, I say to you, you seek me, not because you saw signs, but because you ate your fill of the loaves." So why does everyone chase after Jesus? *'Cause they want another miracle?* Yes, I think so; but Jesus isn't going to give them one. Instead he's going to take advantage of their excitement to do some teaching. Knowing they're still fired up about the free food, Jesus says, "Do not labor for the food which perishes, but for the food which endures to eternal life, which the Son of Man will give to you..." And the crowd thinks, umm...ok! They have no idea what he's talking about yet, but they have miracle food on their minds, and they remember a very old food miracle...in the desert...40 years...*Oh, manna!* Yes! They say, "Our fathers ate the manna in the wilderness; as it is written, 'He gave them bread from heaven to eat." Now that'd be a deal: 40 years of free food, courtesy of Jesus. "What sign can you do, that we may see and believe in you? What can you do?" And Jesus says "my Father gives you the true bread from heaven. For the bread of God is that which comes down from heaven and gives life to the world. So they said to him, "Sir, give us this bread always," as in ok, fine, whatever you say, just give us the miracle bread already.

More Miracle Bread

But Jesus said to them, "I am the bread of life; he who comes to me shall not hunger, and he who believes in me shall never thirst." Enough prophet-talk, please...now, about the bread? "The Jews then murmured at him, because he said, "I am the bread which came down from heaven." They said, "Is not this Jesus, the son of Joseph, whose father and mother we know? How does he now say, 'I have come down from heaven'?" Jesus is puttin' on airs. Now in the Bible, "murmur" is when people grumble and complain to each other about someone else. The j murmured, griped, *whined* about Moses before the manna miracle, and now their descendants, the Jews, are griping about a food miracle again.

But Jesus goes on: "I am the bread of life. Your fathers ate the manna in the wilderness, and they died. This is the bread which comes down from heaven, that a man may eat of it and not die." What? What bread? We don't see any bread! Show us the bread! "I am the living bread which came down from heaven; if any one eats of this bread, he will live for ever; and the bread which I shall give for the life of the world is my flesh." It gets worse by the minute! Now Jesus expects people to eat him like bread?

They...are...getting...*aggravated!* Yes! "The Jews then argued among themselves, saying, "How can this man give us his flesh to eat?" Now, when someone in the Bible says something more than once, they're emphasizing how important it is. Jesus has just said that they must eat heavenly bread, which if it's his flesh means...*they have to eat Jesus?* Yes. Now y'all count out loud each time Jesus says that; he's said it once already. So Jesus said to them, "Truly, truly, I say to you, unless you eat the flesh of the Son of man [*two!*] and drink his blood, you have no life in you" More aggravation: now they have to eat his flesh and...*drink his blood?* Yes. Girls, how about it? *Ewww, gross!* "...he who eats my flesh [*three!*] and drinks my blood has eternal life, and I will raise him up at the last day." Now many Christians believe that Jesus was speaking symbolically: nobody had to literally chew him up and swallow him. But then Jesus says, "For my flesh is *true* food, and my blood is *true* drink," so we know he's not meaning it symbolically. Then, "He who eats my flesh and drinks my blood [*four!*] abides in me, and I in him." What does *abide* mean? *To live?* Yes... *abide* means not just to be alive, but to dwell, like in a house, an *abode*. So if Jesus says we'll abide in him and he in us, what's he mean? *Umm...that we live in each other's house?* Yes, that each one of us dwells in Jesus; and Jesus dwells in us. He'll be at home in us. "As the living Father sent me, and I live because of the Father, so he who eats me [*five!*] will live because of me. This is the bread which came down from heaven, not such as the fathers ate and died; he who eats this bread [*six!*] will live for ever." Living forever- what's that about? Is everyone confused yet?

I don't think anything else in the Bible was said six times in a row, so we can be sure Jesus is as serious as cancer about eating his flesh and drinking his blood. At this point almost everyone is...*aggravated!* Yes. And offended. Disgusted, even. "Many of his disciples, when they heard it, said, "This is a hard saying; who can listen to it? After this many of his disciples drew back and no longer went about with him." This is the first time the Gospels say Jesus lost followers. I probably would have left too. Eating people and drinking blood; it's too awful even to hear about.

But not everyone left: "Jesus said to the twelve, "Do you also wish to go away?" Go on; take off if it's too tough for ya. Guess who answers this question? *Peter?* Yes! "Peter answered him, "Lord, to whom shall we go? You have the words of eternal life." I like Peter...does he understand all this cannibal talk? *No?* Right, he's as disturbed as anyone else. He doesn't understand Jesus, but he has faith in Jesus even if he doesn't understand.

Somebody tell me though where Jesus is bread, and people eat his flesh & drink his blood. *At Mass!* Yes, we know how this all turns out. But on that day, and for another couple of years, the apostles did *not* know how it would turn out, did *not* know how what Jesus said could possibly be true. But they had...*faith!* Yes.

A few days later Jesus asked his disciples, "Who do men say that the Son of Man is?" *Son of Man* is an Old Testament way that Jesus refers to himself. And they said, "Some say John the Baptist, others say Elijah, and others Jeremiah or one of the prophets." Everybody's got an opinion about Jesus: he raised the dead and performed food miracles like Elijah, baptized like John, and aggravated the scribes and Temple staff like Jeremiah. "He said to them, "But who do *you* say that I am?" Who's gonna answer this? *Peter!* Yes, as usual the Gospels show Peter is the #1 apostle. "Simon Peter replied, "You are the Christ, the Son of the living God." Tell me, what's the Hebrew word for Christ? *Anointed!* Yes, in English, good; what's the Hebrew? *Messiah!* Yes, so Peter is saying Jesus is...*the Messiah?* Yes, the one all the Jews have been waiting for. "And Jesus answered him, "Blessed are you, Simon Bar-Jonah! For flesh and blood has not revealed this to you, but my Father who is in heaven." Notice Jesus doesn't call him Peter. And Peter didn't figure this out on his own like a genius, but what? *God told him!* Yes; God is giving Peter some special guidance that he isn't giving the other 11. Tell me what Jesus says next. Thou art Peter...*and upon this rock I build my church!* Yes! At this moment Jesus changes Simon's name to Peter, which means...*rock.* Right. Do we ever say, "Peter broke the window with a peter?" *What?* Do we say, "I stubbed my toe on a peter"? *Ha! We say rock.* Right. We might also say *stone*, as in the cornerstone of a building.

'Peter' is just a name to us in English. But let's see... ¿Quién aquí habla Español? Who speaks Spanish? Me! OK m'ija, digame, cómo se llama Peter en Español? How do we say 'Peter' in Spanish? *Pedro.* Yes...who already knew 'Pedro' is Spanish for 'Peter'? Almost everybody, good. [I write Peter and Pedro on the board] Hija, when Jesus changes Simon's name to Pedro, how does he say 'rock'? *Roca.* Oops, sorry, how does he say 'stone'? *Oh...piedra! He says "piedra".* Yes, 'piedra' [piedra goes on the board beside Pedro]. Y'all see, it's more clear in Spanish that Peter is the Rock, the Stone, the words are almost the same. And by the way, how do the French say Peter? *Pierre?* Yes, Pierre, which is also exactly how they say stone [Pierre goes on the board under Peter, Pedro, and piedra]. It's perfectly clear to the French that Peter is the Stone. In French you *can* say, "Pierre broke the window with a pierre." And at the port in Charleston there are *piers;* what do think they're made of? *Stone?* Yes; well, nowadays they're concrete, but you see where the word comes from.

[For you catechists, here are the translations:

In Spanish: "tú eres Pedro, y sobre esta piedra edificaré mi iglesia" (Reina-Valera)

In French: "tu es Pierre, et que sur cette pierre je bâtirai mon Église" (Louis Segond)]

Again with the Key Business

Now we know that a name-change in the Bible is a big deal, from Abram to...*Abraham,* yes; from Sarai to...*Sarah,* and Jacob to...*Isaac?* Close, starts with an *I...Israel!* Yes. In each case they got blessings and authority. So when Simon's name changes to Rock, he gets...*blessings and authority.* Yes. And about his Church Jesus says, "the powers of hell shall not prevail against it;" which means...*bad stuff won't happen to* the Church? Almost. It means that even though bad stuff may happen, that in the end...*the Church will be ok?* Yes. Then Jesus tells Peter: "I will give you the keys of the kingdom of heaven, and whatever you bind on earth shall be bound in heaven, and whatever you loose on earth shall be loosed in heaven." Honorary sons & daughters, what's the business with St. Peter and the keys? *Well, Jesus gave him the keys.* Yes, to his car? [I show my keys.] *Jesus didn't have a car! Peter got the keys to heaven.* Oh yeah, heaven. I bet they were huge keys, heaven being so big and all. *They weren't real keys.* Well, put it this way, heaven is a *spiritual* place, so the keys would be *spiritual* not *physical*, but they might still be *real.* If I give you the keys to my car or my house, then you're in charge and you can do....*whatever I want?* Yes; but if you are trustworthy you'll try to do what's right. Somebody tell me the story about King Hezekiah...the story about the keys we acted out a couple of months ago...*where he gave the keys to the other guy?* Yes, the names are hard to remember. King Hezekiah took his key back from Shebna, the dishonest prime minister, and gave it to Eliakim. King Hezekiah said, "I will place on his shoulder the key of the house of David; he shall open, and none shall shut; and he shall shut, and none shall open." This is like Jesus telling Peter, "I will give you the keys of the kingdom of heaven, and whatever you bind on earth shall be bound in heaven, and whatever you loose on earth shall be loosed in heaven." And when the apostles heard Jesus say that to Peter, it reminded them that King Hezekiah put Eliakim in charge of his kingdom in the same way. I bet they were thinking, "Ooh, Jesus is quotin' Isaiah again... he's putting Peter in charge of everything!" Now did Jesus put Peter in charge of the kingdoms of Judea or Israel? *No, he was in charge of the kingdom of heaven.* Yes. It's amazing that Jesus would put a sinful human in charge of heaven, and let him bind and loose "whatever." How could Jesus be ok with that? *He'd watch out for him?* Yes, we saw how God gave only Simon the knowledge that Jesus was the Messiah; and then Jesus changed Simon's name to Peter to indicate his new authority. So it's reasonable to think Jesus will provide his new prime minister with some guidance so he won't make a mess out of heaven or Jesus's church, and the gates of hell won't prevail against it.

Praised be Jesus Christ! *Now and forever!*

Class over!

Chapter Twenty-One: Blinder then Blind

(Gospels 8)

Matthew 17, Transfiguration: Moses (law) & Elijah (prophets) [Sheol, heaven not yet available]. Coming of Elijah; John. John 9, Jesus heals a blind man using clay: healing through physical media. The stiff-necked Pharisees. Pride, humility and blindness. John 10, the good shepherd: sheep don't hire and fire shepherds.

Last week we were talking about how Simon's name was changed to Peter, the Rock, the Stone; and how his name was changed in Spanish to *Pedro*, which is like *Piedra,* stone. And then Jesus gave Peter the keys to heaven, which were invisible, or symbolic, or both; and quoted from Isaiah, so the other apostles would know that Jesus was putting Peter...*in charge!* Yes, just as Hezekiah's prime minister got the King's keys, so does Peter. Then Matthew's Gospel says, "From that time Jesus began to show his disciples that he must go to Jerusalem and suffer many things from the elders and chief priests and scribes, and be killed, and on the third day be raised." Now imagine the apostles: what? *what*? Why would the scribes want Jesus dead...and what's this raising after 3 days stuff? Jesus, *pleeeze* stop talking strange and upsetting us! "And Peter took him and began to rebuke him, saying, "God forbid, Lord! This shall never happen to you."

What's rebuking? No guesses, that's ok, it's an old word. It means to chew someone out, severely correct someone. It means Peter is going to straighten Jesus out! "But [Jesus] turned and said to Peter, "Get behind me, Satan! You are an obstacle to me. You are thinking not as God does, but as human beings do." So Jesus actually straightens out Peter, and calls him Satan! But why? No guesses, don't worry. I don't think the apostles understood Jesus either. "Then Jesus told his disciples, "If any man would come after me, let him deny himself and take up his cross and follow me." Tell me, if you are taking up, carrying, a cross in those days, what does that make you? *A criminal?* Yes, and what will happen to you? *You'll be crucified?* Yes. I imagine the apostles are more confused than ever. They aren't criminals and neither is Jesus; why is he saying this? *'Cause he'll get crucified later?* Yes, Jesus is making some prophecies that the 12 won't figure out for a while. "For whoever would save his life will lose it, and whoever loses his life for my sake will find it." More prophet-talk, more confused apostles. "For the Son of Man is to come with his angels in the glory of his Father, and then he shall reward every man according to his works." Now the first part of that sounds like the prophet Daniel. A few months ago we looked at one of his prophecies which included "behold, with the clouds of heaven there came one like a Son of Man...And to him was given dominion and glory." So the apostles would have thought, "Jesus is quoting Daniel...about himself!" And they might've calmed down some, thinking that later on all those other strange prophecies Jesus made over the last few days would make sense: eating him, drinking his blood, taking up crosses. And after the Son of Man, that is Jesus, comes in glory with *his* angels, "he shall reward every man according to his works." What are works? *What you do?*

Yes. So, does Jesus care about what you believe, or what you do? *What you do!* Well, he cares about both; remember when Peter stepped out on the water, he was doing, acting. But why did he start sinking? *He stopped believing!* Yes! Peter had to act...and...*believe!* Yes, because Peter was made of a *body'n'soul*, so he had to act...in...*faith!* Yes. So when Jesus says "he shall reward every man according to his works," does he mean he doesn't care what you believe? *No...he just means you have to do good things too.* Yes. Hey, do y'all know anyone (don't say any names) who believes it's important to wear a seat-belt in the car, but never does? *Yes.* Why don't they want to wear a seatbelt? *They're uncomfortable.* Uh-huh...who agrees it's more comfortable not to wear them...everybody. OK: if someone believes seat-belts are important, but never wears them, tell me about their belief. *They don't really believe it.* Oh...did you look into their soul? *No, I see they don't wear the seatbelt.* Yes...they may believe it a little, but not enough to matter, to change what they do. That's why Jesus always reminds those creatures that have a body'n'soul, that's us, that if we truly believe what he teaches, we can tell we believe it by...*what we do.* Yes. Soul and Body; Faith and Works; Believe and Do; Act in Faith.

About a week later, "Jesus took with him Peter and James and John his brother, and led them up a high mountain." Why bother going to the top of a high mountain? Try this: is it better to offer a sacrifice in a hole, or on a mountaintop? *A mountaintop!* Because? *It's closer to God.* Yes, so Jesus took them up...*to be closer to God.* Yes. "And he was transfigured before them, and his face shone like the sun, and his garments became white as light." The apostles may have remembered that after Moses visited God on Mount Sinai, his face shone, too. "And behold, there appeared to them Moses and Elijah, talking with him." Now Elijah is the #1 prophet who raised people from the dead and performed food miracles like Jesus. And Moses made the Covenant with God, and brought the 10 bananas...*10 commandments!* oh yeah, right, to the Israelites. This shows the apostles that Jesus is *at least the equal* of these two very important guys. And if that's not enough, "a bright cloud overshadowed them, and a voice from the cloud said, "This is my beloved Son, with whom I am well pleased." Tell me, when John the Baptist baptized Jesus, what did God say? *The same thing?* Yes, so once again, God in Heaven quotes from Isaiah. "When the disciples heard this, they fell on their faces, and were filled with awe." Y'all may remember when Manoah and his wife saw the angel zoom up to heaven, they fell on their faces, too. And tell me about the overshadowing cloud. *It's the Shaboobie!* Close...the Shekhinah, which overshadowed...*the Ark!* Yes, good!

A few seconds later they looked up, and Moses and Elijah were gone.

Trick question: were Moses and Elijah in Heaven? *Yes!...No!* Well? *No!* Right, why not? *Jesus hadn't died yet!* Yes. Heaven was closed to sinners. Were Moses and Elijah in Hell? *No?* Right, they weren't in Hell either. *Purgatory?* Good guess, but there's no Purgatory yet. They were in S-h-e-o-l [on the board], a place where the souls of the dead stayed before heaven was available. It's pleasant enough, but it's not Heaven. In Greek stories, who knows where dead people went? *Hades?* Yes, H-a-d-e-s [on the board], good. Sheol and Hades are similar. Well see later on that Jesus visits Sheol.

Malachi Redux

136

On the way back down the mountain, the apostles have Elijah on their minds. They asked Jesus, "Why do the scribes say that Elijah must come first?" Now, what sort of jobs did the apostles have before they followed Jesus? *Fishermen?* Yes, and other regular jobs. They didn't spend their workdays studying scripture like the scribes and Pharisees. So they ask Jesus, who they know is the Messiah, to explain to them about Elijah coming before the Messiah. Jesus probably reminds them of the last prophecy of the Old Testament, when Malachi says "Behold, I will send you Elijah the prophet before the great and terrible day of the LORD comes." Jesus said "Elijah does come, and he is to restore all things; but I tell you that Elijah has already come, and they did not know him, but did to him whatever they pleased." He means the scribes and Pharisees. "Then the disciples understood that he was speaking to them of John the Baptist." (Matt 17) Of course the scribes and Pharisees knew who John was, but their pride blinded them to John's significance, that he fulfilled Malachi's prophecy.

Speaking of blindness, our next story, which is the whole chapter 9 in John's gospel, is one where Jesus heals a blind man. *I'll be the blind man!* Alright; and you two volunteers are his parents. The rest of y'all are the crowd and the Pharisees. "As he passed by, he saw a man blind from his birth." Blind man, is that true? *Yes?* Parents, true: blind from birth? *Yes.* How would you know? *We're his parents!* Yes, just checking. "And his disciples asked him, "Rabbi, teacher, who sinned, this man or his parents, that he was born blind?" The disciples have the common understanding of sin in those days: that if you sinned, or your parents sinned, or your ancestors sinned, God would punish you here on Earth. And they're half-right: if not for sin, would *anybody* be blind? *No!* So Jesus answered, "It was not that this man sinned, or his parents, but that the works of God might be made manifest in him." Jesus means the man isn't blind because of his or his parents' sins, but so that Jesus can turn this into yet another teaching opportunity.

Then Jesus said "I am the light of the world." I suppose then that he can make blind men see. Now, I'm Jesus; blind man, stand by me. Shut those eyes! Now does anyone want to guess how I heal him? *You lay hands on him!* Good guess, that's sort of right. I do touch him. First I reach down and get some dirt. Now what do I do? No guesses? *ptoo...ptoo...*I spit in the dirt...*ptoo.* Close those eyes blind man! Now I make mud out of the dirt and spit...and...*you rub it on his face?* His face? What's his problem, that he's ugly? *No, on his eyes!* That's better. Hold still blind man, you volunteered for this; besides, this is make-believe spit-mud...there. Now go wash it off...open your eyes...well? *I can see!* Yes. See your way back to your desk. Crowd, tell me about the mud...is it magic? *No.* Right. Was Moses' stick magic? *No!* Was the tassel of Jesus's cloak magic? *No!* Elijah's cloak? *No!* Remember watching the comedian on TV...is the TV funny? *No, the comedian!* Right. The TV has no sense of humor, it's just the thing in the middle that conducts the humor from the comedian to you. So the mud is just another physical thing-in-the-middle, a medium, to carry God's power in our physical world from God to us. Because we're made of a...*body'n'soul*, yes, so God comes to us spiritually and...*physically!* Yes.

But everyone isn't happy about this miracle: "The neighbors and those who had seen him before as a beggar, said, "Is not this the man who used to sit and beg?" Some said, "It is he"; others said, "No, but he is like him." He said, "I am the man." "They brought to the Pharisees the man who had formerly been blind. Now it was a Sabbath day when Jesus made the clay and opened his eyes." Uh-oh, Jesus is healing on the Sabbath again, doing doctor's work. "The Pharisees...asked him how he had received his sight. And he said to them, "He put clay on my eyes, and I washed, and I see." Some of the Pharisees said, "This man is not from God, for he does not keep the Sabbath." But others said, "How can a man who is a sinner do such signs?" There was a division among them. Oh dear, once again people are...getting... *aggravated!* Yes! "So they...said to the blind man, "What do you say about him, since he has opened your eyes?" He said, "He is a prophet." Well, let me assure you as a Pharisee that no blind man can recognize a prophet. I'm the expert in that department, and I don't see no prophet no how in Jesus. Why, I bet this is a scam, a trick, and he was never blind in the first place!

Let's ask his parents. Parents, "Is this your son, who you say was born blind? How then does he now see?" Parents, speak up! *We don't know!* Do y'all still say he was blind from birth? *Yes?* The parents were afraid of the Pharisees, who "had already agreed that if any one should confess him to be Christ, he was to be put out of the synagogue." What's Christ in Hebrew? *Messiah!* Yes, so the Pharisees would throw anyone out of the synagogue who said Jesus was the Messiah. The parents aren't any help, so the Pharisees ask the man again how he was healed. He says, "I have told you already, and you would not listen. Why do you want to hear it again?" He wonders if the Pharisees want to follow Jesus! They must love that. "They reviled him, saying, "*You* are his disciple, but *we* are disciples of Moses. We know that God has spoken to Moses, but as for this man, we do not know where he comes from." And the man says, "Why, this is a marvel! You do not know where he comes from, and yet he opened my eyes...Never since the world began has it been heard that any one opened the eyes of a man *born blind*. If this man were not from God, he could do nothing." The formerly blind man now can see, and not just physically; he can see spiritually, too, and believes that Jesus is at least a prophet, and comes from God. Now the Pharisees go nuts! "You were born in utter sin, and would you teach us?" And they cast him out of the temple area. See, this is plain old pride in action, just like Adam and Eve's in the Garden. The Pharisees just assume that the man is a worse sinner than they are, and that they know God better than any beggar.

"Jesus heard that they had cast him out, and having found him he said, "Do you believe in the Son of man?"....He said, "Lord, I believe"; and he worshiped him. This reminds me of Isaiah's Christmas prophecy: "The ox knows its owner, and the ass its master's manger; but Israel does not know, my people does not understand." The Pharisees are too proud to recognize the Messiah, but a blind, illiterate, humble beggar can.

Jesus said, "For judgment I came into this world, that those who do not see may see, and that those who see may become blind." Now the Pharisees are smart, and they know that Jesus's remark is aimed at them in some annoying way: "some of the Pharisees near him heard this, and they said to him, "Are we also blind?" Which is their way of saying their eyes work just fine, and if Jesus means they can't see spiritual truth, well, he's flat wrong. Now what Jesus said is hard to understand, which makes it a bit of a prophecy. But can someone tell me, in this story, can the blind man now see? *Yes.* And can his parents? *Yes.* And the Pharisees? *Yes...No!* No? Don't their eyes work? *Yes, but they can't see Jesus is the Messiah.* Yes, they *won't* see; and this prophecy of spiritual blindness won't be limited to the Pharisees.

And finally Jesus said to them, "If you were blind, you would have no sin; but now that you say, 'We see,' your sin remains." Uh-oh. Refusing to accept Jesus' authority isn't just a matter of opinion, it's a *sin.*

Y'all are still kids, and someone always has authority over you. Your lives don't have a lot of room for pride yet: your parents feed you, house you, clothe you. Your teachers teach you what you don't know. You can't drive, can't make money, can't reach things on high shelves. Depending on others for so much tends to make you humble. But as you get older, you gain the knowledge of how to do all that yourself, and that makes adults proud...real proud in some cases. But every adult, even a king or president, is still under God's authority, and still depends on God even if they won't admit it to themselves, just like the Pharisees. It's always a struggle for adults to be humble; if pride's not a problem for you now, it will be a problem soon enough. Even nowadays one adult will tell another, "Your pride is blinding you to the truth." So always remember the Pharisees in this story: they weren't obviously evil like King Herod, killing babies. But refusing to humble their intellects before God's authority was a big enough sin to keep them out of heaven.

That was the whole chapter 9 of John's gospel. Speaking of being humble and letting God be in charge, let's look a bit at chapter 10 and that'll be it for tonight.

In this chapter Jesus calls himself the Good Shepherd; in Spanish, *el Buen Pastor*. Remind me, *pastor* is Spanish and Latin for...*shepherd,* yes. Remember last week the crowd looked "like sheep without a shepherd" to Jesus; and part of the Loaves and Fishes miracle was to show the people that the apostles had Jesus's authority. In this chapter Jesus has more to say about his sheep, his flock. Tell me about "sheep without a shepherd"...are they safe? *No.* Why not? *Other animals would eat them.* Yes. And if they're hungry, do they hunt rabbits? *Ha, no they eat grass!* Yes...does the shepherd just follow them around the countryside like a baby duck following the momma duck? *No, I think he takes them to where they can eat good grass or something.* Right, he leads them to food and water. So shepherds have two main responsibilities...which are...*protecting the sheep?* Yes, and...*getting them food?* Yes. Jesus says the shepherd will "find pasture" for the sheep. And he also says "I am the good shepherd. The good shepherd lays down his life for the sheep." So if a wolf attacks the sheep, the shepherd runs off? *No he fights the wolf.* Yes the shepherd will risk his own life to save the flock. Jesus is making a prophecy about his own death.

Now Jesus is a Jew, a descendant of David under the covenant God made with Moses, and preaches to Jews. So when he talks about his sheep, who's he talking about? *The Jews?* Yes, God's Chosen people, the Sons of Abraham. But he also says, "And I have other sheep, that are not of this fold; I must bring them also, and they will heed my voice. So there shall be one flock, one shepherd." This is a prophecy, too. Who would those other sheep be? Are y'all Jews? *No.* But are you part of Jesus's flock? *Yes!* So...*we're the other sheep?* Yes, all the people who believe in Jesus but aren't Jews.

So how many shepherds are there? *One!* Yes, who is...*Jesus.* Yes. So why does every parish have a pastor, a shepherd, if Jesus is the one shepherd? *'Cause Jesus is in heaven?* Yes, he's not physically here for the time being. And centuries before Jesus, Jeremiah prophesied "I will give you pastors, shepherds according to my heart, which shall feed you with knowledge and understanding." So even though there is one shepherd in heaven, he has lots of assistant shepherds on earth.

Now tell me about sheep and shepherds: who is in charge? *The shepherd.* Who knows best? *The shepherd.*

Who has authority? *The shepherd.* Yes, it's very obvious. Suppose the sheep decided they didn't like their shepherd; could they fire him, run an ad in the paper and hire a new shepherd? *Sheep can't do that.* OK, how about Jesus's flock, we're people. If we don't like our priest or bishop can we fire him and hire another one? *No.* Right. We don't hire our pastor, he's appointed. Like the apostles: *Jesus* picked them, not his followers. He even picked Judas, who betrayed him; so shepherds aren't always saints. Catholics sometimes murmur and grumble like Israelites and Pharisees about not being able to fire their pastor and get one they like better. But if the people can fire the pastor, is the pastor really in charge? *No.* Who would really have the authority? *The people!* Yes, the flock, the sheep. And suppose half the flock liked the pastor and half wanted a new one...what then? *Well, the unhappy people could get their own I guess.* Yes, and split the flock. That is not what Jesus taught, and not what Jeremiah prophesied. If God "gives us pastors according to his heart, who shall feed us with knowledge and understanding," how can we hire or fire them?

Real sheep are naturally humble; they know they depend on the shepherd. But we prideful humans like to think we know better than God, or his appointed shepherds.

Praised be Jesus Christ! *Now and forever!*

Class is over 13, 12, 11 seconds early!

Chapter Twenty-Two: Straight Down the Toilet (Gospels 9)

Luke 15, the Prodigal Son: selfishness, repentance, forgiveness, happiness [Confession], the older son. Rembrandt's painting of the Prodigal Son.

Hey before we pray, Madam Bouncer has a handout for y'all....everybody got one? [It's Rembrandt's *Prodigal Son* with the Act of Contrition beneath it.] Look at the prayer at the bottom, you've heard it before, but now you can read it. Here we go: "In the name of the Father and of the Son and of the Holy Spirit:

O my God, I am heartily sorry for having offended Thee,

and I detest all my sins because of Thy just punishments; but most of all because they offend Thee, my God, Who art all good and deserving of all my love.

I firmly resolve, with the help of Thy grace, to sin no more and to avoid the near occasion of sin.

Amen.

Rembrandt & Reconciliation

OK...now look at the painting on the handout; it was done a few centuries ago by an artist named Rembrandt. He was Dutch, so what country did he live in? *Holland?* Yes. What is Holland famous for? *Windmills! ...Wooden shoes!* And what flower? *Tulips!* Yes, geniuses! Rembrandt painted lots of Bible stories, like this one. Can you guess the story? No? Actually it's a painting of one of Jesus' parables. I like this painting because it reminds me of how I feel when I go to confession. Any guesses yet on the story? No? Y'all have heard the story before, and now you're gonna hear it again, but with cartoons. Won't that be all the fun you can stand? *No.* Oh cheer up, your suffering comes to an end in a couple of months.

Pretend Jesus is telling you the story (all from Luke 15):
"There was a man who had two sons. And the younger of them said to his father, 'Father, give me the share of property that is coming to me.' And he divided his property between them."

[I draw two faces without mouths] This is the younger Son....and his Father, he's old like me...needs a beard & some wrinkles...there. *Where are their mouths?* I'll put some in later. What do you call it when a parent's property is divided among the children? *Inheritance?* Yes, the part each child (usually they're adults, like the son) gets is his inheritance. Do my kids have their inheritance yet? *Ha, no.* How do you know? *Because*

141

you're not dead yet. Yes; not quite yet. And you're right, a father's estate doesn't get divided among the kids 'til he's dead. So how would the father feel when the son asks for his inheritance? *Sad?* [I put a sad mouth on the Father] Yes, the Son can't wait around for his Father to die so he can get the goodies. But the Father goes ahead and gives the Son his share, which today might be a million dollars or so. The Father allows the Son to exercise his free will, even if it's gonna be a big fat mistake. How does the Son feel? *He feels great!* [happy mouth on the Son] He's an *ingrate,* but he *feels great* (haw!). I bet he has tons of self-esteem, but not a lick of self-respect. He's very proud of himself, and all the money he has that he didn't earn. Now who is the Son thinking about? *Himself?* Yes [arrow from the Son's head back around to his own head]. Who's the Father thinking about? *Himself?* Well, if he were thinking of himself he'd've thrown his son out of the house with nothing; so I suppose he's thinking of...*his Son?* Yes [arrow from Father to Son].

Then Jesus says: "Not many days later, the younger son gathered all he had and took a journey into a far country, and there he squandered his property in reckless living." What's that mean, to "squander property in reckless living?" *To waste all his money!* Yes, but how? *Buying lots of stuff, cars and things!* Yes, and? *Parties?* Yes, probably getting drunk, gambling and behaving badly with women like King David did...what today we might call Sex, Drugs and Rock'n'Roll. *What's wrong with Rock'n'Roll?* Well, sometimes it's ok; other times, especially if people aren't behaving well, it can make it easier to behave even worse. *Like what?* Like, ask your parents; this isn't a Rock'n'Roll class. It's a Learn About God class. Yes? *Is he the Prodigal Son?* Yes, you got it.

Prodigal means 'wastefully extravagant.' He just blew that money right out the window! Do you think the Son would've done that if he'd earned the money himself? *No!* That's right! Hey, tell me what the lottery is. *It's when people buy a ticket to win a lot of money!* Yes. There are some people who win millions of dollars in the lottery, and within a couple of years it's all gone. People tend to disregard things they don't work for. You should always carefully spend the money you're given as though you had to work for it yourself.

Then Jesus says: "After he had spent everything, there was a severe famine in that whole country, and he was hungry. So he went and hired himself out to a citizen of that country, who sent him to his fields to feed pigs." Now ever since Moses at least, Jews couldn't have anything to do with pigs, which were unclean: no bacon, no ham, no barbecue. Mmm...I love pigs. But for the Son, and the Jews hearing the story, this is just the nastiest situation. "He longed to fill his stomach with the swill that the pigs were eating, but no one gave him anything." Have y'all ever seen what pigs eat? No? When I was kid, my uncle kept pigs. He'd collect leftovers from the schools in big buckets: food, milk, juice, just a dreadful stinky glop. He'd pour out that smelly slop and the pigs went snortin' crazy for it. I can't imagine being as hungry as the Son; to want to eat that mess.

How does the younger Son feel now? *Sad.* You bet he does [I erase the Son's smile, replace it with a sad mouth]. Who does he feel sad for? *Himself.* Yes. And notice how Jesus says "no one gave him anything." Who's the only person who gave him anything? *His Father!* Yes, who loves him. But he was mean to his Father, so too bad for him now.

Then Jesus says: "When [the Son] came to his senses, he said, 'How many of my father's hired men have food to spare, and here I am starving to death! I will set out and go back to my father and say to him: Father, I have sinned against heaven and against you. I am no longer worthy to be called your son; make me like one of your hired men."

Justice or Mercy?

Now this is starting to look a lot like My Favorite Sacrament...which is? *The Eucharist?* Well...that's not my favorite right now. Another guess? *Baptism?* Baptism!? No! You're just throwing out answers now. It's Confession. The son at last realizes he's sinned against his Father; we'd say he's examined his conscience. Y'all know what that is, right, examining your conscience? *When you think about your sins.* Yes, I try to do it every night before I go to sleep. Before Confession you should do it too, so you don't get in there and say, "Umm I have some sins I think....just a second." So the Son has decided to go confess his sin to his Father. And why is he doing this, why does he now realize he's offended his father? *Because he's hungry!* Yes, he's still thinking about himself, but he's thinking about his father as well, so that's progress [new arrow to the Father]. And is he still prideful? *No, he's humble.* Yes. That's progress, too. And he knows he doesn't deserve to be treated like a son since he's already wolfed down his big slice of pie in one huge bite. How's he gonna pay all that money back? *He can't!* That's right! A million bucks flushed straight down the toilet, *squoosh!* So he can't make amends! What's the only thing he can hope for? *That his father will forgive him!* Yes; the Son doesn't want *justice.* He wants what? *Forgiveness!* Yes, he wants a merciful Father. As we say, "Have mercy on me Lord, a sinner."

Then Jesus says: "So he got up and went to his father. But while he was still a long way off, his father saw him and was filled with compassion for him..." What does the Father do? Put on his kicking boot? *No he runs out to his Son!* Yes! "...he ran to his son, threw his arms around him and kissed him."

I think the Father is surprised his Son is even alive, and runs out to hug and kiss him. How does the Father feel? *Happy!* Yes [Father now smiles] But isn't the Father the offended party? *Yes.* So why is he glad to see his good-for-nothing-blow-a-million-bucks younger son? *'Cause he loves him anyway!* Yes....and who is the father thinking about? *His son!* Yes. If he thinks about himself, and how thoughtless his Son had been to him how would he feel? *Sad.* Yes. Now does the Father know the Son's sin, how the son offended him? *Yes!* Can he tell the Son is as sorry as he can be? *Yes!* But instead of saying, "hush now, you don't have to apologize," he lets the Son confess his sin out loud, even though he already knows what he's going to say. Just as we do in Confession, the younger Son repeats out loud his Examination of Conscience: "Father, I have sinned against heaven and against you. I am no longer worthy to be called your son." Why does the father let the Son confess? *So the Son will feel better!* Yes. Confessing our sins out loud to a priest isn't for God's benefit- he knows our sins before we do...who's it for? *It's for us.* Yes. And who is the Son thinking about now? *His Father.* Yes...a little about himself too; he's miserable, who can blame him?

Now let's look at Rembrandt's painting again. The poor Son is exhausted by his sins and his guilt. His shoes are falling apart; he's penniless. Just a poor, forlorn sinner like me. This is just how I feel when I'm in Confession and the priest tells me Jesus has forgiven my sins. The Son looks peaceful and relieved and sorry all at once. And the father is patient and affectionate....he can stand there and comfort his Son and welcome him home for as long as the Son needs him to. Rembrandt was one of the world's greatest painters, and he knew it. Like most adults he committed some spectacular sins, and wallowed in pride like a pig. Rembrandt painted this when he was old and near death, like me. He's showing how he hoped God would forgive him his sins. He didn't want justice, he wanted...*forgiveness!* Yes, just like me.

OK, back to the story: the Son just wants to be treated like a hired hand, not a son. But Jesus says: "...the Father said to his servants, 'Quick! Bring the *best* robe and put it on him. Put a ring on his finger and sandals on his feet. Bring the fattened calf and kill it. Let's have a feast and celebrate. For this son of mine was dead and is alive again; he was lost and is found.' Was the Father always ready to accept his Son back? *Umm...yes?* Yes, as long as the son...*apologized?* Yes, he had to *be* sorry, and *say* he was sorry, and repent. It was up to the Son, not the Father. Do you think the Son will be this mean to his father again? *No!* Right; like Ezekiel said, he has a heart of flesh now, not one of stone.

So the Son, having confessed, is forgiven by the Father, who restores him to an even better situation than before he left, as we'll see in a minute. At this point how does the Son feel? *Happy!* Yes, maybe happier than he's ever been [happy mouth on the Son]. And the Father? He's happy too! [two happy faces] And the Father is thinking about...*the Son!* And the Son....*his Father!* Yes, they're not selfish, but.....*selfless!* Yes [arrows from each face toward the other face].

Remind me, how many sons did the father have? *Two?* Yes. Now Jesus says: "So they began to celebrate. Meanwhile, the older son was in the field...and he heard music and dancing. A servant said 'Your brother has come, and your father has killed the fattened calf because he has him back safe and sound. The older brother became angry and refused to go in the house."

And who's this [new face]? *The older son.* Which person is he in the painting? *The one in the back?* Good guess, but no. How do you think the second older son feels? *Mad!* Yes. So? *The man on the right?* Yes, and both he and his father are wearing red, an expensive color. And you can tell he's not happy that his worthless brother's back in town; his Daddy may be an old softie, but he's not. He ain't huggin' nobody! *Who're the other people?* Servants probably. So the older Son is mad [angry face] and won't come in the house...what do you think the Father does? *He goes outside?* Yes! Who's he thinking about? *His son!* Yes.

"So his father went out and pleaded with him. But he answered his father, 'Look! All these years I've been slaving for you and never disobeyed your orders. Yet you never gave me even a young goat so I could celebrate with my friends." Now, who is the older Son thinking about? *Himself.* Yes [arrow from his face that curves back around to his face]. "But when your son returns who swallowed up your property with prostitutes, for him you slaughter the fattened calf." I love that...it's not "my brother," but "*your* son."

Then the Father says: "My son, you are always with me, and everything I have is yours. But we had to celebrate and be glad, because your brother was dead and is alive again; he was lost and is found." And let's see...who's happy? *The Father and the younger Son.* And who are they thinking about? *Each other!* And the older Son is...*thinking about himself!* and....*is unhappy.* Yes. And the story ends with the older son staying away from the celebration.

Now the older Son is a problem for most people: he says he's obeyed his Father, isn't it reasonable for him to be annoyed? *Yes!* Maybe so....but my guess is he's like most of us. I say, oooh, that Prodigal Son, he was *so* bad. He needed to apologize big time to his Dad. But me, *I've* never been that bad, *I* don't need to apologize, *I* do what God wants...more or less. But like me, the older Son is a sinner, too. He has things he should apologize for to his Father; we all do, even saints. But he wants to focus on his brother's sins. That way he can keep his pride, and not have to examine his own conscience; he'd rather examine his *brother's* conscience. He doesn't want to apologize out loud like his brother. Plus he sees his father and younger brother are closer than they used to be....he's jealous of that, but doesn't want do what's necessary to have that closer relationship with his Dad: to admit out loud he's sinned, too. It's harder for him to ask forgiveness for his *small* sins than for his younger brother to apologize for his *big* ones. So the lesson we learn from the older brother is as important as the one we learn from the younger one. Sometimes I'm like the younger Son: I know I need forgiveness. But other times I'm like the older Son: I think I've been pretty good, I don't need forgiveness, I haven't been too bad. But God doesn't care how big your sins are; he cares that you repent and confess your sins out loud so He can forgive you.

And we're made of what...? *Bodynsoul!* Yes, we have two natures: spiritual and...*physical!* So we need to confess spiritually and....*physically!* Yes, so God can forgive us spiritually and.....*physically!* And in Confession, how do we get physical forgiveness? *The priest tells us we're forgiven!* Yes, right in our ears. Just like King David heard the words of forgiveness from Nathan's mouth.

This is a great gift, sons & daughters, but like the Prodigal Son we have to *use* it: to confess, repent, and be forgiven even our worst sins through the Sacrament of Reconciliation.

The handout's to help you when you and your family go to confession: the Act of Contrition is there so you don't have to be embarrassed if you don't remember it. And while you're waiting in the line & feeling uncomfortable, you can look at Rembrandt's painting and remind yourself how great you'll feel after you tell God out loud you're sorry, and you hear Jesus tell you through the priest that he forgives you, and loves you more than you know.

Praised be Jesus Christ! *Now and forever!*

Class over!

Chapter Twenty-Three: House of Prayer, Den of Thieves (Gospels 10)

Matthew 19, Mark 10, the Rich Man: the decalogue; Jesus loved him, why? Matthew 21, Jesus enters Jerusalem: Hosanna, donkey, Christos (Greek) & Mashiah (Hebrew from Egyptian), anointed. Matthew 21, Mark 10: Jesus Cleanses the Temple and quotes Jeremiah & Isaiah; what does he mean by that?

Y'all remember a couple of weeks ago we talked about Jesus and the children (Mark 10)? *Yes.* We covered that a little out of order to compare those kids going straight to Jesus to the boy with the loaves and fishes only getting access to the Apostles. Remind me please, who brought those kids to Jesus? *Their parents.* Yes, the parents knew Jesus was some kind of prophet, miracle-worker, maybe even the Messiah. What'd the parents want? *They wanted Jesus to bless the kids.* Yes, by...*laying his hands on them!* Yes! Did Jesus tell the kids, "Hey now, your parents put you up to this; y'all come back when you have some faith of your own, and then I'll bless ya." *No, he just blessed them!* Yes, because the *parents* wanted it for their children; the *parents* had faith. It's the same with Baptism: do babies know anything about Jesus? *No.* Right. Babies don't know anything; but their parents do. Babies are baptized because their parents intercede for them.

The Twelve Commandments

Shortly after blessing the kids, Jesus started on a journey, probably to Jerusalem. (Mark 10) "And as he was setting out on his journey, a man ran up and knelt before him, and asked him, "Good Teacher, what must I do to inherit eternal life?" And Jesus says, "You know the commandments: 'Do not kill, Do not commit adultery, Do not steal, Do not bear false witness"...which means? *Don't lie!* Yes..."Do not defraud, Honor your father and mother." (Mk 10) *What's defraud?* Tricking someone out of his money, stealing. Jesus is sort of teasing him, saying, "What's the matter? Don't you know the 10 Commandments?" And the man says, "Teacher, all these I have observed from my youth." And Jesus, looking upon him loved him..." Why do you think Jesus loved him? *Because he wanted to be good?* Yes! And because he felt like observing the 10 Commandments *wasn't enough...*there was more he should be doing, but he couldn't say what. Jesus said to him, "You lack one thing; go, sell what you have, and give to the poor, and you will have treasure in heaven; and come, follow me." Uh-oh...I don't know if *I* could do that. Following Jesus means more than checking off the 10 Commandments every day. "At that saying [the rich man] went away sorrowful; for he had great possessions." Jesus didn't let people stop with the 10 Commandments, he had two more: love your...*neighbor?* Yes, as yourself; and love your...? No guesses? Jesus told us to turn the other cheek if someone hits us, and to love...*our enemies!* Yes! I think those two are tougher than the first Ten. And Jesus said, "Children, how hard it is for those who trust in riches to enter the kingdom of God! It is easier for a camel to go through the eye of a needle than for a rich man to enter the kingdom of God." And they were exceedingly astonished..." Tell me, in Jesus's day, how could you tell if God had super-blessed someone? *They were rich?* Yes, God blessed people with lots of kids and goodies. And if God *didn't* bless you, you might be afraid you'd wind up with a son who was blind from birth. But now Jesus says being rich is more of a *problem* than a *blessing*. But if it's hard for the rich, who enjoy God's favor, to get to heaven, what chance do the poor Apostles have? They said to him, "Then who can be saved?" Jesus looked at them and said, "For men it is impossible, but not for God; for all things are possible with God." Jesus means that whether someone is rich or poor, he still can't get to heaven on his own; we all have to trust in God.

Now y'all may remember Peter had a mother-in-law, which means...*he was married?* Yes. And I know how much I miss my wife if I don't see her at lunch every day. But Peter had to leave home to follow Jesus all around the Judean countryside for a couple of years now. Peter said to Jesus, "We have given up *everything* and followed you." I think Peter's reminding Jesus that he didn't just give up being a fisherman, which would make him poor; but he gave up being with his wife and family, which is even worse! Jesus said, "Truly, I say to you, there is no one who has left house or brothers or sisters or mother or father or children or lands, for my sake and for the gospel, who will not receive a hundredfold...and in the age to come, eternal life." Jesus is telling Peter he knows what Peter has sacrificed. People like Peter, who trust in God and let go of whatever they have to to follow Jesus, will have eternal life, which is what the rich man was looking for at the start of the story. The rich man was afraid to completely trust in God. He also wanted to trust in his possessions and money; but that may keep him out of heaven. I know how he feels; I like to trust in that stuff too.

NTHNGBTCNSNNTS

Shortly after this episode, Jesus enters Jerusalem during the time of Passover, as we saw last week. One of the first things he does in Jerusalem is to go aggravate the scribes and priests at the Temple. Tell me about it. *He went in and knocked over the tables and whipped people!* Yes! "The Passover of the Jews was at hand, and Jesus went up to Jerusalem. In the temple he found those who were selling oxen and sheep and pigeons, and the money-changers at their business. And making a whip of cords, he drove them all, with the sheep and oxen, out of the temple; and he poured out the coins of the money-changers and overturned their tables." Now Jesus didn't go into the holy part of the Temple where only priests could go; he was in the outer court where people could come in to make their Passover offerings. If they came from far away they might have to change their money to pay a Temple tax and buy animals for sacrifice. Imagine cows peeing and pooping and farting in front of our church: smelly, noisy, and completely irreverent. "And he...said to them, "Is it not written, 'My house shall be called a house of prayer for all the nations?" What's that mean? *That people should be respectful?* Yes. Then he says "But you have made it a den of thieves." Tell me about it. *They shouldn't steal people's money?* Yes, maybe the moneychangers were taking advantage of poor people who didn't know what a fair deal would be; *defrauding* them. That's how most of the people who heard Jesus would understand what he said. But the scribes and Pharisees and priests understood Jesus even more, which made them decide to get rid of Jesus, and soon.

Let's see...who can read this [on the board]: NTHNG. *Nothing?* Yes, good! Keep going if you can...NTHNGBT. *Nothing but?* Yes again...this is harder...NTHNGBTCNSNNTS. *Umm...nothing but consonants?* Yes, genius! Very good. Sometimes even grownups can't figure that out. The Old Testament Scriptures were first written in Hebrew. The Hebrew alphabet didn't have vowels, and there were no spaces between the words, or punctuation, or lower case letters, or paragraphs. Like God's name, spell it. *Y-H-W-H!* Yes. Don't say it! *We weren't going to!* OK. So a book in the Bible was one long stream of consonants on a scroll. What's a scroll? *A rolled-up book?* Yes, one long page rolled up. Reading was hard to do, and the only people who could read well were Pharisees, and scribes, who could also write. They made a living out of reading, studying, and memorizing the Scriptures. They knew them very well; all of the important parts from memory, much better than the average person, even the Apostles. So when they heard Jesus say "My house shall be called a house of prayer for all the nations" they knew right away he was quoting Isaiah. And when he said "den of thieves" they remembered Jeremiah had said it first. We covered both of these quotes a couple months ago during our prophet classes; let's see what Jesus was telling the scribes, Pharisees, and other Temple staff.

First off, Jesus quotes Isaiah, who had spoken at the Temple centuries before. But when the scribes hear "house of prayer," they don't think about just those words, but the whole passage. Isaiah prophesied that someday God's House would be for all people, not just Jews: "Also the sons of the stranger, that join themselves to the LORD, to be his servants, every one that keepeth the Sabbath, and taketh hold of my covenant. Even them will I bring to my holy mountain, and make them joyful in my house of prayer: their burnt offerings and their sacrifices shall be accepted upon mine altar; for mine house shall be called a house of prayer for all people." Jesus reminds the scribes and Pharisees that being Chosen won't matter so much if God will accept non-Chosen people into his Covenant.

Then Jesus quoted Jeremiah while standing in the Temple Court, where Jeremiah had stood when he chewed out the Temple staff centuries before; Jesus was showing he had the same authority as Jeremiah. When he said "den of thieves" the Pharisees recalled the whole passage, part of which is: "Will you steal and murder, commit adultery and perjury, burn incense to Baal and follow other gods you have not known, and then come and stand before me in this house, which bears my Name, and say, "We are safe to do all these detestable things? Has this house, which bears my Name, become a *den of thieves* to you?" Now I don't think the Temple staff of Jesus' day was doing all the bad stuff Jeremiah's talking about, but Jesus' point is they were just as unfaithful in their own way. And then they'd remember the next thing Jeremiah said: "Go now to the place in Shiloh where I first made a dwelling for my Name, and see what I did to it because of the wickedness of my people Israel." Tell me about Shiloh and the Ark. *They took the Ark to a battle and everybody died, and they lost the Ark.* Yes, and when they got the Ark back, did they return it to Shiloh? *No?* Right. God abandoned Shiloh; God and his Ark never dwelled there again.

Now these two prophecies together are very insulting to the Temple staff. Jesus, speaking through Isaiah and Jeremiah, prophesies that being a Jew won't matter much, and that non-Jews may be dearer to God than Chosen People. Then he compares them to adulterers and worshipers of Baal, the baby-eating false god. And finally he says that this place, the beautiful Temple in Jerusalem, will be abandoned by God just as Shiloh was: that God won't live there anymore. As fast as the scribes and priests figure all this out, they are livid! What's livid? *Real mad?* Yes, you might say killing mad.

Then "...the blind and the lame came to him in the temple, and he healed them." Healing is how Jesus shows his authority to prophesy. "But when the chief priests and the scribes saw the wonderful things that he did, and the children crying out in the temple, "Hosanna to the Son of David!" they were indignant; and they sought a way to destroy him; for they feared him, because all the multitude was astonished at his teaching." When people say "Hosanna to the Son of David!" to Jesus, who do they think he is? *The Messiah?* Yes, and a Son of David Messiah would be a...*king?* Yes. So how would Caesar like for the Jews to get themselves a new king like David? *He wouldn't like it.* So what would he do? *Have a war?* Yes. And the Temple staff doesn't want a war: the Romans would go crazy and kill half the country. So they have both a political reason and a religious reason to get rid of Jesus.

And a few years after Jesus ascended to Heaven, the Jews rebelled against the Romans, who defeated them, captured the Ark, and destroyed the Temple, which hasn't been rebuilt even until today.

Y'all remind me what Jesus did in Jerusalem when he was a kid. *He was teaching the grownups?* Yes, at the camel store? *Ha, no, at the Temple!* Yes; he was discussing the Scriptures with the teachers there (probably scribes, Pharisees, and Levites), and they were impressed with his knowledge. I like to imagine that on this day when grownup Jesus quoted Isaiah and Jeremiah at the Temple, some of the older men there would have remembered him when he was a smart kid 20 Passovers ago.

Praised be Jesus Christ! *Now and forever!*

Class over!

Chapter Twenty-Four: Just Do It

(Gospels 11)

Matthew 21, The Two Sons: faith & works, body & soul. Matthew 22, Wedding Feast parable: proper attire and behavior. Chosen people vs. Gentiles [Mass, Revelation Wedding Feast of the Lamb]. Matthew 25, Judgment of nations through least of my brothers: works matter. See Jesus in others.
Soul & body /faith & works.

Y'all remember last week Jesus drove the Temple staff crazy right in front of the Temple? *Yes.* Imagine someone coming into your house and yelling at your parents...who would stand for that? The scribes & priests got so fed up with Jesus that they wanted him dead. Tell me again, who ran Judea? *Caesar?* Yes, and who did Caesar put in charge of Judea? He washed his hands at Jesus' trial...*Pontius Pilate!* Yes, the Roman Governor, who had the power to sentence criminals to death. So the priests told Pilate that Jesus wasn't just a religion problem, but a political problem, too. Crowds of people thought Jesus was the Messiah, a new King like David; that would make Jesus a rebel. So after knocking over tables in the Temple Court and chewing out Pharisees, Jesus had only a few more days to live.

In these last days Jesus was still busy telling parables; let's look at a couple of them. Remember when I read parables, imagine ya'll are in ancient Jerusalem listening to Jesus tell 'em.

"What do you think? A man had two sons; and he went to the first and said, 'Son, go and work in the vineyard today.' And he answered, 'I will not'; but afterward he repented and went. And he went to the second and said the same; and he answered, 'I go, sir,' but did not go. Which of the two *did the will* of his father?" *The first one!* Yes, that's easy. Jesus isn't too interested in what people *say* they believe, he's interested in what their faith makes them...*do!* Yes, because Jesus expects us to act...in...*faith!* Yes. Then Jesus told the chief priests and Pharisees, "Truly, I say to you, the tax collectors and prostitutes go into the kingdom of God before you." I bet their heads were about to explode! Tax collectors and prostitutes weren't part of decent society...but they're going to heaven first? Jesus means that people like the Prodigal Son who repent of huge sins will do better than people like his older brother, who won't repent of their small sins. Then Jesus says, "John the Baptist told everyone to repent; and humble sinners did repent. But y'all are too proud." And without repentance, there's no...*forgiveness?* Yes. And no forgiveness means...hair on fire...pitchfork in the butt...*Hell!* That's it! Yes? *What's a prostitute?* Ask...your...*parents!* Yes!

Tonight my favorite Sacrament is Marriage, because it figures in this next parable. "The kingdom of heaven may be compared to a king who gave a marriage feast for his son..." OK, this is a parable, so tell me who the

King is...*God?* More specifically...*God the Father.* Yes...and the son is...*Jesus.* Yes. The father "sent his servants to call those who were invited to the marriage feast; but they would not come." OK, this half of the class is Chosen People, Sons of Abraham; the other half are non-Jews, what we call Gentiles. Which group is invited to the wedding feast? *Chosen People!* Yes, but they didn't come. This doesn't mean *every last person* didn't come; it just means a lot of them didn't, even though they were God's family.

"Again he sent other servants, saying, 'Tell those who are invited, Behold, I have made ready my dinner, my oxen and my fat calves are killed, and everything is ready; come to the marriage feast.' But they made light of it and went off, one to his farm, another to his business, while the rest seized his servants, treated them shamefully, and killed them." Now, who might one of these messengers be, whose message the Pharisees ignored? *Jesus?* Good guess, but who is the son in this story? *Jesus.* Yes, so he can't do two parts. Who was the messenger who came before Jesus...his head got cut off...it was put on a plate...*John the Baptist?* Yes. "The king was angry, and he sent his troops and destroyed those murderers and burned their city. Then he said to his servants, 'The wedding is ready, but those invited were not worthy. Go therefore to the highways, and invite to the marriage feast as many as you find.' Which group is this? *Us!* Yes, the Gentiles, people not part of God's Covenant. And those servants went out into the streets and gathered all whom they found, both bad and good; so the wedding hall was filled with guests. "But when the king came in to look at the guests, he saw there a man who had no wedding garment..." Who has been to a wedding feast, what we call nowadays a reception...lots of y'all...tell me about it. *It's fun and there's good food.* And? *People dance and there's music.* Yes, a great time. And how do people dress...like they're gonna cut the grass? *No they dress nice!* Why? *Because it's special!* Yes...I mean, why do people dress nicely when they attend something special? *You just have to dress special if you're going to something special.* Yes, that's how we show with our bodies that our minds and souls believe it's special. Daughter, if I came to your wedding in a t-shirt & flip-flops, how would you feel? *I wouldn't like it.* But suppose I said I know this is your special day, and I'm so glad I came, but I don't like wearing a suit and tie, they're not comfortable like jeans. *I wouldn't care.* Right. You wouldn't want someone to behave badly at your wedding. *But clothes aren't the same as behaving!* Well, in some ways, clothes *are* a kind of behavior. How you act, smell, sound, and look are all parts of behavior. But the guest isn't thrown out just because he isn't wearing the right clothes. It's because he's not repentant; he wants to eat at the banquet, but he wants to do it his way, not...*God's way!* Yes.

And the king says to this guy who had no wedding garment, "Friend, how did you get in here without a wedding garment?" I love that: *"how did you get in here?"* The king can tell just by looking that the man doesn't have respect for the king, and how wonderful the feast is. "Then the king said to the attendants, 'Bind him hand and foot, and cast him into the outer darkness; there men will weep and gnash their teeth." What's the outer darkness? *Hell?* Yes. Now what banquet is the parable about? We have it on Sundays....*Mass!* Yes. But something is missing from this wedding feast...we have the groom...we have the father of the groom...*there's no bride!* Yes! Who or what is the bride...who is Jesus' bride? *Jesus didn't get married.* Yes, you are right. But this is a heavenly, spiritual marriage; like when Isaiah said Israel's husband was God. Jesus' bride is the Church. He loves the Church like I love my wife; well, actually it's the other way around, which is... *You love her like Jesus loves the Church.* Yes. And that's why we call the Church "she," like a ship. Do priests get married? *No.* Right: they imitate Christ, who had no bride on Earth. But who is Jesus' heavenly bride? *The Church?* Yes, so if priests imitate Christ, they marry...*the Church too?* Yes. *How can she have a thousand husbands?* It's not identical to an earthly marriage. By the way, speaking of spiritual marriage, whom do nuns marry? *Nobody.* I said *spiritually. Ummm, the Church?* Is the Church a bride? *Yes.* Do women marry brides? *No.* So do nuns marry the Church? *No.* Women marry...*men.* Yes; so nuns marry...*ummm, Jesus?* Yes. Priests give themselves to the Church and nuns give themselves to Jesus; and my wife and I give ourselves to each other. It's all very romantic.

Faith'n'Works

Here's our last parable from chapter 25 of Matthew's gospel: "When the Son of Man comes in his glory, and all the angels with him, then he will sit on his glorious throne." That's Jesus quoting Daniel again. "Before him will be gathered all the nations, and he will separate them one from another as a shepherd separates the sheep from the goats, and he will place the sheep at his right hand, but the goats at the left." So the sheep go to...*Heaven,* and the goats...*to Hell.* Yes. And he says to the sheep, "I was hungry and you gave me food, I was thirsty and you gave me drink, I was a stranger and you welcomed me, I was naked and you clothed me, I was sick and you visited me, I was in prison and you came to me.' Once again, Jesus wants to know what you do, not just what you say you believe.

"Then the righteous will answer him, 'Lord, when did we see thee hungry and feed thee, or thirsty and give thee drink? And when did we see thee a stranger and welcome thee, or naked and clothe thee? And when did we see thee sick or in prison and visit thee?' And the King will answer them, 'Truly, I say to you, as you did it to one of the least of these my brethren, you did it to me.'

When Jesus says "the righteous" in this way does he mean people who are really, truly righteous? *No, people who just think they're righteous.* Yes; people who think they aren't bad enough to need to repent, and do good works. And in this parable, how does Jesus expect us to take care of him? *By taking care of other people?* Yes, because Jesus is in all of us.

Scabby People & the Grumpy Nun

Who's this? [I pull out a picture book about Mother Teresa] *Mother Teresa.* Yes, nice to see some of y'all know who she is; tell me about her. *She takes care of sick people.* Yes, she used to; she died a few years ago...the Church may make her a saint in your lifetimes. [I show some pictures in the book] She lived in India, where very poor sick people may lie on the sidewalk until they die. She made it her business to take care of as many of them as she could. She had been a schoolteacher; but one day on a train Jesus spoke to her. He asked her to love him by loving the least of his children, just like Jesus said in this parable. So her life permanently changed at that moment.

Who's Jay Leno? *He has a TV show!* Yes, the Tonight Show. About 30 years ago, I saw Mother Teresa on the Tonight Show. In her photographs she always looked grumpy, but I was surprised to see how lively and happy she was in real life. I couldn't understand why she was happy, since she spent all her time dealing with scabby, smelly, sick, dying people. But she said she saw Jesus in all those people; and she was happy to do stuff for Jesus. She was just doing what Jesus said to do in the parable. Anyway, for years after watching her on TV, I felt guilty about not doing anything for anybody like Mother Teresa did. One day I told my pastor I liked Mother Teresa's example, but I never saw sick people lying on the sidewalk in Greenville. So he started me going to the hospital to visit sick people and bring them Communion. At first it was odd: I can't stand the hospital, didn't know any of the patients, and felt unworthy of bringing them communion. But after a couple of months I got used to it, and learned to see Jesus in those people...no kidding. Now y'all remember Moses' stick and Jesus' cloak with the tassels, were those things magic? *No, they were just...well, God's power went through them.* Yes; they were *media*, like the TV that mediated Mother Teresa into my house. Well, over the next few years of going to visit the sick, I realized I was being a medium for God's grace; there were times when dying people were so happy to see me, but it wasn't me in particular. I think it was God coming through me to them...like so:

One time I went to see a woman, who of course was a total stranger. I knocked & walked into a dimly-lit room. There was a very old, thin woman in the bed, the skinniest thing you've ever seen. She wasn't moving, but her eyes were open. Her daughter, a grownup like me, was trying to feed her some yogurt; and her two daughters, about your age, were there too. The old woman's daughter was stressing out and getting frustrated because her sick mom wouldn't eat any yogurt, but she was supposed to. And the two granddaughters were worried and stressed because their mom and grandmother were stressed. The whole room was unhappy. I told the daughter I was there to bring her mom Communion if she could receive it; sometimes people are too dehydrated to receive Communion, they can't swallow. The daughter said her mom would want to, but she was too dry, couldn't swallow, and wouldn't eat any yogurt, which would moisten her mouth and throat. I said, do you mind if I try? She said sure, go ahead, and sat in a chair, just exhausted from taking care of her two girls and her mother. I took the cup and spoon. As I got closer to grandma, I saw she was so dehydrated that her lips were cracked and had little scabs on them. I said to her, "Hey darlin', I'm here to bring you Communion if you'd like to receive." She looked right into my eyes and nodded just the littlest bit; she was worn out, too. "OK...do you want to try some yogurt? It'll help you to swallow." Another little nod, kept looking right in my eyes. "OK...here you go, just a little bit...there. Was that too much? OK...another one...let me know when you've had enough...another one, good..." And it went like that 'til she ate the whole container. Then, "Do you think you can swallow a little bit of Communion?" *Yes.* "Would you like to sip some water from a straw to help it go down?" *Yes.* "OK darlin'...the Body of Christ...Amen...here's the water...is that enough? There ya go." We just looked at each other the whole time, and all the tension left the room. I swear she was smiling with her eyes the biggest smile I've ever seen. I could feel God's love flowing out me and into her, and from her into me. We were both seeing Jesus in each other. It was incredible. I said, "I'll see ya next week," and kissed her on the forehead. When I came back the next week she was gone. Yes? *How come she got to have communion right after eating?* Because the rules are different when you are seriously sick.

This is a good example of what can happen if you try to see Jesus in everyone, especially "the least" of his children. Not only can you be a medium of Jesus' love to a stranger, but *surprise*, they can channel Jesus' grace right into you as well. It's amazing what great things happen when a sinner like me lets God use him. And if it weren't for this parable and Mother Teresa, I don't know if I would ever have visited a single sick stranger.

That was our last parable; Jesus is going to be arrested soon. But before the soldiers come for him, he and his Apostles eat the Final Dinner. *The Last Supper?* Oh yeah, that's it. We'll cover that next.

Class over!

Chapter Twenty-Five: Melchizedek Redux

(Gospels 12)

Last Supper: old & new Passover meal, but bread & wine like Melchizedek.

Remember from last week that Jesus had come to Jerusalem a few days before Passover. Now it's Thursday evening and Jesus wants to have dinner with his friends the apostles. "Now the feast of Unleavened Bread drew near, which is called the Passover. And the chief priests and the scribes were seeking how to put him to death ...Then came the day of Unleavened Bread, on which the Passover lamb had to be sacrificed. The disciples came to Jesus, saying, "Where will you have us prepare for you to eat the Passover?" He said, "Go into the city to a certain one, and say to him, 'The Teacher says, My time is at hand; I will keep the Passover at your house with my disciples." And the disciples did as Jesus had directed them, and they prepared the Passover. When it was evening, he sat at table with the twelve disciples." Tell me please, at the first Passover, what did people eat? *A lamb.* Yes, and...*umm, some bread?* Yes, what's called *unleavened* bread. Does anyone know what leavening is? No? How about yeast? No? Yeast or leavening is what makes bread fluffy. If you don't put yeast in bread dough, you get very flat bread. But you can eat sooner, because it can take a few hours for leavened dough to rise and fluff up. At the first Passover, Moses told the Israelites to make unleavened bread and eat quickly, so that when Pharaoh decided to let them leave Egypt, they'd be ready to go. Tell me what pita bread is. *It's flat round bread.* Yes, it has just a little yeast and it doesn't rise for very long before it's baked. Can anybody think of some other round flat bread? No? How about at Mass? *Oh, communion bread!* Yes; it's unleavened bread, too. *It's real flat.* Yes it is.

Again with the Miracle Bread

So what do you expect Jesus and the apostles to eat at this dinner? *Lamb and bread!* Yes, unleavened bread. "Now as they were eating, Jesus took bread, and blessed, and broke it, and gave it to the disciples...." There's the bread. And Jesus said, "This is my body which is given up for you." What? Why would Jesus say the bread was his body? *So we would have Communion?* Yes. But right then the apostles didn't know that. Remember after Jesus fed the crowds and they wanted more miracle food the next day he said some strange things that upset people...about eating weird stuff...*drinking* weird stuff...*oh, eat my flesh and drink my blood!* Yes! Nobody understood Jesus; how could anybody eat Jesus? But then at the Last Supper he says

157

the bread is his body. Would the apostles know how to eat Jesus now? *Yes, they'd eat the bread!* Yes, the bread he turned into his body. Then he said, "Do this in remembrance of me." What did Jesus just do? *Change the bread?* Yes, into...*his body.* Yes. So what should they do to remember Jesus? *Change the bread?* Yes. *How can they do that?* Jesus would work the miracle through them; they would have his authority. When do we still remember this? *At Mass.* Yes. And listen again: "This is my body which is given up for you." What's Jesus mean that his body is given up for them? If say, soldiers give up, what happens? *They surrender.* Yes. Is Jesus going to surrender himself to anybody soon? *The Roman soldiers?* Yes; and what will happen to Jesus? *He'll be crucified.* Yes, he'll be sacrificed for our sins. So when Jesus says his body is given up for them he's making a little prophecy, because nobody's arrested him just yet. And the apostles don't know why he'd give his body up for them anyway. But *we* know he'll be sacrificed. So, did Jesus sacrifice himself? *Yes.* Oh, he killed himself at the Last Supper? *Ha, no!* Right; who *did* kill Jesus? *The soldiers.* Yes. Jesus offered himself as a sacrifice at the Last Supper, but didn't do the actual sacrificing, the killing. That happened the next day, which would be...*Good Friday?* Yes. *Why do we say it's Good?* Because it was good for *us.*

"And he took a cup, and when he had given thanks he gave it to them, saying, "Drink of it, all of you; for this is my blood of the new covenant, which is shed for you." Y'all and the apostles have already figured out how to eat Jesus' flesh; how will they drink his blood? *By drinking the wine?* Yes, by drinking the wine Jesus changed into...*blood.* Yes. Do y'all think at the Last Supper Jesus' body and blood looked like a hunk of meat and a cup of blood? *No it just looked like bread and wine.* Yes; the apostles still needed faith, just like we do at Mass.

Now Jesus and his friends were observing Passover, which began with Moses in Egypt; what have they eaten so far? *Bread?* Yes, anything else? *Well they drank some wine.* Yes; what are they *supposed* to eat at a Passover dinner? *A Lamb!* Yes, sacrificing and eating lambs were signs of the Covenant God made with the Israelites. Tell me about the sign of the lamb's blood at the first Passover. *They splashed it on their houses!* Yes. But Jesus says drinking his blood, not splashing it, is the sign of a *new* covenant. And right about now the apostles are thinking: *what new covenant?* Isn't this a Passover meal like people have eaten for centuries? But maybe the apostles remember one of Jeremiah's prophecies that we looked at a couple of months ago: "Behold, the days are coming, says the LORD, when I will make a new covenant with the house of Israel and the house of Judah, not like the covenant which I made with their fathers when I took them by the hand to bring them out of the land of Egypt, my covenant which they broke, though I was their husband, says the LORD...." (See how important marriage is?) "I will put my law within them, and I will write it upon their hearts; and I will be their God, and they shall be my people." It's like a romance between God and his people. Do my wife and I have a bunch of rules on paper? *No.* Why not? *Because if you love somebody you don't need rules.* Yes. Boys never answer that question, but the girls always get it right. Boys, pay attention to what the girls say. Anyway, I imagine the apostles thinking, "Wow, is Jesus talking about that new covenant that Jeremiah prophesied? I wonder how that's gonna work?" Somebody tell me how it's gonna work. No takers...what do we expect the apostles to eat that they haven't eaten? *A lamb.* Yes. Tell me what John the Baptist called Jesus...Jesus was coming to be baptized...behold the Banana of God...*Behold the Lamb of God!* Yes, who... *takes away the sins of the world.* There ya go! So if Jesus is a Lamb, what kind of Lamb...a Christmas Lamb....Little Bo Peep's Lamb...*a Passover Lamb!* Yes. How are the Apostles going to eat this Lamb? What's the bread? *Jesus.* What's the Lamb? *Jesus.* So if you eat the bread you...*eat the Lamb!* Yes. This is a new kind of covenant meal; but it's like the old one, too.

Now who was it that made that first Passover covenant with God? *Moses.* Yes. Moses was a very big deal for Jews: he got their ancestors out of Egypt, brought them the 10 Commandments, set up the Ark and Meeting Tent, got them to the Promised Land. So why would anybody dump that covenant and listen to Jesus talk about a new covenant? *'Cause Jeremiah said there'd be a new one?* Ooh, good guess, but Jeremiah isn't as big a deal as Moses. He doesn't outrank Moses.

Now tell me yet again what they have at this Final Din-Din? *The Last Supper.* Yes...what did they have? *Bread and wine.* Yes. And thinking way back this year, y'all may remember this guy [on the board] M-e-l-c-h-i-z...*Melchizedek!* Yes. Tell me. *He was a priest?* Yes. A king *and* a priest. What did Melchizedek bring out to Abraham...chips & dip? *Umm, bread and wine!* Yes. We don't know exactly how Melchizedek offered up the bread and wine, but Genesis said he was a priest. And Abraham gave him a tenth of the stuff he had just won in a battle. Sort of like the way we give money on Sunday to support the Church. So if Melchizedek blesses Abraham, and then Abraham makes an offering to Melchizedek, who ranks higher? *Melchizedek?* Yes, why? *Well...Abraham had to give him stuff.* Yes. And because Melchizedek outranks Abraham, he also outranks Abraham's descendants, like Isaac and Moses. So when Jesus offers bread and wine like Melchizedek, he's showing that his new covenant outranks Moses' covenant.

When Jesus offered the same things that Melchizedek did, I bet the apostles were thinking, "is this like Melchizedek?" And then "does it matter?" because they didn't figure things out right away, and Jesus had given them a lot to think about.

After supper was over did they go out bowling? *They went to pray!* Yes, in...a...bowling alley? *Was it the Garden of Eden?* No, good guess; another Garden... *the Garden of Gethsemane.* Yes, good. But time's up, we'll start here next week.

Praised be Jesus Christ! *Now and Forever!*

Class over!

Chapter Twenty-Six: The Prodigal Thief

(Gospels 13)

Matthew 26, Mark 14: Gethsemane, prayers answered, sometimes God's answer to prayer is "no." Apostles fall asleep 3 times. Jesus' arrest thru Crucifixion: Pilate washes hands, Peter breaks oral contract, denies Jesus 3 times. New Passover Lamb with no broken bones per Old Passover & Leviticus; blood, water & hyssop; forgiveness of Good Thief.

Remind me where we left off last week. *They had the Last Supper!* Yes.

So after the Last Supper, where did everyone go? *To the Garden.* Yes, the Garden of...G-E-T-H... *Gethsemane!* Yes. And what did Jesus do? *He prayed.* And what did Jesus ask the Apostles do? *To pray too.* Yes, to watch and pray. And what did Jesus pray for? *He didn't want to die.* Yes. "He advanced a little and fell prostrate in prayer, saying, "My Father, if it is possible, let this cup pass from me; yet, not as I will, but as you will." And what was God's answer to this prayer? *No?* Right, God said *No.* I remind myself when I pray for something that if God could tell Jesus *No,* he can tell me *No,* too.

Then Jesus went to check on the apostles; guess what they were doing. *Sleeping?* Yes! "...he said to Peter, "So, could you not watch with me one hour?" Then he went to pray some more; "again he came and found them sleeping, for their eyes were heavy." Guess how many times he found them sleeping? *3 times!* Yes! Tell me, doing or saying something 3 times makes or breaks a...*contract!* Yes! So the apostles made it perfectly clear they'd rather snooze than pray with Jesus. Does anyone know what Adoration of the Blessed Sacrament is? No? Who knows what this gold thing is [I draw a monstrance]...yes? *It's what they put Communion in.* Yes, it's called a monstrance; not like *monster,* but like *demonstrate.* It means *to show* in Latin. This center part is glass so it shows Jesus in the Eucharist. Some parishes have what's called an Adoration chapel, usually about the size of a big dining room. It's open 24 hours a day, and has a monstrance placed on a little altar. People sign up for an hour at a time to watch and pray in these chapels with Jesus, partly because the apostles were too sleepy on that Thursday night. If anyone in your family does Adoration, you might go with them sometime; it's very peaceful, and the hour passes quicker than you might think. You can help make up for the snoozing apostles.

Right after Jesus found them sleeping for the third time, he was arrested and taken to the chief priests of the Temple, who wanted the Romans to get rid of Jesus. How did the authorities know where to find Jesus?

Judas showed them. Yes. He did a bad thing. But hadn't Jesus picked him to be an apostle? *Yes.* How could an apostle be so bad? *Well, everybody can be bad.* Yes, even people personally picked out by Jesus can sin. Even popes and saints sin and go to confession.

So they took Jesus to the Temple. The High Priest said "tell us if you are the Christ, the Son of God." Remind me, Christ is Greek for...*Messiah!* Yes, in English the...*Anointed One!* Yes. "Jesus said to him, "You have said so. But I tell you, hereafter you will see the Son of man seated at the right hand of Power, and coming on the clouds of heaven." Jesus is quoting Daniel again about himself: sitting beside God the Father, coming down from heaven. It's like Jesus saying he's God. The high priest goes nuts! "Then the high priest tore his robes, and said, "He has uttered blasphemy. Why do we still need witnesses? You have now heard his blasphemy. What is your judgment?" They answered, "He deserves death."

Then Jesus was taken to the Roman governor...P-O-N- *Pontius Pilate,* yes. But Pilate didn't think Jesus was a threat to Rome. He sent Jesus to King Herod, the son of the King Herod who killed all the babies when Jesus was born. Herod was the King of Judea, the King of the Jews, but Pilate outranked him. Herod didn't have a problem with Jesus either, and sent him back to Pilate. Pilate was ready to release Jesus, but the priests said no. What did Pilate do to Jesus, hoping the priests would feel sorry for him and agree that Jesus could be let go? *He whipped him!* Yes. And tell me the mean stuff the soldiers did to Jesus. *They hit him.* Yes, and? *Put the crown of thorns in his head.* Yes, and? *Spit on him.* Yes. Remember this Isaiah prophecy: "...many were astonished at him-- his appearance was so marred, beyond human semblance, and his form beyond that of the sons of men..." Why does that matter? *Because that's how Jesus looks.* Yes. Isaiah prophesied a suffering Messiah, not a fighting Messiah like David.

Then Pilate let the people choose between letting Jesus go, and letting a criminal go. Now what day is this? *Thursday?* That was the night before. *Friday?* Yes, and the next day is...*Saturday.* In Hebrew please...*the Sabbath.* And this is a special Sabbath...the Lamb business...*Passover!* Yes! "Now at the [Passover] feast the governor was accustomed to release for the crowd any one prisoner whom they wanted. And they had then a notorious prisoner, called Barabbas." What's notorious? *Bad?* Yes...famously bad. "So when they had gathered, Pilate said to them, "Whom do you want me to release for you, Barabbas or Jesus who is called Christ?" For he knew that it was out of envy that they had delivered him up." What's envy mean? *Jealous?* Yes. The priests were jealous that people followed Jesus, and thought he was the Messiah; and that he knew the Scriptures better than they did; and that he was righteous when he knocked over the tables earlier in the week. Jesus had aggravated them and they were fed up. But Pilate didn't want to do what was right, which would have been...*to let Jesus go!* Yes. He wanted to do what was convenient. Tell me what happened next. *They picked Barabbas.* And what did the crowd yell about Jesus? *Crucify him!* Yes. So Pilate let the crowd choose between Jesus and Barabbas and they chose Barabbas. And what did Pilate do to show it wasn't his problem? *He washed his hands?* Yes. He wanted to show that his hands were clean of this dirty business; he said, "I am innocent of this righteous man's blood," but he was the person in charge, not the crowd; he wasn't innocent.

Now when Jesus was arrested on Thursday night, what did the apostles do? *Run away!* Yes, they were all scared. Later that night some people recognized Peter as a friend of Jesus. What did Peter say? *He wasn't*

Jesus' friend. Yes...how many times did he say that? *Three times!* Yes, so... *he's breaking a contract!* Yes...what contract? *Umm, to be Jesus' friend?* Yes, to be his disciple, his follower; Peter had told Jesus at the Last Supper he'd stick with him and even die for him. But Peter, whose name means...*Rock,* yes, ran off and even told people he didn't know who Jesus was. Some rock. More like Silly-Putty.

I probably would have run away too.

About noon on Friday the Roman soldiers took Jesus up to a hill called Golgotha to be crucified between two thieves. And Jesus didn't make a fuss even though he was innocent. But Isaiah had said as much: "...he was harshly treated...Like a lamb led to the slaughter...he was silent and opened not his mouth." While he was hanging there on the cross people made fun of him: "Hey Jesus, if you're the Messiah, why don't you get yourself off that cross; why don't you get Elijah to come save you? Huh? Huh? C'mon Son of God, come down and we'll believe in ya!" Just terrible how mean people were to him. Jesus was treated like the Suffering Servant that Isaiah had prophesied. And "One of the criminals who were hanged railed at him, saying, "Are you not the Christ? Save yourself and us!" But the other rebuked him, saying, "...this man has done nothing wrong." And he said, "Jesus, remember me when you come into your kingdom." The second man is called the Good Thief...why? *'Cause he told Jesus he was sorry?* Yes, genius! He repented of his sins and had a...change...*of heart!* Yes! How do we know the Thief repented? *'Cause he said so?* Yes, he repented out loud; like David, and the Prodigal Son, and like we do in...*confession.* Yes. "And [Jesus] said to him, "Truly, I say to you, today you will be with me in Paradise." I like to imagine the Good Thief and Jesus on their crosses: hot, sweaty, thirsty, dirty, bloody, big nails hammered into them, flies buzzing around their heads. And how happy they would both be: the Good Thief repents, and Jesus forgives him. I bet for a few minutes they were as happy as the Prodigal Son and his Daddy.

Then Jesus saw his mother Mary with the youngest apostle, John. John was pretty brave to be with Jesus; he was the only apostle there. Because Jesus didn't have any brothers or sisters, who would take care of his mom when he died? *Didn't he get John to do it?* Yes, what did Jesus say? *Umm...behold your mother?* Yes, and to Mary he said...*behold your son?* Yes, good. We understand Jesus was showing that Mary wasn't just going to be John's mother, but the mother of everybody; and the Church's mother, too. Then Jesus said he was thirsty...tell me. *They gave him some wine in a sponge?* Yes, how'd they get it up to his mouth? *On a spear?* Close, but no. *A stick?* Yes. A particular stick as we'll see in a few minutes.

At about 3 o'clock Jesus died. Remind me why Jesus died. *He died for our sins!* Yes, remember Isaiah said, "Because he surrendered himself to death...he shall take away the sins of many, and win pardon for their offenses." And he died silently, like a...*lamb!* Yes. Later that day, "Since it was the day of Preparation, in order to prevent the bodies from remaining on the cross on the Sabbath (for that Sabbath was a high day), the Jews asked Pilate that their legs might be broken, and that they might be taken away." If tomorrow is the Passover feast what's being prepared today? *The food?* Yes which includes...*lambs?* Yes, so what's the first step with the lambs? *To cook them!* Before that. *To kill them?* Yes. And John the Baptist called Jesus...*the Lamb of God,* yes and at the same time that the Old Covenant lambs are being killed, the New Covenant Lamb...*is being killed too!* Yes. And when Jewish people had the Old Covenant Levites kill and offer up a lamb for their sins, what would happen? *They'd be forgiven?* Yes; in Leviticus we saw that sacrificing the

163

lamb *imperfectly* atones for the sin. And how about when the New Covenant Lamb was sacrificed on the cross? *Our sins are forgiven?* Almost: the sins are *perfectly atoned* for. We still have to ask for forgiveness, though. Trick question: who offers sacrifices for sinners? *Priests.* Yes; trickier question: who offered up the New Covenant Lamb? *Well, the Romans killed him.* Yes, but as Jesus said, they didn't know what they were doing; when was Jesus' body and blood *offered* to God, not killed? *Umm, at the Last Supper?* Yes. So who was the priest? *Jesus?* Yes. *But how can he do that?* Do what? *Be the priest if he gets killed.* Well, we understand that Jesus is the priest *and* the victim. That way we have a perfect priest and a perfect victim to atone for all sins forever. But they're the same person. It's different from sacrificing an animal.

Back to the story: the Jews don't want these crucified guys "hanging around" on Passover, it's not dignified. They ask the Romans to break their legs so they'll hurry up and die before Passover starts. "So the soldiers came and broke the legs of the first, and of the other who had been crucified with him; but when they came to Jesus and saw that he was already dead, they did not break his legs." I think the soldiers beat the thieves' shinbones like you'd hit a baseball with a bat, just as hard as you can until their legs were broken like toothpicks. *Ewww, gross!* No kidding. But Jesus looked dead so they didn't break his legs. That way he'd be a perfect lamb; remember, God wouldn't accept lambs that were sick, mangy or had broken legs. Then what did a soldier do to be sure Jesus was dead? *Stick a spear in him?* Yes; and what came out? *Blood and water!* Yes, genius, you remembered the water. Does anyone remember what Moses and Levite priests used to sprinkle blood and water on people? *It was a bunch of sticks.* Yes, remember what kind of sticks? H-Y-S- *Hyssop!* Yes. Before Jesus died, John's gospel says a hyssop stick was used to raise the wine-soaked sponge up to his mouth. So there's hyssop, blood and water when Jesus is sacrificed. That's like those Old Testament rituals when a priest would kill a bird over a pot of water, and use hyssop to sprinkle the blood and water on people or homes, like so: "take the...hyssop...along with the living bird, and dip them in the blood of the bird that was killed and in the running water, and sprinkle the house seven times." John's Gospel is careful to show these same things at the crucifixion so people will know Jesus' sacrifice relates to the old way of sacrificing. Trick question: how do we get sprinkled with the blood of the New Covenant Lamb? When do get sprinkled with anything? *At Mass we get sprinkled sometimes.* Yes. Any other time water gets on us? *At baptism?* Yes. In both those cases we're sprinkled with water, but the blood is included in the water because...what came out of Jesus? *Blood and water!* Yes. So if we're sprinkled with the water, it includes...*the blood.* Yes, the blood of the...*Lamb!* Yes.

Later on Friday Jesus was taken down and placed in a tomb: "After this Joseph of Arimathea, who was a disciple of Jesus...asked Pilate that he might take away the body of Jesus, and Pilate gave him leave. So he came and took away his body. Now in the place where he was crucified there was a garden, and in the garden a new tomb where no one had ever been laid. So because of the Jewish day of Preparation, as the tomb was close at hand, they laid Jesus there."

(Class continues in the next chapter.)

Chapter Twenty-Seven: No Loitering

(Gospels 14)

John 20, Resurrection up to Ascension: Anastasis (Greek) image of Jesus in Sheol; Mary thinks He's a gardener? The apostles receive another dose of the Holy Spirit, authorized to forgive & retain sins [Confession]. The apostles' faith & doubt, especially Thomas.

After Jesus was buried on Friday evening, the apostles hid out; they worried they'd wind up on crosses themselves. What happened on Saturday? *Nothing?* Well, Saturday was a feast day...what feast day? *Easter!* Easter? There's no Easter just yet; when's the first Easter? *The next day.* Yes, Sunday. So what's the Saturday/Sabado/Sabbath Lamb feast? *Passover!* [on the board] Yes. What's the Hebrew word? No guesses? *It starts with a P. Pesach!* Yes, P-E-S-A-C-H, [on the board under Passover] that's ok, it's not easy to remember. So what happened on Sunday? *Jesus was alive again!* Yes, we call that particular Sunday...*Easter Sunday.* Yes. What word does *Easter* have in it? *Umm....east?* Yes, and where does the sun rise? *In the East.* Yes. The word Easter refers to Springtime, it's an old pagan word, but now we use it for a Christian holy day...we baptized it so it's a Christian word now. *You can't baptize a word!* You're right, I don't mean it literally. Hey, cómo se llama Easter en Español? What's Spanish for Easter? *Pascua!* Yes, P-a-s-c-u-a [on the board under Pesach]. That's how the Spanish say Pesach. In Italian they say Pasqua; in French Pâques; in Holland it's Pasen; in Danish it's Påske. Most countries say "Pesach" when we say "Easter" because the whole 4 days from the Last Supper on Holy Thursday to Easter Sunday make the Passover, the Pesach, of the New Covenant. We miss out on that in English; but we do call Jesus the *Paschal Lamb*, which means what? *The Passover Lamb?* Yes, the Lamb of the *New* Passover.

So when did Easter start? *Sunday morning.* What happened? *Jesus was alive again.* Yes, that's called the...Res...*Resurrection!* Yes. Somebody ask me how Jesus resurrected. *How did He do that?* I...don't...know! It's...a...*miracle!* Yes! Humans can't figure it out. Now, Super-duper trick question: what was the first thing Jesus did after he was buried? *Walk out of the tomb?* Good guess, but listen:

I believe in God,
the Father Almighty,
Creator of Heaven and earth.
I believe in Jesus Christ, His only Son, our Lord,
who was conceived by the Holy Spirit,
born of the Virgin Mary,

suffered under Pontius Pilate,
was crucified, died and was buried.
He descended into Hell.
On the third day, He rose again...

So before Jesus rose? *He went to Hell!?* Yes, but remember when Lazarus, the dog-licked-scabby-man died, he rested in the bosom of...*Abraham!* Yes. Was he in Heaven? *No.* Was he in Hell with the Devil? *No.* So where was he? *The other place that starts with an S.* Yes, S-H-E...*Sheol!* Yes, like Hades in Greek. English uses the word *Hell* for both Sheol and 'regular' Hell.

Let's look at this handout of Jesus descending into Sheol:

The Anastasis fresco, Chora church, Istanbul

This event is called the "Anastasis" [on the board] in Greek. It means "standing-back-up;" just like "Resurrection" means "erecting-up-again" in Latin. By the way, Anastasia (ah-nah-STAH-zi-ya) is a girl's name in Russian and Greek; it comes from Anastasis. How about that name, girls? *It's pretty!* I think so, too. Boys? *Who cares?* Boys- wise up to what girls think.

What would you expect a picture of the Resurrection to show? *Jesus coming out of the tomb with the soldiers and all.* Yes. The Eastern Churches also remember that Jesus first went to Sheol, like the Creed says.

Hey, let's check out the Greek on the picture: over Christ's head is HANAcTACIC [on the board], which means...*Anastasis?* Yes, good. *It looks weird.* Yes, the Greek alphabet is a bit different from ours, but sometimes you can still read it. To the left is IC, short for IECUC [on the board], "Jesus"; to the right, XC for...*Christ!* XRICTOC [on the board], yes, "Christos". *Why don't the C's sound like C's?* They do, like the C in "cereal". And the X shows why we abbreviate Christmas as *Xmas.* Now look at Jesus; what's he up to? *He's pulling those people out of Sheol.* Yes, pulling them to where? *Heaven?* Yes. And he's *yanking* them out by the wrists, he's fired up! Time to get out! Now who are these people? *Good people who couldn't go to Heaven?* Yes, but now they can, because...*Jesus died for their sins?* Yes! How long have they been there? *A long time?* Yes, that's why Jesus is in a hurry, they don't need to be in Sheol one more second. Tell me who the first two people are that Jesus is yanking out...are they two monkeys? *It's a man and a woman.* Yes, and the man has the longest beard so...*he's the oldest?* Yes, and so...he's been there...*the longest?* So, who would this man and woman...*Adam and Eve!*...be, yes, Adam and Eve! They're getting out first because...*they went there first.* Yes. And behind Eve, who's the guy with a stick who comes next? What's the stick? *A shepherd thing.* Yes, a crook. So he's...*a shepherd.* Yes, so? Who's a shepherd after Adam and Eve? *Abel!* Yes! And behind Adam, who are the two men with crowns? *Kings?* Yes... Kings Herod senior and junior? *No, they were bad.* So? *David and Solomon?* Yes, which is which? *David is the older one.* Yes, and his son Solomon is younger. And how about the man with the ragged hair and dull outfit...it's not obvious... *John the Baptist?* Yes, genius! Messy hair, a long beard, and plain clothes are some of John's attributes. An *attribute* is something an artist paints into a saint's picture so we can recognize him. Does anyone remember how St. Stephen was martyred? *He was stoned to death!* Yes. So what might his attribute be? Umm...*a rock?* Yes, that's how it works. And Jesus gave Peter... keys, yes, so...*Peter pictures have keys?* Yes, good.

Now I'm just guessing about the other people in the Anastasis, but they may be Abraham, Moses, Elijah, Ezekiel, Jeremiah, & Isaiah...prophets & patriarchs, y'all know 'em. Now look at the bottom, what's that busted-up stuff? *Locks?* Yes, why? *'Cause Jesus unlocked Sheol?* Yes, and those broken doors show people can't be shut up in Sheol anymore. Can y'all see that tied-up man down there? Who might that be? *A bad person who won't go to Heaven?* Good guess...or maybe he represents Death, or the Devil. This painting is in a church in Istanbul, Turkey, so if you ever travel there, you might go see it. Yes? *We just learned about Istanbul in school!* Yes? Tell us about it. *There's a big church there called Hagia Sophia and it was built by Justinian.* Yes, I've been to Hagia Sophia a few times, it's the best, it's incredible! *Hagia Sophia* means "Holy Wisdom" in Greek; Istanbul used to be a Greek city. Here's a word y'all probably know [on the board]: *philosopher.* It's Greek for someone who "loves wisdom;" the *soph-* is the same in Hagia *Soph*ia and philo*soph*er. Do y'all know any girls named Sophia? *I do!* Sophia's another pretty Greek name.

Back to the story: after Jesus "descended into Hell," then what? *He rose up out of the grave.* Yes, the tomb. "Now on the first day of the week Mary Magdalene came to the tomb early, while it was still dark, and saw that the stone had been taken away from the tomb. So she ran, and went to Simon Peter...and the other disciple...Peter then came out with the other disciple, and they went toward the tomb. They both ran, but the other disciple outran Peter and reached the tomb first; and stooping to look in, he saw the linen cloths lying there, but he did not go in. Then Simon Peter came, following him, and went into the tomb..." Why did young John let Peter go in first? *'Cause Peter was older?* Yes, and because Jesus had changed Peter's name, the apostles knew Peter was #1; so he should go first. But John and Peter thought someone must have stolen Jesus' body: "as yet they did not know the scripture, that he must rise from the dead." They didn't have any idea that Jesus would come back to life. "Then the disciples went back to their homes. But Mary stood weeping outside the tomb...turned round and saw Jesus standing, but she did not know that it was Jesus... (She supposed him to be the gardener)." Mary was so sure Jesus was dead that she didn't recognize him! "Jesus said to her, "Mary." She turned and said to him in Hebrew, "Rabbi!" (which means Teacher)." Once Jesus spoke to Mary, she knew who he was. She must've tried to hug him, because "Jesus said to her, "Do not touch me, for I have not yet ascended to the Father." Don't touch me? What?

Later that evening "Mary Magdalene went and said to the disciples, "I have seen the Lord." They probably thought she was just seeing things. But "On the evening of that day, the first day of the week, the doors being shut where the disciples were, for fear of the Jews, Jesus came and stood among them and said to them, "Peace be with you." Can you imagine how excited they would have been? And Jesus appeared to them in a shut room- how'd he manage that? "And...he breathed, (he *respired)* on them;" tell me the Spanish word. *Respirar!* Yes, like 'spirit.' And Jesus said to them, "Receive the Holy Spirit. If you forgive the sins of any, they are forgiven; if you retain the sins of any, they are retained." Y'all remember earlier in Jesus's ministry, he stopped doing Baptisms. If you wanted to get baptized, what would happen? *One of the apostles would do it.* Yes, Jesus put...them...*in charge!* Yes, in charge of...*baptisms!* Yes. Well, when Jesus tells them "If you forgive the sins of any, they are forgiven" what's he putting them in charge of now? *Forgiving sins?* Yes; so if we want to get our sins forgiven...*we get an apostle?* Yes. *But they're all dead.* Yes. Jesus put the apostles in charge, and they knew they'd die; so in turn, the apostles put...*somebody else in charge?* Yes, bishops and priests. So if you want sins forgiven...*you go to a priest?* Yes. *But can't we pray to Jesus if we're sorry for our sins?* Yes, we can, and do. But we're made of a...*body'n'soul,* yes. And which parts sin? *Both parts!* Yes, and for both our soul *and* our body to experience forgiveness, we go to Confession. We have to confess body and soul to an authorized person, like King David confessed to Nathan.

"Now Thomas, one of the twelve, was not with them when Jesus came. So the other disciples told him, "We have seen the Lord." But he said to them, "Unless I see in his hands the print of the nails, and place my finger in the mark of the nails, and place my hand in his side, I will not believe." We call him Doubting Thomas. He didn't want to have faith, he wanted to...*see!* Yes, people say seeing...is...*believing!* Yes! "Eight days later, his disciples were again in the house, and Thomas was with them. The doors were shut, but Jesus came and stood among them...he said to Thomas, "Put your finger here, and see my hands; and put out your hand, and place it in my side; do not be faithless, but believing." Thomas answered him, "My Lord and my God!" How much faith did Thomas need to stick his fingers in Jesus? *Well, not any.* Right, and Jesus said to him, "Have you believed because you have seen me? Blessed are those who have not seen and yet believe." But I feel better knowing Thomas did stick his fingers in the holes.

Remind me please, on Good Friday, what happened? *Jesus died on the cross.* Yes, he was dead. Totally dead: not sorta dead, or nearly dead, or faking-it dead. Completely alive on Thursday; completely dead on Friday.

And then on Easter he rose from the dead, much to everyone's surprise. Completely dead on Saturday; completely alive on Sunday! But the Risen Jesus, the new Jesus, wasn't like the old Jesus: chewing out Pharisees, driving out demons, knocking over tables, drawing crowds. It would've been ok to hug the old Jesus. But the Risen Lord didn't want Mary to even touch him.

On one occasion Jesus runs into two apostles on a road, the Road to Emmaus. They talk and walk with Jesus for a long time, and don't recognize him until dinnertime; as soon as they recognize him, he disappears!

Then two times the Apostles were laying low in the upper room, with the door shut. Each time, Jesus appears among them without coming through the door, and apparently leaves without going through the door.

Sometimes Jesus eats; sometimes he doesn't. Sometimes he doesn't want to be touched, as Mary Magdalene learned; but what did Jesus tell Thomas to do? *Stick your fingers in the holes!* Yes! Sometimes he's here, then vanishes, then he's somewhere else. People have no idea when or where Jesus will show up, or how long he'll stay if he does. Sometimes he says important things; other times he hardly makes a peep.

Trick question. Remember Adam & Eve in Eden: sick? *No!* Old? *No!* Hang out with God all day? *Yes!* What messed up this good deal? *Sin!* Yes. Now, before the Resurrection, could Jesus get sick? *Yes!* Get old? *Yes!* Die? *Yes!* Good. Trick question...was Jesus a sinner? *No!* So how come he could have bad stuff happen to him? No guesses? Go back to Eden: in Eden could a lamb get eaten by a lion? *No!* How about after Eden? *Yes!* Did the lamb become a sinner, and so that's why it could get eaten, get sick, and die? *Ha, no, animals can't sin.* So why did bad stuff happen to animals? *'Cause Adam & Eve messed everything up?* Yes, the whole world suffered because of sin. So why did bad stuff happen to Jesus? *Well 'cause he was in the world?* Yes. Even the innocent suffer. How about after he rose again; could bad stuff still happen to Jesus? *Ummm...no?* Right, why not? *Well, he had risen from the dead.* Yes, so? OK, if we die in a state of grace, where do we go? *Heaven.* Yes, our *souls* go to heaven; our bodies go...*into the ground!* Yes. When Jesus died on the cross, where'd his soul go? *Heaven?* Well, he did *open* heaven. But Jesus' soul couldn't just stay in heaven while his body decomposed in the tomb. Why not? *Umm, he had to show people he was God?* Yes. When Jesus rose physically, he showed that all that stuff he'd been saying for the last 3 years was true; that he had conquered sin, body'n'soul. But his new glorified body was different...y'all guessed right that he couldn't get sick, grow old or any of that. Who does that sound like: no sickness, no growing old, no death...? *Adam and Eve?* Yes, in Eden. So Jesus' risen body is free from the bad things that come from sin. But even though he's risen, he still appears in the sinful world. If your body'n'soul are free from sin, where should they be? *Heaven?* Yes, and that's where Jesus is going to wind up, just like we hope to, but he has to tie up some loose ends. He appears to a few people (especially Thomas) so they can be sure he really rose from the dead; he eats a little food so they see he's not a ghost; Jesus shows the Apostles how the Old Testament is full of prophecies about himself; and he gives them an extra dose of the Holy Spirit so they can forgive sins. The Bible doesn't say, but maybe he also visited Mary, his mother. But Jesus doesn't stick around more than necessary. Living in the sinful, fallen world just isn't comfortable if you should be in heaven; it's not normal. Jesus doesn't want to get very involved in the world like he used to, it's not his home anymore. He just lingers a bit here and there....he's *disengaged*, that's a good word for y'all to learn. Remember Jesus told

Mary Magdalene right after he'd risen, "don't touch me; I haven't yet ascended to the Father." He wasn't used to his glorified body yet, and didn't want to be touched by the sinful world; I think he just wanted to be in heaven. Later on, he did let Thomas touch him, but I imagine Jesus had to prepare himself for that. So during the forty days after Easter, he visits people only now and then, and never for very long. Some people think he may have visited his mother Mary when he wasn't with the apostles. Jesus appears and disappears, but he's not a ghost. Remind me about 'forty days,' please. *It means a long time.* Yes, a long time of what? *Preparation!* Yes. So this 40 days is about Jesus preparing to do what? *Umm, go to heaven?* Yes, where he belongs.

Next week Jesus will go back to Heaven; and the apostles will get fired up about their new job: setting up the Church.

Praised be Jesus Christ! *Now and forever!*

Class over!

Chapter Twenty-Eight: Building the Church

(Acts 1)

Luke 24, Jesus explains OT prophecies to the apostles. John 21, Jesus restores the oral contract with Peter, who 3 times professes love. Acts 1, Ascension anticipates Second Coming [Assumption]; recall Elijah and Enoch. Jesus physically goes to Heaven. Jesus exists physically right now [Eucharist]. Replacing Judas with Matthias [Apostolic Authority, Office, Isaiah]. Saul, Paul, Ananias, and authority.

Y'all remember from last week Jesus rose from the dead on...*Easter Sunday,* yes, and after a certain amount of time...*40 days,* yes again, will go to...*heaven.* Yes. Let's look at two more things Jesus did before He "ascended to His Father."

What did the apostles do for a living? *They were apostles.* I mean before they followed Jesus, what did they do? What did Peter do? *He was a fisherman.* Yes. They were regular guys with regular jobs, not Scripture experts like the scribes, priests, and Pharisees. So after Jesus was alive again, "beginning with Moses and all the prophets, he interpreted to them in all the scriptures the things concerning himself." Jesus had to explain to the apostles how prophecies (like all the Christmas prophecies) made by men such as Isaiah were true about Jesus. "...he said to them, "These are my words which I spoke to you, while I was still with you, that everything written about me in the law of Moses and the prophets and the psalms must be fulfilled." Then he opened their minds to understand the scriptures..." I don't think they would have figured it all out on their own.

Remember that even though the Risen Jesus was on earth between Easter and the Ascension, he wasn't with the apostles the whole 40 days, only occasionally. And He didn't give the apostles clear instructions about what they should be doing. They were at loose ends. One evening Peter was with some of the disciples. "Simon Peter said to them, "I am going fishing." They said to him, "We will go with you." Doesn't that sound sad? "Guess I'll go fishing, go back to my old job..."

"They went out and got into the boat." How many fish do you think they caught? *Not any!* Yes. "...but that night they caught nothing. Just as day was breaking, Jesus stood on the beach; yet the disciples did not know that it was Jesus. Jesus said to them, "Children, have you any fish?" Well? *No!* Right. "He said to them, "Cast the net on the right side of the boat..." Then what? *They caught a lot!* Yes! "So they cast it, and now they were not able to haul it in, for the quantity of fish." Then they recognized Jesus- why? *'Cause they caught all the fish.* Yes; it was like the first time Peter met Jesus three years before, after fishing all night and catching nothing.

After they got all the fish to shore, they had breakfast with Jesus. Remind me, on the Thursday night Jesus was arrested, what did Peter do when people recognized him as a friend of Jesus? *He said he wasn't His friend.* Yes, how many times? *Three!* Yes, which means Peter... *broke the contract!* Yes: "I ain't no Rock, I'm Silly-Putty!" Poor Peter. But "When they had finished breakfast, Jesus said to Simon Peter, "Simon, son of John, do you love me more than these?" He said to him, "Yes, Lord; you know that I love you." Peter is so sorry he abandoned Jesus. How many times...*three!* Yes, Jesus asked Peter three times. And how many... *three times!* Yes, three times Peter said he loved Jesus. Which means? *They have the contract again.* Yes, in front of witnesses. And each time Peter said he loved Jesus, Jesus said, "Feed my lambs." So the contract is pretty specific now. Who is the Good Shepherd? *Peter!* Is he? *...no, Jesus is!* Yes! Is Jesus going to be around much longer? *No!* Where's he going? *Heaven.* And while Jesus will be away he...*puts somebody in charge!* Yes. By the way, did Jesus give all the apostles his authority to forgive sins? *Yes?* Yes, they were all together in one room when he breathed on them. But did Jesus tell them all to feed his lambs? *No, just Peter.* Yes, Peter is the #1 apostle-in-charge.

That's the end of the Gospels.

The next book in the New Testament is about the things the Apostles did. What's the name of this book? *The Acts of the Apostles?* Yes. Whatta gimme that was. As we know from the Gospels, Jesus has resurrected, but he really belonged in...*Heaven.* Yes. Chapter 1 of Acts says: "So when they had come together, they asked him, "Lord, will you at this time restore the kingdom to Israel?" See, even after all this Resurrection business, the apostles are still expecting Jesus to restore the kingdom that had been built by...*King David,* yes, and...*King Solomon.* But Jesus wants them to quit obsessing about politics. "He charged them not to depart from Jerusalem, but to wait for the promise of the Father, which, he said, "you heard from me, for John baptized with water, but before many days you shall be baptized with the Holy Spirit." "...you shall receive power when the Holy Spirit has come upon you; and you shall be my witnesses in Jerusalem and in all Judea and Samaria and to the end of the earth." And when he had said this, as they were looking on, he was lifted up, and a cloud took him out of their sight." *Bam,* just like that, gone.

Imagine the apostles standing there, with their mouths open, gaping at the sky: wow...wouldja just look at that. "And while they were gazing into heaven as he went, behold, two men stood by them in white robes..." who would be...*angels?* Yes. They said, "Men of Galilee, why do you stand looking into heaven? This Jesus, who was taken up from you into heaven, will come in the same way as you saw him go into heaven." How did Jesus go up? *On a cloud.* So how will he come back? *On a cloud?* Yes, we assume so: "in the same way."

The apostles went back to Jerusalem and waited for the Holy Spirit. In the meantime, they had a problem. How many apostles were there? *Twelve?* Oh. Who betrayed Jesus, a monkey? *No, Judas!* Yes, who was a monkey? *No, an apostle!* And was Judas the slimy traitor still part of the Apostle Club? *No, he killed himself.* Yes, so how many ap...*eleven!* Yes, there were only eleven apostles now. How many should there be? *Twelve.* So they have to...*make another apostle?* Yes. "Peter stood up among the brethren..." see, Peter's in charge; and he says, "May another take his office." Tell me, if my brother dies, can I get another brother? *No.* But if the mayor or the president dies, what then? *We get another one.* Yes. Being a mayor or a president makes someone an office-holder. Even if the person in the office dies, the office goes on. And Peter says being an apostle is an office, so they should get another. "So one of the men who have accompanied us during all the time that the Lord Jesus went in and out among us, beginning from the baptism of John until the day when he was taken up from us; one of these men must become with us a witness to his resurrection." They pick from the disciples who had been with Jesus the whole three years. "And they put forward two, Joseph...and Matthias. And they prayed and said, "Lord, who knowest the hearts of all men, show which one of these two thou hast chosen to take the place in this ministry and *apostleship*..." (Acts 1:25) And they cast lots for them, and the lot fell on Matthias; and he was enrolled with the eleven apostles." Casting lots is like drawing straws or rolling dice. I think the apostles weren't too sure of themselves yet to just out-and-out pick someone.

Remind me how many days it was from Easter Sunday to the Ascension. *40.* Yes. So the Ascension is always on a Thursday. There's another event 10 days after the Ascension...? What's 40 plus 10? *50.* Yes. What's this called [I draw a pentagon]? *A pentagon.* Yes; P-e-n-t-e [on the board] means...*five!* Yes, so the event 50 days after Easter Sunday is...*Pentecost?* Yes, Pentecost Sunday, it's the birthday of the Church; like the Last Supper was the birthday of the priesthood. Let's look at Pentecost now.

"When the day of Pentecost had come, they were all together in one place. And suddenly a sound came from heaven like the rush of a mighty wind, and it filled all the house where they were sitting. And there appeared to them tongues as of fire, distributed and resting on each one of them. And they were all filled with the Holy Spirit and began to speak in other tongues, as the Spirit gave them utterance." (Acts 2:1-4) Y'all have probably seen paintings of the apostles with the little birthday-candle sort of flames above their heads...I think of them as getting FIRED UP with BIG FIRE over their heads! No more "Jesus, we're too scared to stick with you; Jesus, we're too tired to watch and pray; Jesus, which one of us is your favorite apostle; Jesus, explain that to us again; Jesus, we don't know what to do next." Instead, like John the Baptist said, they were baptized with fire and the Holy Spirit. From then on they spread the Gospel, the Good News, fearlessly; so fearlessly that they were all eventually martyred except for John.

"Now there were dwelling in Jerusalem Jews, devout men from every nation under heaven. And at this sound the multitude came together, and they were bewildered, because each one heard them speaking in his own language. And they were amazed and wondered, saying, "Are not all these who are speaking Galileans? And how is it that we hear, each of us in his own native language?" People can't believe these hicks from Galilee know any foreign languages. This is one of their gifts of the Holy Spirit, to spread the Good News in other languages.

So the Church started in...*Jerusalem,* yes. Before too long there were so many new Christians that the apostles needed some help with the daily work of the Church, such as feeding the poor. "And the twelve summoned the body of the disciples and said, "It is not right that we should give up preaching the word of God to serve tables. Therefore, brethren, pick out from among you seven men of good repute, full of the Spirit and of wisdom, whom we may appoint to this duty. But we will devote ourselves to prayer and to the ministry of the word." And what they said pleased the whole multitude, and they chose Stephen..." and six others. "These they set before the apostles" and what did the apostles do? *Lay their hands on them!* Yes!

"...they prayed and laid their hands upon them." They "handed" over some of their authority to these helpers.

Now let's learn about a man who is sometimes called the 13th apostle. His name is Saul...Yes? *His name got changed to...*Stop! Don't give it away yet! So, there was this man named Saul. He may have been a Pharisee: knew the Scriptures up and down, back and forth, way better than the apostles did. And he knew all the rules about the Sabbath and so forth. Well, Saul didn't like this new Christ-Messiah business that the apostles wouldn't shut up about. They were aggravating scribes, Pharisees and Levites at the Temple just like Jesus used to do! So Saul had it in for the Christ-followers, the Christians: "...Saul was ravaging the church, and entering house after house, he dragged off men and women and committed them to prison." And if that's not bad enough, he was there when Stephen, who was just made one of the apostles' helpers, was stoned to death. The book of Acts says "And Saul was consenting to his death."

Stephen is the first of many martyrs.

Then "...Saul, still breathing threats and murder against the disciples of the Lord, went to the high priest and asked him for letters to the synagogues at Damascus, so that if he found any belonging to the Way, men or women, he might bring them bound to Jerusalem." Saul wasn't satisfied with catching Christians in Jerusalem; he had to go root them out in Damascus, which is still the capital of Syria, right next to Israel. "Now as he journeyed he approached Damascus, suddenly a light from heaven flashed about him. And he fell to the ground and heard a voice saying to him, "Saul, Saul, why do you persecute me?" And he said, "Who are you, Lord?" So...who was it? *Jesus?* Yes. "I am Jesus, whom you are persecuting; but rise and enter the city, and you will be told what you are to do." The men who were traveling with him stood speechless, hearing the voice but seeing no one. Saul arose from the ground; and when his eyes were opened, he could see nothing; so they led him by the hand and brought him into Damascus." (Acts 9:1-8)

Some paintings of the moment that Jesus appeared to Saul in that blinding flash of light show Saul knocked off a horse he had been riding. Acts doesn't say if he was on a horse or not, but I like the idea that Jesus knocked Saul off his high horse to get his attention and teach him some humility.

After a few days, Jesus sent a disciple named Ananias to heal Saul's blindness... how'd he do it? *Laid hands on him!* Yes. Where did Ananias get the authority to lay hands on Saul? *Umm... the apostles?* Yes, probably... did they send him a text message? *No, they laid hands on him!* Yes! "Ananias departed and entered the house. And laying his hands on him he said, "Brother Saul, the Lord Jesus who appeared to you on the road by which you came, has sent me that you may regain your sight and be filled with the Holy Spirit." And immediately something like scales fell from his eyes and he regained his sight. Then he rose and was baptized, and took food and was strengthened. For several days he was with the disciples at Damascus. And in the synagogues immediately he proclaimed Jesus, saying, "He is the Son of God." Saul was converted to faith in Jesus in just a few days; of course it helped to have Jesus personally appear to Saul and knock him silly.

And today if someone has a rapid change of heart about something important, people will say they had a

Damascus Road conversion.

Saul was such a great preacher about his new faith in Jesus that he aggravated people in Damascus; some were aggravated enough to...*kill him?* Yes. But his friends lowered him over the city walls in a basket, and he made it back to Jerusalem. But Saul needed some time to persuade the Christians in Jerusalem that he had had a change...of...*heart!* Yes, and that he could be trusted. But once the Church was satisfied, Saul and his friend Barnabas were sent out on their own: "While they were worshiping the Lord and fasting, the Holy Spirit said, "Set apart for me Barnabas and Saul for the work to which I have called them." Then after fasting and praying they laid their hands on them and sent them off." Being "set apart" means Saul is especially dedicated to his job of evangelizing. In Saul's case, being set apart meant that like John the Baptist and Jesus, he never got married. What people are like that today? *Priests?* Yes, and ...*nuns.* Yes. Priests, nuns, and Saul all imitate...*Jesus.* Yes.

Now after Saul got hands laid on him and was set apart, the Bible never calls him Saul again. OK you can tell me, from now on he's called...*Paul!* Yes, his name was changed, like Simon's named was changed to...*Peter,* yes which means...*rock*, or...*stone.* Yes.

Praised be Jesus Christ! *Now and forever!*

Class over!

Chapter Twenty-Nine: The Living Chain

(Acts 2)

Acts 13, Hands laid on Paul. 2Timothy 1, Paul's hands laid on Timothy & Titus: authority physically transmitted [Isaac and Jacob, Ordination]. Acts 14, appointing presbyters. Acts 2, Pentecost [Confirmation], yet another dose of the Holy Spirit. Acts 15, Council of Jerusalem [Church Authority, Holy Spirit]; Jews and Gentiles. Oral teaching: no New Testament, but a Church with structure and authority.

After hands were laid on Paul, he went to Cyprus and Greece to evangelize. Y'all know about Greece, right? *Yes.* It's still a country, and Cyprus is a copper-mining island near Greece. The word *copper* comes from *Cyprus*. Paul intended to bring the Gospel to Jews living in Greece and Cyprus, but he had better luck with Gentiles, people like us who weren't Jews. Let's imagine Paul coming to a new town, let's say Corinth in Greece. What would you call people who live in Corinth? *Corinthians?* Yes. Paul would go to the synagogue or the marketplace, and start preaching about Jesus to whichever Corinthians would listen. As people came to believe in Jesus, Paul would baptize them and their households. After a couple of months, there would be enough new Christians to start a small church; usually people would meet in someone's house. But was Paul's job to stay in one town and run a parish? *No, he had to go to other places.* Yes, why? *Well, to tell everybody about Jesus.* Yes. Now when Paul would leave a new flock of Christians, what would they need? *A shepherd!* Yes, and would the sheep hire their own shepherd? *No, Paul would pick one!* Yes. He might ask the flock to suggest someone to be in charge of them, but it was his decision to *appoint* a shepherd. Yes? *I thought Jesus was the shepherd.* He is, but remember how Jesus gave his authority to the apostles to feed the multitudes, baptize, forgive sins, and so on? *Yes.* Well, the apostles laid hands on Paul to give him their authority; and in turn, Paul laid his hands on men he would authorize. Just like Isaac "handing" down his authority to Jacob. Let's jump ahead a bit since you bring this up now. Later on in his travels, Paul makes bishops of two men named Timothy and Titus. In a letter he wrote to Timothy, Paul said, "I remind you to rekindle the gift of God that is within you through the laying on of my hands." And what do people rekindle? *A fire.* Yes, in this case *spiritual* fire. And he wrote to Titus, "I left you in Crete, that you might...*appoint* elders in every town as I directed you." Paul is always careful to *appoint* shepherds or bishops by laying hands; people don't vote for them. And he expects those bishops...*to lay hands on people too.* Yes, in this example, to "appoint elders." In those days if someone claimed to be an elder, he might say, "The apostles laid hands on Paul; who laid hands on Titus; who laid hands on me." That way people could see that he shared the authority of the apostles. The Bible doesn't say one way or another, but I expect that Jesus laid his hands on the apostles to start the chain.

Speaking of all this hands-laying, what will happen to y'all next year or so? *We get confirmed.* More specifically, please. *The Bishop lays his hands on us?* Yes. He's at the end of a 2,000-year-old living chain of authority and hand-laid blessings and going back to Jesus. So in a couple of years when you're confirmed, you'll become a part of that chain.

And when y'all are Confirmed, are y'all going to be bishops? *Ha! No!* Oh....are you going to be priests or deacons? *No, we just stay the same.* Well, actually you don't stay the same; there is a change, but the change isn't obvious.

When a baby is born, what's the first thing Christian parents do? *Get the baby baptized.* Yes, when the priest squirts ketchup on its head? *No! He uses water!* Oh yeah, water....what does the water wash away? *Original sin!* Yes...and if the priest prays real hard but doesn't pour water on the baby, does that work? *No!* Right; Jesus said you have to be born again of water *and* spirit. So the water and the Holy Spirit *together* change the baby. Can you tell the baby is different? *His head's wet.* Uh-huh, thank you for your contribution.....after his head dries off, he seems exactly the same as before, but the Holy Spirit's made a big *spiritual* change. Original sin is gone, and the baby is permanently changed, even if he sins when he gets older. He can never be un-baptized.

Through Baptism the baby is cleaned of Original Sin by a big first dose of the Holy Spirit.

But in the New Testament we see the Apostles get *extra* doses of the Holy Spirit *after* Baptism. The second time is when the resurrected Jesus breathed on them and says, "Receive the Holy Spirit. If you forgive the sins of any, they are forgiven them; if you retain the sins of any, they are retained." (Jn 20) Then on Pentecost Sunday the Apostles got *a third* dose of the Holy Spirit. What did that dose look like? You could see it above their heads.... *Oh, fire!* Yes, fire; they were...*fired up*! Yes! So we know the Apostles got at least three separate doses of the Holy Spirit. I doubt they looked any different after any of them, so don't be disappointed if you look the same after Confirmation.

Later in Acts, the Apostles 'hand' out doses of the Spirit like so: "Now when the apostles in Jerusalem heard that Samaria had accepted the word of God, they sent them Peter and John, who went down and prayed for them, that they might receive the Holy Spirit, for it had not yet fallen upon any of them; they had *only* been baptized in the name of the Lord Jesus. Then they laid hands on them and they received the Holy Spirit." (Acts 8:14-18) The Bishops today lay hands that same way. And their blessing is like Isaac's: so special that it makes a *permanent difference.* You can usually tell a blessing is special when someone with *authority* puts his hands on the head of the person being blessed.

The dose of the Holy Spirit we all receive at Confirmation doesn't authorize us to forgive sins, but it *is* a bit like the Apostles' last dose on Pentecost. You'll be spiritually strengthened, and receive what are called Gifts of the Holy Spirit. Everyone doesn't get the same gifts: like St. Paul said, a body has different parts, but they all work together. But you'll get something, and it may be years before you realize what it is. It took me about 30 years. My gift is making 6th graders suffer! *We know that already!* Oh.

And what else will the Bishop do? No guesses, that's ok. You'll get treated like King David...you'll get...*anointed?* Yes, genius! *We will?* Yes, no kidding. Remind me please, *Messiah* [on the board] is the

178

Hebrew word for *anointed*, yes, and *Christos* [on the board], or Christ would be...? *Greek for anointed!* Yes. They both mean *anointed*. At Baptism a baby gets oil put on its head, it's called *Chrism* [on the board], the Greek word for oil. See how Christ and Chrism are related? And when priests are ordained, their hands are anointed with...*Chrism*. Yes.

All these anointings with Holy Chrism mark a permanent change in the anointed people: the King is permanently King; a baby becomes a member of Christ's family; a priest is permanently a priest. When you are Confirmed, you'll be anointed with Holy Chrism, marking a permanent change in you. Sort of a spiritual tattoo...it doesn't come off. By the way, the Greek-speaking churches call Confirmation *'Chrismation'*...why is that? *Because that's Greek for Anointing?* Yes, genius at work, you are right!

These are the things that will happen to you at Confirmation: the Bishop, who is a successor to the Apostles, will lay his hands on you in blessing. You'll be anointed with Holy Chrism. You'll receive another dose of the Holy Spirit, giving you Gifts to help to live your Christian faith. All these things have been done for God's children for thousands of years, and soon you'll be a new link in that living chain of spiritual fire. So when the bishop lays his hands on you, don't just think about the bishop. Think of the apostles on Pentecost Sunday getting fired-up with Gifts of the Holy Spirit; the apostles handing that fire on to the bishops; and the bishops keeping the fire alive for 2,000 years so that those Gifts can be handed on to you.

But suppose I said you can skip all that Confirmation business; I'll rub some oil and lay hands on you right here in class? How about that? *It wouldn't work.* Why not? *You aren't a bishop.* Right; I don't have...*authority?* Yes. I don't have *apostolic* authority.

Back to Paul. Remember he converted more Gentiles than Jews to Christianity. The problem was that Gentiles did things Jews didn't do: eat pigs, oysters, lobsters, food that was unclean for Jews; do whatever they wanted on Saturday, ignoring those 39 rules the Pharisees were so obsessed with; and paid no attention to all that Levitical sacrifice business at the Temple in Jerusalem. Well, the Jewish Christians thought the Gentile Christians needed to do all the Jewish stuff in order to be Christians. After all, Jesus followed all the Mosaic laws; shouldn't his followers do the same? And weren't the scriptures God's Word? Who could ignore them? Trick question: what did Paul decide? *That they didn't have to do that stuff?* Good guess, but no; Paul didn't make a decision on his own. "Paul and Barnabas and some of the others were appointed to go up to Jerusalem to the apostles and the elders about this question..." Even though Jesus had *personally appeared* to Paul, spoke to him, blinded him, and knocked him down, that didn't give Paul authority to make this big decision by himself. "When they came to Jerusalem, they were welcomed by the church and the apostles and the elders, and they declared all that God had done with them...But some believers who belonged to the party of the Pharisees rose up, and said, "It is necessary to...charge them to keep the law of Moses."..."The apostles and the elders were gathered together to consider this matter." Did the whole flock of sheep get together? *No, just the shepherds!* Yes, genius; just the shepherds. And guess which apostle spoke first? *Peter!* Yes, "...after there had been much debate, Peter rose and said to them...why do you make trial of God by putting a yoke upon the neck of the disciples which neither our fathers nor we have been able to bear?" Then James said, "Therefore my judgment is that we should not trouble those of the Gentiles who turn to God..." And so the apostles and elders decided, "For it has seemed good to the Holy

Spirit and to us to lay upon you no greater burden..." So the shepherds as a group decided that people who belonged to the *New* Covenant didn't have to obey the rules of the...*Old Covenant?* Yes. And they understood that the Holy Spirit would guide them to the right answer. The apostles didn't cast lots or draw straws to find out what God wanted, like they did when they replaced Judas with Matthias; they were more confident now about making decisions together with the Holy Spirit. And even though some of the sheep didn't like the apostles' decision they had to accept it, because the shepherds had...*authority?* Yes. Neither Paul nor the sheep could decide for themselves what Scripture means, or what the Church should do.

When all the shepherds meet to make big decisions for the whole flock, it's called a *council.* Because this council was held in Jerusalem, it's called the...*Council of Jerusalem?* Yes. And there have been many other councils in other cities since then. That first council was held by Peter and the apostles, but they're all dead. Who would be at a Church council now? *Umm, the Pope?* Yes, and? *Bishops?* Yes. The most recent council was held in Rome when I was about your age, the Second Vatican Council. Bishops came from all over the world to that council; it was exciting even for kids.

That's it for tonight...praised be Jesus Christ! *Now and Forever!*

Class over!

Chapter Thirty: Bishops & Epidemics

(Acts 3)

Greek terms: papa, episkopos, presbyteros, diakonos; *Catholic hierarchy. Offices and authority; cathedra.*
[Ordination] Other denominations: Episcopalians, Presbyterians, Baptists.

Last week we saw how the apostles set up the Church so that it would keep running after they all died. Let's look at a picture of that [I draw]. Here's Jesus...and somebody else. What's Jesus doing? *Laying his hands on the other guy!* Yes, is Jesus laying hands on a monkey? *No, an apostle!* Yes. Remember, the Bible doesn't say whether or not Jesus laid his hands on the apostles to give them his authority; but that was the standard Old Testament way to do it. I don't want to draw all 12 apostles...which apostle do you think this one is? *Peter!* Yes, because Jesus changed Simon's name to...*Peter, yes, and because Jesus told only Peter to...feed...his sheep!* Yes. So Peter represents all 12 apostles in this picture. Now Jesus goes to heaven [Jesus is erased]. The apostles know they're going to die, so...*they lay hands on other people.* Yes, just like the way Paul laid his hands on Timothy and Titus, who became...*shepherds!* Yes, what's the church word for them, you had it last week...*bishops!* Yes.

So who is this guy [I draw] with this pointy hat? *A bishop.* Yes, and he's got his bent stick, a crook...because...*he's the shepherd!* Yes, *a* shepherd. And the apostles get old....and...*they die!* Yes [apostle is erased], but it's OK, because...*they made bishops.* Yes, and when these bishops get old...*they make more bishops!* Yes, all the way down to today. And bishops also make...*more bishops?* No, I mean *besides* more bishops. Who runs our parish, the bishop? Does he run around the state every Sunday saying Mass as fast as possible in all the churches? *Ha, no!* So, who takes care of business at the parishes? *Oh, the priests!* Yes, bishops make priests...by...*laying hands!* Yes, and...*anointing?* Yes.

But what about Peter? *Huh?* Peter got special authority from Jesus...and he died...so...*they made another Peter?* Yes, what do we call his office? What do we call men who replace Peter? *Popes?* Yes, popes. But when St. Luke was writing Acts of the Apostles, was St. Peter dead yet? *No.* Right, he was alive and doing things that Luke wrote about. So there's nothing in there about replacing Peter in particular; it wouldn't have come up yet.

And remind me, where'd Peter get his authority? *Jesus.* And when Peter died, was that it? Did his authority disappear? *No, they picked another pope.* Yes. By the way, in Rome they don't say Pope, they say Papa [on the board]. Why is that? *Because he's the father?* Yes again, and because fathers have authority....trick question: what language does 'Papa' come from? *Latin?* Good guess. It's Greek, the Romans got it from the Greeks! But yes, the Pope is the Holy Father, the Papa. In Italy, Greece and Spain they still say *papa* for pope.

It's All Greek to Me

Time for some more Greek...what do you use to see things far away? *A telescope?* Yes; in Greek it's spelled like this: tileskopos [on the board] (τηλεσκόπος, fyi). And to see very small things? *A microscope!* Yes; mikroskopos [under tileskopos] (μικροσκόπος, fyi). And to see out of a submarine? *A periscope!* Yes; periskopos [under mikroskopos] (περισκόπος, fyi).

So what does *tile* mean? *Far away?* Yes, and *mikro?* *Small!* And *peri?* *Up?* Good guess; it means *around*. On subs they use the periscope to look around. And *skopos?* *See!* Yes [on the board]! My, my, geniuses at work; how'd y'all know all this Greek? *We're smart!* Uh-huh.

What's an epidemic [on the board] (επιδημία, epidimia)? *When everybody gets sick!* Yes. Epi-demic is Greek for *over-people* [*over* goes under epi]. It's a disease that's over all the people.

Now I write *epi-skopos* [under Papa] (επίσκοπος, fyi).

OK, what's *epi* mean again? *Over!* And *skopos?* *To see!* And if someone is an epi-skopos what are they? *Umm...an over-seer?* Yes, genius! [overseer goes next to episkopos] And is an overseer a monkey that gets told what to do? *No, he's the boss, he tells the* monkeys *what to do!* Yes. An *episkopos*, an overseer, is someone who is in charge. Who's in charge of our diocese, all the Catholics in South Carolina? *Bishop Macaroni!* That's very funny, his name is Guglielmone, goo-lyel-MO-neh. It's Italian. But we're not talking about Italian tonight, we're talking about...*Greek!* That's right.

Now watch the magic finger [I erase *episkopos* down to *piskop*]; how do we say *episkopos* in English? *Umm, bishop?* Yes! ¿Quién aquí habla Español? *Me!* How do you say bishop in Spanish? *Obispo?* Yep. 'Obispo' comes from episkopos, too [*bishop* and *obispo* go beside *piskop*]. Most Bibles say 'bishop' and some new translations say 'overseer,' but it's the same job: being a bishop.

Y'all can see how the old word *episkopos* changed into the new words over 2,000 years. That's how old the office of Bishop is, about 2,000 years old. The New Testament talks about bishops a lot, and what language was the NT written in? *Greek!* Yep. And the Old Testament? *Hebrew!* Yes, mostly Hebrew; you remembered.

Hierarchy

Bishops are so important to the church that the word *bishop* shows up in the New Testament six times, which shows you that there were bishops even before the Bible was finished. Now, there are Christians who go to churches that don't have bishops. They may tell you bishops aren't necessary, or are just overseers, nothing special. But appointed bishops are in the Bible, so the Bible agrees with the Church. Y'all may remember last week the apostles had to pick another apostle to replace Judas? *Yes.* Peter said, let another person take his... *office!* Yes. In an older Bible translation, Peter says let another person take his *bishoprick* [on the board]. What does that tell you? That *being a bishop is like being an apostle?* Yes, good. To be a bishop is to hold an *apostolic* office.

Where is our Bishop? *In Charleston.* Yes. At his church there's a special chair for him to sit in called a *cathedra* [on the board]...yes? *Is that why the church is a cathedral?* Yes, you are too fast! A Catholic church with a bishop's chair, a..*cathedra*, yes, is called a... *cathedral.* Yes, a cathedral church.

OK let's review a bit, who's in overall charge of feeding the sheep of Jesus' flock while he's away? *The Pope!* How do we say that in Greek? *Papa!* And who helps the Papa take care of the flock? *Bishops!* And what's 'bishop' mean? *Overseer!* Yes. And next comes what the Bible calls 'presbyters.'

I have *presbyopia* [on the board]; I can't see stuff close-up anymore. Presbyopia is Greek, it means *old-eye*. What might 'presby-' mean? *Old?* Yes, old. The Greek word for an old man, an elder, is presbyteros [on the board under 'episkopos,' restored from 'piskop'] (πρεσβύτερος, fyi). You may remember St. Paul and the apostles didn't just appoint bishops, but also elders. Presbyteros is a very old word, a few thousand years old or so. We use it all the time in English but it's changed so much we don't recognize it anymore. It's gotten shorter, watch the magic finger: [I rub letters out of presbyteros so that it reads presbyter]. That's like what word? *Presbyterian?* Yes. But it got even shorter: [more rubouts] pres--ter. Nowadays it's real short: pres--t...what's that word now? *Is it priest?* Yes, good. So when we say 'priest' we also are saying....*elder?* Yes. Some Bibles will say 'presbyter;' some will say 'elder.' Hey, have y'all ever heard of Chicago? *Yes.* Well, in Chicago's government there are elders, who are right under the mayor. They call them 'aldermen', it's just a way to say 'elder-men'. Kind of like the way our priest-elders are under the...*bishop?* Yes.

Now remember last week we learned from Acts that when the apostles were first setting the Church up in Jerusalem, they needed help feeding widows and orphans. They appointed men who would help them serve the tables. In Greek, the word for that kind of Church helper is *diakonos* [on the board under presbyteros] (διάκονος, fyi). What do we- *deacons!* Yes, we call them deacons. They assist at Mass, funerals, baptize and marry people; they help the priests and bishops, just like in the apostles' day.

So these are all the offices of the Church; say 'em in English from the top: *pope...bishop...priest...deacon.* Yes. The Catholic Church has all of these offices, but not all Christian churches do.

What church's name sounds like episkopos? *Episcopal?* Yes. Who do you think is in charge of that church? *Umm...bishops?* Yes. Episcopalians don't accept the Pope's authority, which Jesus gave to Peter.

How about presby- *Presbyterians!* Yes, do they have bishops? *No.* Right; Presbyterian churches have elders and deacons, but not bishops or popes.

And last are churches that don't have presbyters, but have...*deacons?* Yes. For example, most Baptist churches have a Board of Deacons which is in charge.

So tell me, which Church has all the offices that we see Jesus and the apostles setting up in the New Testament? *The Catholic Church.* Yes.

May Jesus Christ be praised! *Now and forever!*

Class over!

Chapter Thirty-One: Rags & Aprons

(Acts & Epistles)

Acts19, Paul healing through facecloths & aprons (using a dishrag as a prop); faith & works/ body & soul; healing through physical media [Relics, Sacraments] Epistles treated collectively, general intro: letters written to people or churches that are having problems. Paul comes to a town, teaching, appointing overseers, moving on, writing letters later to clear up problems [Laying hands, Hierarchy, Authority]. 1 Corinthians 3: Paul discussing burning away of dross, works matter. Malachi 3, purifying fire, Isaiah's sinful lips [Purgatory].

Relics in the Making

One more bit from Acts of the Apostles and we'll move on. I need volunteers. I need... a mother! That's you! And if I need a mother...*you need a father!* Yes, you, sitting right next to mom. And this [I put my rubber fetus on mom's desk] is your little girl. *But it's not born yet!* Well, pretend she's been born and she's bigger. *It looks weird.* She looks just like you did when you weren't born yet, so stop whining. How old are you? *12.* Then pretend it's your 12-year-old-daughter. And I need a St. Paul...yes, come on up here. Now, mom & dad, your daughter is deathly sick. But look, who's in town? *St. Paul?* Yes. St. Paul, show the rest of the class your preaching skills, but silently...that's it, bring them the Good News. Parents, what are you going to do about your dear, sick little girl- stay home and pray? *No, we're going to take her to St. Paul so he can lay hands on her!* Great plan parents, but your daughter is so near death you don't dare move her. Here you go mom, here's one of your dishrags [an old rag from my house] from the kitchen, don't argue! *But what is-* be patient, mom! Father, your wife has to stay home with your daughter, but she's giving you the dishrag...go on, hand it over. Father, what are you gonna do? *Mmm...take it to Paul?* Well, go on, time's a wastin'. St. Paul, here comes the sick girl's daddy [Paul takes the rag, wads it up in his hands a few times, breathes on it, and hands it back. These kids are so smart.] What now, dad? [He goes back home and gives it to the mother] Well, mom? [She covers the baby with the rag] Somebody tell me what happens? *The baby gets better!* Yes indeed she does! Why? *'Cause the rag had touched Paul!* Yes! Acts says, "God did extraordinary miracles by the hands of Paul, so that handkerchiefs or aprons were carried away from his body to the sick, and diseases left them and the evil spirits came out of them." By the way, back in the Book of Exodus, how'd the Israelites get water in the desert? *Moses hit the rock with a stick!* How'd Jesus heal the blind man? *Put mud on his eyes!* How'd the old woman with the bleeding problem get healed? *She touched Jesus's clothes!* Yes, a tassel, the littlest piece of his cloak. How do we get sins washed away? *With water!* How do we eat Jesus? *Bread and wine!* Yes, when they become... *body'n'blood!* Yes; is any of this stuff magic? *No!* God's power goes through the stuff, because we are made of a...*bodysoul,* yes, so even today Jesus still comes to us spiritually, and...*physically!* Yes.

Now tell me about this rag, which is *not* a magic rag. Do you think it might heal someone else later on? *I guess so.* Sure, there's no rule that says God's power is exhausted with that one healing; who knows, maybe people's faith could keep it charged up like a holy battery. [Out comes the chicken bone] It might work like Elisha's bones, which did what? *Made that man come back to life when they threw him on the bones.* Yes, and even though Elisha had been dead for a good while, nothing but bones, God's power still went through his dead body parts. That's why Catholics respect the bodies of saints; or even parts of their bodies, like a finger bone. What do we call bits of saints' bodies? *Relics?* Yes.

That's it for Acts of the Apostles. Now let's recall how Paul would come to a new town, and set up a new church. I'm Paul, y'all are the congregation of new Christians; some Jews, some Gentiles. OK y'all, I have to bring the Gospel to another town now. Goodbye, flock! Is there anything missing? *You have to lay hands on somebody!* Yes. Can y'all recommend anyone? *Him.* OK, let's see, your name is... Timothy. Yes, I know Timothy, I agree he's a good choice. [I lay hands on Timothy] Timothy, I hand over to you my authority to shepherd this flock, and pray that you be strengthened by the Holy Spirit. 'Bye now, I'll probably never see y'all again.

Things may go fine for a while for Bishop Timothy, but problems will likely arise. The Jewish Christians might insist that the Gentiles quit eating pork. Or some Gentiles might want to sacrifice an animal to Zeus every now and then just to be on the safe side. Or they might disagree about keeping the Sabbath on Sunday, in honor of Easter, instead of Saturday. Timothy, do you want to figure this stuff out on your own? *No!* So what's the fix? *Can you come back?* No, sorry, I'm far across the sea. Flock, how can I give Timothy some guidance? *Well...could you write him a letter?* Yes, geniuses, that's exactly what Paul did! In fact, St. Paul wrote two letters to Timothy, called the First and Second letters to...*Timothy.* Yeah...another gimme.

The Greek word for letter is *epistoli* [on the board] (επιστολή, fyi); what is it in English? *Epistle.* Yes. Let's look briefly at the Epistles, which follow Acts in the New Testament. Paul wrote most of the Epistles because he set up so many new congregations, which then needed his guidance. But other apostles wrote letters, too, such as Peter and James. Let's look at a few things in the Epistles before we move on; we'll see more of the Epistles when we learn about the Mass in a couple of weeks.

To start, here's a short bit I like from the Letter to the Hebrews: "Therefore, since we are surrounded by so great a cloud of witnesses, let us also lay aside every weight, and sin which clings so closely, and let us run with perseverance the race that is set before us..." The part I like is the "cloud of witnesses." What's a witness? *Someone who sees what happens?* Yes, and if the witnesses are in a cloud, what are they? *People flying?* No, it's more like when a cloud took Jesus to Heaven...what sort of witnesses would be on those clouds? *Oh... angels?* Yes, and... saints! Yes. I like this passage because it reminds me that we're never alone [I look around the room at the top of the walls]; we're surrounded by these cloud-witnesses...hey y'all, how ya doin'? *That's funny.* Hey, I'm serious, they're here. The angels & saints love us and want us to get to heaven, too. They'll pray for you if you ask them. That's why you have a guardian angel, and should have a patron saint by the time you're confirmed. They want to help you "run the race." Anyway, I especially think about the cloud of witnesses at Mass. Remembering the statues in church, what witnesses in particular might be with us at Mass? *Mary?* Yes, and? *Joseph?* Yes, and? *Angels.* Yes. A priest was ordained in our church a few years ago, and I imagined all the saints packing the church that day. What a cloud of witnesses that was. By the way, where do you usually hear about witnesses? *When people have a jury?* Yes, in court. Sometimes guilty people don't want a witness to testify, and the witness may be murdered if they won't keep quiet. The Greek word for witness is *martyr* [on the board]. Why do we call some saints martyrs? *'Cause they were killed?* Yes. Martyrs, God's witnesses, were, *and still are*, being killed because they won't keep quiet about Jesus. *You mean like today?* Yes, even today Christian witnesses are martyred for their faith.

Faith'n'works

Now I need someone to tell me what Jesus taught about the hungry and the naked and the sick and so forth. *We have to give them clothes!* Yes, clothe the hungry, and- *no, feed the hungry!* Oh, OK, and... *clothe the naked.* Yes, and... *visit sick people.* Yes. That's because Jesus doesn't just care about what you believe, but also...*what you do!* Yes, your works. And in his Epistle, St. James wrote, "What good is it, my brothers, if a man says he has faith but has not works? Can his faith save him? If a brother or sister is ill-clad and in lack of daily food, and one of you says to them, "Go in peace, be warmed and filled," without giving them the things needed for the body, what good is it? So faith by itself, if it has no works, is dead." St. James means we have to act...in... *faith!* Yes. He goes on: "Was not Abraham our father justified by works, when he offered his son Isaac upon the altar?" Tell me about it. *God had to make sure Abraham believed in him.* Yes, and how did God make sure? *He let Abraham almost kill Isaac.* Yes. And finally James writes, "You see that a man is justified by works and not by faith alone. For as the body apart from the spirit is dead, so faith apart from works is dead." So we can't say "la-la-la, I believe in Jesus" and do nothing; we have to act... *in faith.* Yes.

Purgatory

Speaking of body and soul separating, tell me about that bit in Isaiah when the angel put the burning coal on Isaiah's unclean lips? *It cleaned his lips!* Yes, so he...could...*say good things!* Yes, so he could speak for God. What do we call it when something's burned 'til it's clean and pure? *Purgatory!* Close...it's called purging, but that's where the word Purgatory comes from. The angel told Isaiah, "see, your lips are purged." Now let's look at something Paul wrote about burning away the bad in order to save the good. It's in the first epistle he wrote to the flock in Corinth, Greece, who were...*Corinthians?* Yes. It's from First Corinthians. Paul says that each one of us is a part of the spiritual building of the Church; and that the building's foundation is Jesus.

Paul writes, "Now if any one builds on the foundation with gold, silver, precious stones, wood, hay, straw...each man's work will be made known..." So Paul is comparing our work, what we do, to different stuff, like so [on the board]:

Gold
Silver

Gems

Wood

Hay

Straw

The best work is...*at the top*, yes, and the junk, the sins...*at the bottom.* Yes. Paul says our works "will be revealed with fire, and the fire will test what sort of work each one has done." Starting at the bottom, the magic finger should erase...*straw, hay and wood!*...yes, when our works are tested by fire. And what doesn't burn up? *The good stuff.* Yes, the good things we do. Paul writes, "If any man's work is burned up, he will suffer loss; though he himself will be saved, but only as through fire." So the bad things we do will get burned away, and we'll be saved "as through fire." What happens to saved people? *They go to Heaven?* Yes. So where do we have our sins burned away and we are saved through fire? Does that happen on Earth? *No...is it Purgatory?* Yes. But it's not physical fire: where are our bodies if our souls are in Purgatory? *In the ground!* Yes! So Purgatory's a spiritual purging, which might still be painful.

Hey, if your body and soul are separated at death, what eventually has to happen? *They get put back together again?* Yes. The last book in the Bible, the Book of Revelation, talks about that. We'll learn about that book next week. Yes? *Is next week the end of class?* No, we still have classes on the Mass; your suffering doesn't end until the last week of April.

Praised be Jesus Christ! *Now and Forever!*

Class over!

Chapter Thirty-Two:

Nomads or Pilgrims?

(Revelation)

Revelation 20, the Second Coming: resurrection of the dead (body & soul reunited), General Judgment, judged by works. Rev 21, Pilgrims vs. Nomads: pilgrim church reaches destination, New Jerusalem, no temple, restoration of status quo ante, i.e., an Earthly Paradise. Body & soul restored, Eden-like dwelling with God restored; the Lamb's Supper.

Class, we have come to the last book of the Bible (please, don't cry), in which the last things are finally *revealed.* This book is called...*Revelation?* Yes. It was written by St. John, the only apostle who wasn't martyred. Among other things in this book, St. John explains what will happen at the end of the world. But to understand this last book, let's do a quick review of the Bible using the timeline on this handout:

Start on the left. This would be the beginning of the Bible...the first book... *Genesis.* Yes. Who were the first people we met in Genesis? *Adam and Eve.* Yes, Adam & Eve dwelled with God in Eden. And even though God the Father has no body, they still experienced him in some physical ways, such as hearing him moving around in the garden, and speaking to them. In the beginning, in Eden, Adam & Eve weren't separated from

God. Why not? *They hadn't eaten the apple yet!* That's right, they hadn't sinned. Speaking of separation, what do we call it when souls separate from bodies? *Death!* And could souls separate from bodies in Eden? *No!* And why not? *There was no sin there.* Right. So nothing was dead in Eden.

But what messed this up? *Sin!* Yes. And after Adam & Eve sinned, how were they separated from God? *The angel threw them out of Eden!* And not only were they separated from God, they would eventually have their souls separate from their bodies, and die. Man was created to be with God, but since we left Eden, we've been separated. That's what we see next, the situation in the world before Jesus. Can people die? *Yes.* Do souls die? *No they stay alive.* Yes; can they go to Heaven? *No .* Why? *Because it's before Jesus.* Yes. So the souls of people such as Abraham go to...*Sheol.* Do souls in Sheol dwell there with God? *I don't think so.* Me neither. And peoples' bodies go...*in the ground.* Yes, they turn back into earth.

Now in the middle of the timeline there's B.C and A.D. What's B.C. mean? *Before Christ.* Yes, this is the situation before Jesus comes, as you said. And what's A.D.? *After Death?* Wow, good guess, but no. It's Latin: Anno Domini [on the board]. *Anno* means "in year," like the ann- in *annual*; *Domini* means "of Lord" like the dom- in *dominate.* In English we say "In the Year of Our Lord," which means what? *When Jesus was alive?* Yes, the time after he was born; and what event is right on the line between B.C. and A.D.? *When Jesus was born?* Yes, Christmas. And after Jesus dies for our sins, where do happy souls go in the third part of the timeline? *Heaven.* Yes, which is wonderful, because who is there? God. Yes; our souls dwell with God, with Jesus. But where do happy bodies go? *Well, they still go in the ground.* Yes; even though Jesus redeemed us, our bodies don't share in the happiness of Heaven.

Now we come to the last part of our timeline; it's still in the future. Tell me, does Heaven go on forever? *Yes!* Well, look again at the timeline. *Umm...no?* Right...what follows Heaven? *New Jerusalem?* And what about our dead bodies? *They go up to be with the souls?* Yes, so the whole person, bodynsoul, lives in the New Jerusalem. What is it, the New Jerusalem? *A city?* Yes, a pure, holy city, not like cities we know in the sinful world. Yes? *How can there be a city instead of heaven?* Good question, we'll find out.

Nomads

But first, a new topic: what's a nomad? *Somebody who wanders around.* Do they live in houses? *No, tents.* Trick question: where do nomads start from? *Nowhere, they just wander.* Yes- like the Israelites in the desert. There are still nomads on earth...think of some. *Gypsies?* Yes, good. Any more? Do y'all know about Lapps [on the board]...no? They're nomads north of the Arctic Circle, they follow reindeer herds. There just aren't many wanderers anymore. Next trick question: where do nomads finish? *They just wander, they don't start **or** finish!* Yes.

Pilgrims

Who were the Pilgrims, the Thanksgiving Pilgrims? *They were people from England who came to America.* Yes. And they came here on a schoolbus, right? *Ha! They came on a boat, the Mayflower!* Yes, a ship. They were traveling; were they nomads? *Sort of.* And being sort of nomads, they just wandered around the ocean until they bumped into Massachusetts? *No, they were coming here on purpose.* I see...and when they arrived, did they grab tents and horses and take off for California? *No, they stayed where the Mayflower dropped them off.* Oh. They *weren't* wandering. Then what makes pilgrims different from nomads? *They have a destination?* Yes. So pilgrims *aren't* nomads; pilgrims don't wander.

Where did the Pilgrims start? *England.* And they stopped in...? *America.* Yes, in Massachusetts. Did they vacation there & then go back home to England? *No, America was their new home.* And if you live in one place, but journey to another place to live you aren't wandering, or vacationing either. So what do we call *any* group of people who journey from an old home to a new one? *Pilgrims?* Yes, the word doesn't refer only to the English Pilgrims who came to America. But those English people called themselves Pilgrims because they did not wander; they knew where they were headed, and when they got there, their journey was over.

Tell me, at Mass, have you ever heard the priest say, "Strengthen in faith and love your *pilgrim* Church on Earth?" *Ehh...I think so...?* Of course you *heard* it, but if you were daydreaming you wouldn't *remember*. Mass is more interesting when you pay attention and know what's going on.

So, the Church is a pilgrim Church...if it's a pilgrim Church, what is it doing...is it *wandering? No.* Right, it's not a *nomad* Church. So...if it's not wandering, what *is* the pilgrim church doing? *It's going somewhere.* Yes, it has...*a destination.* That's right...where's it going? No guesses? That's OK. Look at the back of the Bible again: this last book....is called....*Revelation.* Yes. Revelation tells us, *reveals* to us, where the Church is going. And are we part of the Church? *Yes.* Right, all the faithful make up the Church. So if we're part of the pilgrim church that means we are....? *Pilgrims.* Who are on a...? *A trip!* Yes, on a journey. Just like the American Pilgrims, we and the Pilgrim Church will end our journey at our...*destination.* Yes. Let's see what Revelation says about that destination.

The first thing we'll look at is the Second Coming [on the board]. Tell me, who is coming the second time? *Jesus.* And when was the First Coming? *What?* When did he come the first time? *Oh...Christmas?* Yeah, at Christmas. And later, at the Ascension when Jesus rose up on a cloud, angels told the apostles, "why do you stand here looking into the sky? This same Jesus, who has been taken from you into heaven, will come back in the same way you have seen him go into heaven." So, how do we know Jesus will come back? *Well, the angels said so?* Yes; just checking. And how is Jesus going to come the second time? C'mon, the same way he went up. He rose up to the sky on clouds, so...? *Umm,* down *from the sky on clouds?* Yes. Or something equally impressive; I expect everyone will know what's going on. St. John says, "Then I [saw] a white cloud, and seated on the cloud, one like a son of man, with a golden crown on his head..." St. John is quoting Jesus and Daniel; y'all have heard "son of man coming on clouds" a few times this year. Who's the Son of Man? *Jesus.* Yes, and also the Son of God. Fully human and fully divine. By the way, in Revelation, Jesus is never called by his name; instead he's called the Lamb. Why? *Because he's the Passover Lamb.* Yes, the *New* Passover Lamb.

Now if I die tomorrow, the first thing I'll do once I'm dead is meet Jesus. We'll review all my sins, and I'll find out where I'm going. Let's be charitable and say heaven. This is called the Particular Judgment, when each person is judged individually right when he or she dies. On the timeline I'd be in the third spot: soul in Heaven, body in the ground. But that's not the end of me being judged.

The Second Coming will signal that it's time for the Last Judgment, when all the souls in Heaven, Hell, and Purgatory get their bodies back. People who are alive at this point are still bodynsouls. Yes? *How does God do that if your body is all, you know...*all decomposed and turned back in to earth? *Yeah.* Well, I don't know, but how'd God make Adam in the first place? *From dirt!* Yep, and remind me, why do we call that first man *Adama* in Hebrew? *'Cause it means dirt!* Yes, earth. So whatever God did that first time with earth, he'll probably do it again. Then St. John says, "And I saw a great white throne, and him that sat on it... And the sea gave up the dead which were in it; and death and hell delivered up the dead which were in them: and they were judged every man according to their works." (Rev 20:12-13, DR) This rising again of every dead person is what we mean when we recite the Creed on Sunday: "I believe in the Holy Catholic Church, the communion of saints, forgiveness of sins, the...Res...*Resurrection of the Body!* That's it! Then St. John says again "all were judged according to their works." St. John says it twice just to remind you, it matters what you do, not just what you believe. Now, what is every human made of? *A bodynsoul!* Yes, and which part actually does the 'works'? *The body!* Yes, and if part of the Last Judgment involves what you did with your body, would it make sense to have just souls there? *Huh?* If a person is going to get judged by his faith *and* his works, then his soul *and* his body should both be judged. Imagine just my soul is at the Last Judgment, and I'm going to get in trouble because I did bad things while I was alive, but I say, "Oh dear, that sinful body, it's all rotten and laying in the ground somewhere, don't blame me for what that dirty old thing did. My soul never did anything wrong, I swear!" A whole person is a bodynsoul, so if Jesus is going to judge the whole person...? *The whole person needs to be there?* Yes, genius!

So everyone goes to Heaven or Hell with their bodies & souls no longer separated. Adam & Eve's sin caused body & soul to separate, but in the end they become one again. And those who go to Heaven are no longer separated from God by Adam and Eve's sin, but are reunited with Him. Ever since Genesis, people have suffered separation, but in Revelation, *everything good* is reunited: Creation, Man, and God are all together again, just as they were in Eden. Everything bad is thrown into a "lake of fire," which would be...*Hell.* Yes, a physical Hell.

Because all the saints, who will dwell with God, have their bodies back, they'll have to live somewhere physical. But not on Earth as it is now, with hurricanes, earthquakes, and diseases. Could weather kill people in Eden? *No, there wasn't any bad weather.* Why not? *Because there was no sin.* Yes. Sin doesn't just mess up the spiritual world, but the physical world, too.

And here's what St. John says about this physical place: "And I saw a *new* heaven and a *new* earth: for the first heaven and the first earth were passed away... " So we'll have a new home. And not only will Earth be new, but heaven as well, and they will comprise one perfect place like Eden had been. *What's comprise?* It means to put together: a human being is *comprised* of a bodynsoul. Should body and soul be separated? *No.*

Right. Well, Heaven and Earth shouldn't be separated either, with God dwelling in one place and people dwelling somewhere else.

Then John says, "And I John saw the holy city, new Jerusalem, coming down from God out of heaven, prepared as a bride adorned for her husband." And I know exactly what John means. I remember how beautiful my wife was when she was walking down the aisle to marry me. Why, let's look at my wedding picture [I show the photo]. She looks like she came down out of heaven just like the New Jerusalem. So, where are we going to live? *The New Jerusalem!* Yes. Then John says, "Behold, the tabernacle of God is with men, and he will dwell with them, and they shall be his people, and God himself shall be with them, and be their God." (Rev 21, DR) Does anyone remember another time when God told someone "you will be my people, and I will be your God"? OK, this is from Exodus: "I will take you as my own people, and I will be your God. I will bring you out of Egypt and to the land I promised to give to Abraham, to Isaac and to Jacob." Who was God talking to? *Moses?* Yes, Moses and the Israelites. But when God says it in Revelation, it means more. God brings us out of a land of *sin*, and brings us to a *perfect* land, a perfect home. And when God says, "you will be my people, and I will be your God," It's like marriage, when the man and wife give themselves to each other...not a contract...*a covenant!* Yes! It's very romantic.

Here's a question: Jews worshiped God in a temple in Jerusalem; where do Christians worship? *In a church!* Yes. Now about the New Jerusalem, John says, "I did not see a temple in the city." Why wouldn't there be temple or a church there? That's a hard question, tell me this: in Eden did Adam & Eve go to church to visit with God? *No.* Why not? *They were with God already.* Yes. But after they got thrown out of Eden, we had the Temple and the Church as ways to stay connected to God, even though sin had separated us from Him. In the New Jerusalem will we be separated from God? *No.* So why won't there be a temple or a church? *Because we'll be with God again.* Yes, not separated... like another place a long time ago which would be...? *Eden!* Yes. Imagine we're in the New Jerusalem...I need a volunteer, get up here Jesus! I'm with Jesus, we both have our bodies'n'souls. It's just wonderful being here with you Lord, with my arm around your shoulder. But it's Sunday so I have to go to church now, see you in an hour or so. What's wrong with that? *Well, you're already with Jesus!* Yes.

The Pilgrims' Progress

So back to pilgrims. When the pilgrims were sitting at home in England were they pilgrims yet? *No.* Right, they were at home, not going anywhere. When they got on the Mayflower were they pilgrims? *Yes!* Once they settled down in their new home, were they *still* pilgrims? *Not really.* OK. Were Adam & Eve at home with God in Eden? *Yes.* But then they had to leave. We know from St. John that they and their children, that's us, will someday have a new home with God, the New Jerusalem. Right now we're on a long journey from our old home, Eden, to where? *Our new home!* Which is called...? *The New Jerusalem!* And when people are on a journey from an old home to a new home they are called...? *Pilgrims!* Yes, and that makes us...? *Pilgrims, too.*

Did the English Pilgrims swim to America? *Ha! We already said they took the Mayflower.* Oh yeah....I forgot. Swimming is cheaper- why did they take a ship? *'cause it's safe.* Yes, to have a safe ocean journey you need a sturdy ship. There's an Italian saint named John Bosco who once dreamed about a ship on a dangerous ocean. The ship is called the Bark of Peter. It wasn't a dog or a tree: the Italian word for 'boat' is 'barca.' The captain was the Pope. What did the ship represent in the dream? A hard question? OK, what's the Pope in charge of in the world? *The Church.* And in the dream he's in charge of the ship, so what's the ship? *The Church?* Yes...the Church is our Mayflower. It carries us safely from our old home to our new one. Is it a wandering Church, a nomad Church? *No, a pilgrim Church.* Yes, just like we hear at Mass.

Alpha and Omega

So, look again at the Bible. One book in the front...*Genesis,* yes, about the old home before the journey became necessary, and one in the back about the new home, and all the middle books are about the pilgrims' progress along the way. A pilgrim's journey is called a pilgrimage; we're on a pilgrimage. We know where we're going, and when we arrive, our journey will be over.

When the pilgrims arrive in the New Jerusalem, they become united with God. Like in Eden, there won't be a Church or Temple...once the pilgrims arrived in America, they didn't need the Mayflower anymore, either. St. John explains why the New Jerusalem had no temple. He says, "the Lord God Almighty and the Lamb are its temple."

Revelation is the end of the Bible, and it marks the end of our pilgrimage. All the things that were messed up and separated by sin are healed and made whole: Man's body and soul are one; God and man are united; even Heaven and Earth are joined forever. John says, "there shall be no more death, neither sorrow, nor crying, neither shall there be any more pain: for the former things are passed away. And he that sat upon the throne said, Behold, I make all things new...I am Alpha and Omega." (Rev 21, DR) What are Alpha and Omega? *The first and last letters in the Greek alphabet.* Yes, genius! What does Jesus mean? *That he's the beginning and the end.* Yes, as we pray, "As it was in the beginning, is now, and ever shall be, world without end." Is that "world without end" this world? *No it's heaven.* Is it? *It's...the New Jerusalem!* Yes, genius! By the way, what's the second letter in the Greek "alpha-bet"? *Beta!* Yes!

Hey, next time y'all are in church, look at the big stained glass windows in front [I do a rough outline of the following window]:

St. Mary's Church, Greenville, SC

See these two little triangles of glass? They have an Alpha and an Omega in them; you have to look closely. They are there to remind you of this passage in Revelation. Not everyone notices the Alpha & Omega windows, so point them out to your parents.

Wedding Party

And there will be a big celebration in the New Jerusalem. An angel said to John, "Come, I will show you the Bride, the wife of the Lamb. And in the Spirit he carried me away to a great, high mountain, and showed me the holy city Jerusalem coming down out of heaven from God, having the glory of God, its radiance like a most rare jewel...clear as crystal." So...who's the Lamb? *Jesus.* Yes, and his Bride is...*the New Jerusalem?* Yes, which St. John said was as beautiful as ....? as....? My wife when we got married! *He didn't say that!* Yes, but he didn't know my wife either. *But I thought Jesus marries the Church.* Yes, but the Church isn't a building, right? It's... *people,* yes. And the people are part of the *pilgrim* Church until it reaches its... *destination.* Yes, and the people *then* live in the holy city...*the New Jerusalem.* Yes. So the Lamb isn't marrying a church or a city so much as he's marrying...*the people?* Yes, the saints.

And we know from the Marriage at Cana that after a wedding, there's a... *party!* Yes, Revelation would say a *feast*.

Speaking of wedding feasts, next week we'll start learning about the Mass. Yes? *Mass isn't the same as a wedding.* Well...let's worry about it next week.

Praised be Jesus Christ! *Now and forever!*

Class over!

Unit 3

The Mass

Chapter Thirty-Three:

Sing Along with King David

(Mass 1)

Greeting through Liturgy of the Word, taught from the Missalette & the Bible

Last week we got to the end of the Bible. For the next 3 classes we're going to learn about the Mass.

Tell me, was Jesus a good Jew? *Huh?* Did Jesus do the things a faithful Jew was supposed to do? *Umm...yes?* Right: he kept the Sabbath, went to Jerusalem for Passover, obeyed the Commandments. Being a good Jew, what did Jesus *do* on the Sabbath? *Go to church!* Well, Jesus hadn't founded the church yet, so where did he go instead? *A sss-synagogue?* Yes, a synagogue. That's Greek for "to bring together." Now, remember the time Jesus visited Nazareth after he had grown up. What did the men ask him to do at the synagogue? *To read?* Yes...to read a comic book? *No...the Old Testament?* Yes genius, good, he read from Sacred Scripture, which did *not* include the New Testament. Why not? *It wasn't written yet?* Yes. But that was what Jews did in synagogue on the Sabbath: pray, maybe sing a Psalm or two, read from Scripture; and then the rabbi, the teacher, would comment on the readings.

After Jesus ascended to heaven, and the apostles were fired up by Holy Spirit on Pentecost Sunday, they went out and began to preach about the Messiah to Jews in Jerusalem. The apostles still considered themselves good Jews; after all, the whole Messiah business was Jewish. So they would tell everyone at the Temple and local synagogues the good news about Jesus. The Book of Acts says "And day by day, attending the temple together and breaking bread in their homes, they partook of food with glad and generous hearts, praising God and having favor with all the people." We can guess that the Christians might still attend synagogue on the Jewish Sabbath, which was...*Saturday,* yes, and then "break bread" on Sunday, Resurrection Day. What else did they remember when they "broke bread"? What does "break bread" mean: to bust up stale bread and watch it crumble all over the floor? *No it means to eat!* Yeah... a snack? *No, dinner.* Yes, a meal. What meal might they remember when they broke bread? *The Last Supper?* Yes, Jesus had said "do this in memory of me." So on Saturday the Christians...*read the Bible?* Yes, the Old Testament; and on Sunday...*they did the Last Supper.* Yes. Because what happened on Sunday? *Easter!* Yes.

Unfortunately, like Christ Himself, the Christians were aggravating the scribes and priests and Pharisees. The temple staff thought that the Romans had taken care of their Jesus Problem. But here it is a couple of months after Jesus was crucified, and now there are a dozen apostles getting everyone at the Temple riled up worse than Jesus did!

One day Apostle #1....*Peter!* yes, and John were at the Temple. "And as they were speaking to the people, the priests and the captain of the temple and the Sadducees came upon them, annoyed because they were teaching the people and proclaiming in Jesus the resurrection from the dead. And they arrested them and put them in custody..." The high priest and the Levites told Peter and John to SHUT UP! about Jesus. Did they shut up? *No!* Right. Even after they were beaten up by the temple guards, "every day in the temple and at home they did not cease teaching and preaching Jesus as the Christ."

But one day Stephen, one of the first deacons, was taken before the high priest and his council and accused of blasphemy, like Jesus had been. He wouldn't shut up either. "Now when they heard these things they were enraged, and they ground their teeth against him...Then they cast him out of the city and stoned him." AS y'all know, Stephen was the first martyr; and Saul witnessed his death.

So the Christians figured out that the Jewish authorities considered them blasphemers, not good Jews at all. And they began to stay out of the Temple and the synagogues, and read from Scripture on their own. Eventually they observed the new Sabbath, which was...*Sunday*, yes. They'd pray, listen to readings from the Bible, listen to comments on the readings, sing a Psalm, and then have a Last Supper meal together. What does that sound like? If you were somewhere on Sunday, and you heard Bible readings and then someone talked about the readings, and you sang a Psalm, and then remembered the Last Supper where would you be? *At church!* More specifically please, what event at church? *Oh, Mass!* Yes, at Mass.

Mass still divides into those two main parts: readings from the Bible, and the Last Supper. The first main part is called the Liturgy of the Word [on the board] because...*that's when they read the Bible.* Yes, and the second main part is the Liturgy of the Eucharist [on the board], because...*that's when we have Communion.* Yes. Let's look at them in order. I'm going to read from the Missalette to keep us moving along. I'm not going to read every word, just parts.

Liturgy of the Word

What happens first at Mass? *There's a song.* Yes, an entrance procession and a hymn. After the hymn, the priest says, "The Lord be with you," and we say...*and also with you.* Yes, it's a greeting. Then we say the Confiteor, a prayer like the Act of Contrition:

" I confess to almighty God
and to you, my brothers and sisters,
that I have greatly sinned, "

...we are reminding ourselves that we're all sinners, which is why we're at Mass.

"in my thoughts and in my words,

in what I have done and in what I have failed to do."

We tend to notice sins of *com*mission more than sins of *o*mission; what's a sin of omission? *If you don't take care of your little brother!* Yes, that's a good one.

"therefore I ask blessed Mary ever-Virgin,
all the Angels and Saints,"

This reminds us that at Mass we're surrounded by St. Paul's "cloud of witnesses," who are...*angels and saints.* Yes.

"and you, my brothers and sisters,
to pray for me to the Lord our God."

So we ask all the faithful in Heaven and Earth to pray for us. How do the saints hear us? *Umm...I don't know.* Me neither, but God makes it possible.

Now that we've told God we've sinned, what do we ask for? *For him to forgive us?* Yes, to be merciful. We usually sing "Kyrie Eleison" which is Greek for...*Lord have mercy,* yes, and Christe- *Christ have mercy,* yes.

Next we sing the Gloria. Who can tell me where the first line comes from:

"Glory to God in the highest,
and on earth peace to people of good will."

No guesses, you've heard it this year...around Christmas...from Luke's gospel...someone said it about baby Jesus...*the Wise Men!* No, close though. *The angels said it to the shepherds!* Yes, good! When you say it, remember the story.

And who first said this about Jesus:

"Lord God, Lamb of God, Son of the Father,
you take away the sins of the world"

John the Baptist! Yes, genius, when Jesus came to be baptized in the...*Jordan River!* Yes.

After the Gloria, the priest says a short prayer, and we...stand on our heads? *We sit down!* Yes. Now the Liturgy of the Word begins. At Mass we *hear* a lot of reading out of the Bible, and maybe even *listen* to it! What's the first reading called? *The First Reading?* Yes [on the board]. Since it's first, what Testament would the readings come from? *The Old?* Yes. So we might hear a reading from Genesis or Isaiah.

Trick question: what's next? *The Second Reading!* Wrong, I win! The Second Reading doesn't come next! The next thing isn't usually read; it's sung. A person in the choir sings part, and we sing part. What is that? King David wrote most of them...*Psalms!* [on the board] Yes, and why do we sing them? *'cause they were songs?* Yes. We looked at some Psalms a few months ago. If you listen to the words you can usually tell what was on David's mind when he wrote each one: he was happy, or sad, or thankful, or feeling remorse. *What's remorse?* It means to feel sad and sorry that you did something wrong. So when you sing a Psalm, imagine King David singing it too. Hey, here's a bit from Psalm 141 that tells us something about Mass: "I call upon thee, O LORD...Give ear to my voice, when I call to thee! Let my prayer be counted as incense before thee, and the lifting up of my hands as an evening sacrifice!" What does incense do? *Smell good?* Yes; what does the *smoke* do? *Go up?* Yes; in a spiritual sense, where is it going up to? *Heaven?* Yes, like our prayers. When you're at Mass and incense is burned, remember your prayers should rise up to heaven like the incense.

After the Psalm comes...the next reading...*The Second Reading!* [on the board] Uh-huh. The lector tells you what the reading will be. He might say, "A reading from the Letter of St. Paul to the Romans;" so would the Second Reading be from the Gospels? *No, the Epistles!* Yes, because "Epistle" is Greek for...*letter.* Yes. And because Paul and the other Epistle-writers usually wrote letters to scold people or correct their mistakes, Epistles aren't as easy to understand as the Old Testament stories are. They'll become more interesting as you get older.

And all this time we've been sitting down. What now? *We stand up?* Yes, and sing the Alleluia. What's the next reading? *The Gospel.* Yes. [on the board] Why do we stand up? *'Cause they're about Jesus.* Yes, that's one way we show respect. Gospel readings are always Jesus stories, and they're easy to follow.

And after the Gospel? *We sit down.* Yes, and the priest...*talks.* Well yes, but it's a *prepared* talk, a homily; and it's usually based on the readings.

This part of the Mass, the Liturgy of the Word, is very much like what Jesus or the disciples would have experienced in the synagogue: prayer, Psalm-singing, Scripture-reading, and comments by the rabbi. We have at least 4 readings every Sunday. Special Masses may have more. For example, the Easter Vigil Mass may have 8 readings, starting in Genesis and ending with the Gospel account of Jesus's Resurrection.

Now tell me: suppose the priest really liked Christmas, so all he wanted to read and talk about year-round was Christmas. Would that be ok? *No.* Why not? *Because it's just once a year?* Umm, yes. Look at the whole Bible: it's huge, but Christmas [I hold the Bible and pinch a few pages toward the back] just takes up a few pages. To ignore the whole rest of the Bible would be wrong. To make sure we get a big picture of the Bible, the Church has a schedule of readings. Every three years we go through the whole Bible with readings picked out by the Church from the Old Testament, the Psalms, the Epistles, the Gospels, and other New Testament books such as Acts and Revelation. Lots of times the readings are connected. For example, suppose you heard this bit of Isaiah for the first reading: "Behold, a virgin shall conceive, and bear a son, and shall call his name Immanuel." (Is 7:14, DR) That's a prophecy; who makes the prophecy come true? *Mary?* Yes. So what Gospel reading would go with it? *Something about Christmas?* Yes, or the Annunciation, when Gabriel told Mary she'd have a baby even though she wasn't married yet. Or how about this bit from Psalm 22: "My God, my God, why hast thou forsaken me?... a company of evildoers encircle me; they have pierced my hands and feet..." What does that match up to in the Gospels? *When Jesus was crucified!* Yes, you see how it works; but you have to pay attention.

Y'all remember that it matters to Jesus not just what we believe, but...*what we do*, yes, our "works," as the Bible says. If the Church wanted to emphasize that one Sunday, she could schedule readings that included these verses [I have these bits sticky-tabbed to preclude fumbling]:

First Reading from Proverbs 24:12; "Rescue those who are being dragged to death...If you say, "I don't know this man!"...[God] will know it, and he will repay [you] according to [your] works."

Psalm 62:12-13: "Power belongs to God; so too, Lord, does kindness...And you reward each of us according to our works."

Second Reading from Paul's Letter to the Romans: "[God] will reward every man according to his works: to those who by perseverance in good works seek for glory and honor and immortality, he will give eternal life..." (Romans 2:4-7)

And for the Gospel reading, Jesus says, "For the Son of man shall come in the glory of his Father with his angels; and then he shall reward every man according to his works." (Matt 16:27) Remember we must act...in...*faith!* Yes. If the soul has faith, the body...*does things!* Yes, good works. Faith'n'works, body'n'soul.

So the readings are never just randomly pulled out of a hat; pay attention to how they go together and Mass will be more interesting to you.

(Class continues in the next chapter)

Chapter Thirty-Four: The People's Work

(Mass part 2)

The Nicene Creed; liturgy.

New topic; what's 'incredible' mean? *Unbelievable!* Yes. 'Incredible' comes from the word 'creed' [on the board]. A creed is what you believe. ¿Cómo se dice "believed" en Español? How do you say "believed" in Spanish? *Creer!* No, believed, the past tense. *Umm...Creido?* Yes [on the board under creed]. Somebody digame en Español, "I have believed in the Creed." *Umm... He creido en el credo?* Yes. In Spanish it's clear that a creed is what you believe.

So, after the sermon what do we stand up and say together? *The Creed?* Yes, the Nicene Creed; and you can tell it's a creed because the first words are what? *I believe in one God?* Yes. Y'all know it already, but let's look at few of the last lines from the Creed before we start on the Liturgy of the Eucharist.

First:

"He will come again in glory
to judge the living and the dead
and his kingdom will have no end."

A couple of weeks ago we learned all about the Second Coming and the New Jerusalem; what book of the Bible was that? *Revelation?* Yes. And we say we believe in the Resurrection of...*Jesus!* Umm, yes, but wait a second and try again. "We believe in the Resurrection of...the...*body!* Yes, which also is described in what book? *Revelation.* Yes.

Next:

"I believe in one, holy, catholic and apostolic Church."

What's that mean, the Church is "apostolic?" *That the apostles started it?* Yes, partly; how do we know the bishop in Charleston is a real bishop? *'Cause they laid hands on him!* Yes, and how far back does laying hands go? *Back to the apostles.* Yes, the Church is apostolic both spiritually and physically.

Let's look at one more line, from the Apostle's Creed. It's very similar to the Nicene Creed. Sometimes we use the Apostle's Creed at Mass instead of the Nicene:

"I believe in the Holy Spirit,

the holy catholic Church,
the communion of saints,
the forgiveness of sins,
the resurrection of the body,
and life everlasting. Amen."

What's the Communion of Saints? *Umm... when saints go to communion?* Good guess; what's a union [on the board]? What's it mean to be united? *To be all together?* Yes. Well, a co-union, a *communion* [comm- is added to union], is when a group of people is so like-minded in what they believe that they're close, like a family. They love each other. So why would we mention the Communion of Saints at Mass? Remind me, who are the Cloud of Witnesses? *The Saints!* Yes, and when *we* are at Mass... *they are too.* Yes, we're 'surrounded' by them. So why the Communion of Saints? *Is it like the Cloud of Witnesses?* Yes, but more. St. Paul calls people who are alive on earth and in God's grace saints, too, not just souls in heaven. So the Communion of saints might include...*us?* Yes, we're part of a huge saint family. We want to get to heaven and the saints already there want us in heaven, too. And they'll pray that God gives us the grace to get there, especially if we ask them to pray for us.

Speaking of the saints in heaven, they're part of what's called the Church Triumphant. Why are they called that? *Because they won, they're in heaven.* Yes. And the saints in Purgatory are the Church Suffering because of course...*they're suffering.* Yes...what? *How can they be in the Church?* Well, where will they end up? *Heaven.* Yes, so they are in the Church, too. And the saints on earth are part of the Church *Militant.* If you're in the military what's your job? *Fighting?* Yes; in the case of the Church Militant, we'd say struggling. Why is that? *Cause we're fighting to get into heaven?* Well, yes, fighting against what... *the Devil?* Yes, we struggle against sin and Satan.

Thanksgiving Dinner

Now the Liturgy of the Eucharist starts. 'Eucharist' is the Greek word for 'thanksgiving.' We use that word because at the Last Supper, Jesus "took a cup, and when he had *given thanks* he said, "Take this, and divide it among yourselves...he took bread, and when he had *given thanks* he broke it and gave it to them, saying, "This is my body which is given for you. Do this in remembrance of me." In Greek "gave thanks" is *eucharisteo* [on the board], it's almost exactly the same as our word Eucharist. So we give thanks, too.

First we have the offertory. What happens? *We put money in the basket?* Yes, but more important, what do the people bring up to the front of the church? *Bread and wine!* Yes. Do they bring it up to the altar? *No, they give it to the priest.* Yes. Why don't the people take it up to the altar? *'Cause they aren't priests!* Yes, they aren't set apart for that job. But why do altar servers get to tootle around the altar, they aren't priests either. *But they might be priests when they grow up.* Yes, or deacons; it's a training period for them.

Now let's have a look at this handout. [See the Image Appendix for larger image]

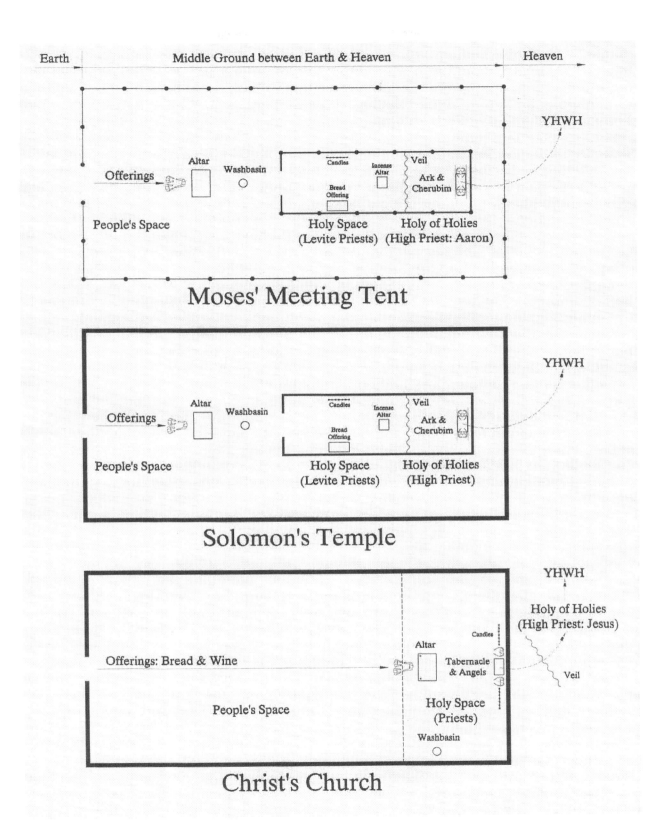

Earth   Middle Ground between Earth & Heaven   Heaven

YHWH

Offerings → Altar   Washbasin   Candles   Incense Altar   Veil   Ark & Cherubim

Bread Offering

People's Space   Holy Space (Levite Priests)   Holy of Holies (High Priest: Aaron)

Moses' Meeting Tent

YHWH

Offerings → Altar   Washbasin   Candles   Incense Altar   Veil   Ark & Cherubim

Bread Offering

People's Space   Holy Space (Levite Priests)   Holy of Holies (High Priest)

Solomon's Temple

YHWH

Holy of Holies (High Priest: Jesus)

Offerings: Bread & Wine →   Altar   Candles   Tabernacle & Angels   Veil

People's Space   Holy Space (Priests)

Washbasin

Christ's Church

You've seen the first two plans before, Moses' Meeting Tent and Solomon's Temple. They're essentially the same, but the Temple is way bigger and made of stone. *It doesn't look bigger.* Yes, the paper is too small to draw the Temple at the same scale as the Tent. This is to show what happens in these spaces, not to be a detailed drawing of the spaces themselves. Let's quickly review the Tent and Temple. On the left, the people bring their offering, let's say a...*lamb.* Yes. They stop at the front of the altar and the priest takes the offering. He washes his hands before he sacrifices and offers the lamb. Behind him is the Holy Space where God's presence dwells. Does Y-H-W-H (don't pronounce it!) have a body? *No!* Right, so he doesn't dwell there physically. There's a bread offering, an incense offering, candles, and a veil so the Levites can't look right at the Ark. Only the High Priest goes into the very back, where the Ark is guarded by no-nonsense cherubs. What's in the Ark? *The Ten Commandments?* Yes, and...the miracle bread...*manna!* Yes, and Aaron's staff. None of those things are God, but they *are* God's stuff.

Now let's look at the church plan; it's very similar to the other two. The people space is bigger because we all come at once, but how it all works is still basically the same. People bring up the offering, which isn't a lamb...*bread and wine!* Yes, and who offered bread and wine for Abraham? *Melchizedek!* Genius, you remember, good. And there are still candles, an incense offering, and a washbasin. *Where's the incense?* Good question, you tell me: is there a piece of furniture in church for burning incense? *No, the altar boy carries it.* Yes, so it's not on the drawing, but incense is still burned.

After the priest receives the bread and wine, he says:

"Blessed are you, Lord God of all creation,
for through your goodness we have received
the bread we offer you:
fruit of the earth and work of human hands,
it will become for us the bread of life."

Speaking of humans doing work, "liturgy" is yet another Greek word. In fact, the Mass is called the 'Divine Liturgy' by the Eastern Churches. Liturgy [on the board] (Leitourgia, λειτουργία), means "people-work;" it's the work the people and the priest do at Mass. What's 'energy' [on the board under liturgy]? *Power?* Yes, power for what? *To make stuff happen?* Yes. Energy is the capacity to do work. The *-urgy* in liturgy is the same as the *-ergy* in energy; it means *work*. So let's look at this people-work; tell me the people-work when you hear it again: "...we have received the bread we offer you: fruit of the earth and work of human hands- *that's people-work!* Yes; and the same for the grapes and the wine.

So we offer bread'n'wine, not wheat'n'grapes. *Yes.* Why not wheat and grapes? *Because Jesus and Melchizedek used bread and wine?* Yes... but maybe there's more to it. If we produce grapes and wheat we work, but the work doesn't change anything. Plant a vine, it makes grapes. Plant a wheat seed, it grows into a stalk of wheat. They're stuff God created. But when we use them to make bread and wine, they stop being wheat and grapes anymore. Human work creates something else in bread and wine: can you get the wheat and grapes back out again? *No.* Right; it's a permanent change, and there's no more wheat or grapes. It's a bit like the change Jesus will work. So if we first do the people-work, then Jesus will do...*the God-work?*

Yes!

The people's work transforms the plant stuff into something new: bread & wine. Then Jesus accepts these offerings, and transforms them into something new again. Now, trick question: can Jesus make his Body'n'Blood out of wheat and grape juice? *Well, can't Jesus do whatever he wants?* Yes, of course... but do you think if we brought up wheat and grape juice at the Offertory, that they'd become the Body and Blood? *No, that wouldn't work.* Right. Why not?

OK, a few years my younger daughter needed to get an old bike in working order so her boyfriend could ride with her. I agreed to fix it, but she had to help me the whole 45 minutes or so. Her help was limited to passing me tools, the oilcan, holding the bike steady, turning the crank, paying attention and making observations (e.g., those chain links need more oil). I could've done it alone, but she does not value the working bike if she doesn't contribute to the fixing. And her contributions, while small, were real. And would I have fixed the bike if she weren't willing to help as best she could? *No!* No indeed. I wouldn't do most of the work if she didn't do a little bit herself. Why not? *Because that's how she shows it really matters to her.* Yes. Could she just sit inside and surf the net and tell me the bike's important? *No, she has to do something, she can't just say it.* Yes. If I do the big fixing, she has to do the... *ummm, the little fixing?* Yes. And at Mass, if Jesus does the *big* transformation, creating his Body & Blood, we have to do the... *little transformation!* Yes. First we do our little work by transforming wheat & grape juice into... bread & wine! Then Jesus does the big work, changing them into... Body'n'Blood! Yes, like so [on the board]:

Wheat > Bread > Body

Grapes > Wine > Blood

The first steps are up to us, and none of the work is reversible. The Liturgy, the people's work, makes it possible for Jesus to do his work. It's like when married people make babies. It's God's creative power that flows through the parents; but if they won't do their part, God doesn't do his part. And at Mass, if the people don't do their work, will Jesus do his? *No!* That's right. He depends on us to do our part. If we don't, nothing will happen. Can you imagine how much Jesus loves us to depend on us? By the way, since Jesus loves us, why does he require us to do something when he's powerful enough to do it all by himself? *It's just good if we help.* Yes, when we help God, it dignifies us. Just like when my wife used to make brownies with our kids: they were dignified by their work, their contribution. Tell me about kids who get everything from their parents without doing anything themselves. *They're spoiled.* Yes. God doesn't want to spoil his kids. God helps those who help themselves as much as they can, just like a loving parent should.

And this is true for other Sacraments. For example, in Confession God will forgive us, but we have to.....*confess out loud to the priest!* Yes...but how about Baptism, what does the baby do? *Ummm....babies can't do anything.* Right. They can't even feed themselves... do they starve? *No, the parents feed them.* So at baptism, if the baby can't decide it wants to be baptized...? *The parents decide for the baby!* Yes, the parents act for the baby. But can parents just drop into church after Mass and say, hey we need our baby baptized quick, or we'll be late for a movie? *No, that's silly!* That's right, the parents and Godparents have to agree to take charge of the baby's Christian life, to do the work until it's old enough to do it for itself.

So y'all see how Catholics first do the People's work, and in response God does His work. And y'all see how my sons & daughters are required to do work for their own good. It's like that in class, too. Honorary sons & daughters, in this class can you just sit there in a stupor? *No!* What work do you have to do? *Pay attention!* Yes, and? *Answer questions!* Yes. I want you to use your brain to... *think!* Yes. When you participate, and do your work, that makes it possible for me to do mine.

Let's stop here. Praised be Jesus Christ! *Now and Forever!*

Class over!

Chapter Thirty-Five: Manoah and the Angel

(Mass 3)

The Eucharistic Prayer; The Holy Tornado.

After the priest receives the bread and wine, he says the Invitation to Prayer:

"Pray, brethren (brothers and sisters),
that my sacrifice and yours
may be acceptable to God,
the almighty Father."

And we reply,

"May the Lord accept the sacrifice at your hands"

What's the sacrifice? *Jesus?* Well, yes, but not yet; what just got brought up at the Offertory? *Bread and wine.* Yes, there's no change yet...but we're getting there. Is the bread nice and fluffy? *No it's flat.* Why isn't it fluffy? *Because Moses couldn't wait for fluffy bread!* Right, for the first Passover the Israelites made their bread without leavening so they could leave Egypt quickly. So our New Passover meal has flat bread, too.

Next we sing the Sanctus, you know it:

"Holy, Holy, Holy Lord God of hosts.
Heaven and earth are full of your glory."

Who was the prophet that saw the angels in heaven saying that? *Jeremiah!* No, close...*Isaiah!* Yes. And then:

"Hosanna in the highest.
Blessed is he who comes in the name of the Lord.
Hosanna in the highest."

Who remembers in the Gospels when people said 'hosanna' to Jesus? He was coming into a town...they were waving palms...*Palm Sunday!* Yes, when Jesus entered...*Nazareth!* No...*Jerusalem!* Yes. People had heard he was the Messiah. Not a meek Messiah, but one like...*King David!* Yes. But when we say 'hosanna' at Mass, we know Jesus isn't an earthly king...where is he king? *In Heaven.* Yes. In fact, the "Holy, Holy, Holy" part of the Sanctus is mostly said in Heaven, not here on Earth. Let's look in Revelation to see what goes on in Heaven while we're at Mass.

In Revelation chapter 4, St. John has a vision of the Heavenly Liturgy: "At once I was in the Spirit, and lo, a throne stood in heaven, with one seated on the throne! And... round the throne was a rainbow..." What's the rainbow for? *It's like when Noah got out of the Ark.* Yes, it reminds us of God's promise. And "Round the throne were twenty-four thrones, and seated on the thrones were twenty-four elders, clad in white garments, with golden crowns upon their heads." [I draw & talk] Here's the throne...who's sitting on it? *God?* More specifically, please. *Jesus?* Good guess, but no. *Mary?* Well, she's Jesus's mom, but no. *God the Father?* Yes. And here are the elders, pretend that's 24 of them....with crowns...there. Who remembers the Greek word for "elder"? *Presby-something?* Yes, *presbyteros*; and we shorten it to...*priest!* Yes; so think of them as priests. And what's a priest's job? C'mon, y'all know this. *To say Mass?* Partly, but *specifically* what do priests do? Aztec priests, Catholic priests, Levite priests, they all...*sacrifice!* Yes, they *offer* sacrifice...they don't always have to kill it.

[Catechist: if you do not want to draw, you may prefer to teach this section from an image of the right-hand panel of the *Triptych of the Mystical Marriage of Saint Catherine* by Hans Memling; and/or the lower central panel of the *Ghent Altarpiece* by Jan van Eyck.]

"And round the throne, on each side of the throne, are four living creatures...the first living creature like a lion, the second living creature like an ox, the third living creature with the face of a man, and the fourth living creature like a flying eagle." Who might these 4 creatures represent? We have an angel, a bull, a lion, and an eagle...four saints, their pictures always show them writing...*MatthewMarkLuke&John!* Yes, who are...*gospel writers!* Yes, evangelists.

"And the four living creatures, each of them with six wings, are full of eyes all round and within, and day and night they never cease to sing, "Holy, holy, holy, is the Lord God Almighty, who was and is and is to come!" We say this at Mass because they're saying it in heaven. "And whenever the living creatures give glory and honor and thanks to him who is seated on the throne, who lives for ever and ever, the twenty-four elders fall down before him who is seated on the throne and worship him who lives for ever and ever..." When they give thanks they 'eucharisteo' in Greek, just like we do with the Eucharist.

Now with all these elders, these presbyters, these...*priests*, yes, standing around the throne, what should they be doing? *Praying?* Hmm...tell me again, what's a priests job? *To offer sacrifices?* Yes, so they...should.... *be offering a sacrifice?* Yes. So what's missing? *A sacrifice?* Yes. What would be a good typical sacrifice? *A lamb?* Yes! John says, "And between the throne and the four living creatures and among the elders, I saw a Lamb standing, as though it had been slain." This Lamb would be...*Jesus?* Yes [I add the Lamb]; how about that? *It looks like a dog.* Please, be charitable. And I need a red marker because the Lamb needs...*blood on it!* Yes...now *that's* a slain lamb! "...and the twenty-four elders fell down before the Lamb, each holding a harp, and with golden bowls full of incense, which are the prayers of the saints...and they sang a new song, saying, "you were slain and by your blood did redeem men for God." So we know the Lamb is...*Jesus,* yes, and the elders are singing, and playing music, and burning incense, and saints are praying, all of which should remind you of...*Mass?* Yes. The communion of saints on earth and in heaven are doing the same things. And which of those things do we do at Mass? *Well...all of them?* Yes. Heaven and earth are *connected* at Mass.

212

So in heaven we have the priest-elders, whose job is to... *offer sacrifice*, yes, and we have a victim, a... *lamb*, who is... *Jesus*, yes. But what's still missing? Do you offer sacrifices on a sofa? *No, an altar!* Right!

John writes, "And another angel came and stood at the altar with a golden censer." So there *is* an altar: "and he was given much incense to mingle with the prayers of all the saints upon the golden altar before the throne; and the smoke of the incense rose with the prayers of the saints from the hand of the angel before God." When we burn incense at Mass, remember that our prayers go up to heaven and mingle with the prayers in heaven. [I add incense and the altar]

Now all of this is like Mass because Mass is like a Passover sacrifice in the Meeting Tent or the Temple. When Moses made the first Meeting Tent, did Moses decide how everything would be? *No, God told him what to do.* Yes, God said the design was based on the pattern in heaven. The Church, Temple and Tent are all patterned on this worship in heaven.

Still More Miracle Bread

Back to Mass on Earth: after the 'Holy Holy' what do we do? *Kneel down.* Yes; this is most important part of Mass, the Eucharistic Prayer. The priest says:

"To you, therefore, most merciful Father,
we make humble prayer and petition
through Jesus Christ, your Son, our Lord:
 that you accept
and bless these gifts, these offerings,
these holy and unblemished sacrifices,"

And what's being offered at this moment? *Bread and wine.* Right, maybe $10 worth of bread and wine. If you were God, would you let that offering atone for our sins? *No!* Why not? *It's not good enough.* That's right.

The priest then reminds us that all of us saints on earth are praying along with all the saints in heaven:

"In communion with those whose memory we venerate,
especially the glorious ever-Virgin Mary,
Mother of our God and Lord, Jesus Christ,
and blessed Joseph, her Spouse,"

That is, Jesus'...*parents.* Yes, and:

"Peter and Paul, Andrew,
James, John,
Thomas, James, Philip,

Bartholomew, Matthew,
Simon and Jude;"

who are...*apostles.* Yes, and:

 "Linus, Cletus, Clement, Sixtus , Cornelius"

...any idea who these guys are? That's ok: they're some of the first saints, and some of the first popes after Peter. And then we hear:

"Cyprian,
Lawrence, Chrysogonus,
John and Paul,
Cosmas and Damian"

who are some of the first martyrs. The Church doesn't name all these people to fill up time, but to remind us of all the saints who are praying with us at Mass.

Now, we are still offering bread and wine at this point, but the priest prays:

 "Be pleased, O God, we pray,
to bless, acknowledge,
and approve this offering in every respect;
make it spiritual and acceptable,
so that it may become for us
the Body and Blood of your most beloved Son,
our Lord Jesus Christ."

The priest is asking God to make the transformation. And when did bread & wine first become Body & Blood? *At the Last Supper?* Yes, so the priest takes the bread, and prays:

"On the day before he was to suffer,
he took bread in his holy and venerable hands,
and with eyes raised to heaven
to you, O God, his almighty Father,
giving you thanks, he said the blessing,
broke the bread
and gave it to his disciples, saying:
TAKE THIS, ALL OF YOU, AND EAT OF IT,
FOR THIS IS MY BODY, WHICH WILL BE GIVEN UP FOR YOU. "

Of course this is straight out of the Gospels. Then he holds the chalice and says:

"In a similar way, when supper was ended,
he took this precious chalice
in his holy and venerable hands,
and once more giving you thanks, he said the blessing
and gave the chalice to his disciples, saying:

TAKE THIS, ALL OF YOU, AND DRINK FROM IT,
FOR THIS IS THE CHALICE OF MY BLOOD,
THE BLOOD OF THE NEW AND ETERNAL COVENANT,
WHICH WILL BE POURED OUT FOR YOU AND FOR MANY
FOR THE FORGIVENESS OF SINS.
DO THIS IN MEMORY OF ME."

And what happens? *They change into body and blood!* Yes. This moment is called the Consecration: when the bread and wine are made sacred, holy.

Then the priest prays:

"Be pleased to look upon these offerings
with a serene and kindly countenance,
and to accept them,
as once you were pleased to accept
the gifts of your servant Abel the just,
the sacrifice of Abraham, our father in faith,
and the offering of your high priest Melchizedek,
a holy sacrifice, a spotless victim."

Tell me quick, Abel offered... *a lamb!* Yes; Abraham offered... *a ram!* Yes, and *before* the ram...*Isaac,* yes, his son. And Melchizedek...*bread and wine!* Yes, and at Mass do we offer bread and wine? *Yes!* And a lamb? *Yes!* And a son? *Yes!* Good. Mass recalls all those earlier offerings.

[The Abel, Melchizedek and Abraham mosaic in St. Apollinare church in Classe, Italy, works well here, and can be combined with the next image on a single sheet of paper.]

Now let's look at this handout:

Is that Manoah's angel at Mass? Maybe it is!

(Permission granted by the Confraternity of the Precious Blood)

Manoah and the Angel Redux

What's that a picture of? *Mass.* Yes, but it's also like the story of Manoah and the Angel. Remember Samson's parents, Manoah and his wife, were told by an angel that they were going to have a baby. They were so happy that Manoah made a Thanksgiving-in-Greek-Eucharist offering to God. "So Manoah took a young goat with the cereal offering, and offered it upon the rock to the LORD, to him who works wonders. And when the flame went up toward heaven from the altar, the angel of the LORD ascended in the flame of the altar while Manoah and his wife looked on; and they fell on their faces to the ground."

And here's what the priest says next:

"In humble prayer we ask you, almighty God:
command that these gifts be borne
by the hands of your holy Angel
to your altar on high
in the sight of your divine majesty"

What does that sound like? *It's like what Samson's parents saw!* Yes, it's like the angel taking Manoah's offering from the altar on Earth up to heaven. But the picture and the prayer are both from....*Mass!* Yes! We don't see the angel who does this, but it's part of our prayer, we believe it happens. Why can't we see this? C'mon, we're blinded by something... *oh, sin!* Yes, and to believe in something we can't see we need... *faith.* Yes. All the saints in heaven can see it, though. And what is the angel taking up? *Well, the offering.* Yes, but what's being offered at this point? *Umm, bread and wine?* No, there's no more bread and wine. *Oh, Jesus is the offering!* Yes. That's Jesus being carried up; not some goat like Manoah offered but a perfect Lamb. And we are offering Jesus to whom? *God.* More specifically, please...*God the Father.* That's it.

"What's everybody doing in the picture? *Well, they're at Mass.* No, I mean their *posture*, they're all bowing their heads; why is that? No takers...let's read the last bit about Manoah again: "...the angel of the LORD ascended in the flame of the altar while Manoah and his wife looked on; and they fell on their faces to the ground." Why'd they fall on the ground? *They were scared when the angel took off.* Yes, a bit scared I'm sure, but they were in the presence of an angel of the LORD, and it made them feel very humble. If I had seen that, I'd have fallen on the ground because I had passed out. People long ago would lie down on the ground in the presence of God, or even a king. Nowadays we just bow our heads, lying on the ground is messy. But notice at Mass, at the Consecration, the altar servers bow *way* down, their heads almost touch the ground when they bow. They bow like Manoah in the presence of God's angel.

And in the picture that's Jesus on the cross: are we nailing Jesus on the cross at Mass? *Umm...no?* No, of course not. He was crucified once. But we offer Jesus' sacrifice at every Mass because Jesus offered himself at the Last Supper. Part of what we "do in memory" of Jesus is offer him when we *co-memorate*, commemorate, the Last Supper at Mass. That way Jesus' sacrifice is always present at the altar at Mass, just like the bloody Lamb is always present at the altar in heaven.

Then we hear,

"so that all of us, who through this participation at the altar
receive the most holy Body and Blood of your Son,
may be filled with every grace and heavenly blessing."

Let's review for a second. At the offertory, what do the people bring up to the priest? *Bread and wine.* Yes, then does the priest right away offer the bread and wine to God the Father: here's ten bucks' worth of bread and wine, Father, please forgive our sins? *Ha, that's silly!* Yes, so the priest offers what? *Jesus.* That's right; that's the perfect sacrifice that atones for our sins. And who turns the bread & wine into Jesus' body & blood? *The priest.* Wow, he must have super powers. Let's remember, Mass isn't mostly about what *people* do, it's about...*what God does,* yes, so who made it happen? *God.* Yes. But God works *through* the priest, so that was a good guess. Then we see in the picture the angel carries our offering from the altar on Earth up to the altar in Heaven...bye! So how do we "at the altar receive the most holy Body and Blood" if it all went to heaven? *Well, some got left behind?* Sort of...think about it this way:

Eucharistic Dinner

When my wife puts on Thanksgiving dinner, she spends a fortune, and does a ton of cooking and preparation. The guests know she worked hard for days. When the guests arrive they usually have something with them, what would that be? *A present?* What kind of present do you bring to a dinner, a power tool? *Ha, no, food!* Good guess, and maybe for the adults something...wet? *Umm... wine?* Yes indeed. Why do guests bring presents? *'cause they are glad you invited them!* You got that right! They are not just *saying* 'thank you' but *showing* it by bringing a thanksgiving offering. Now if someone brings my wife a nice bottle of wine, does she say thanks, and put it away for another occasion? *No, I bet you drink it right then!* Right! She says thank you so much, let's open it right now....here's a glass for you, let's all have some. It's like Mass: she does all of the important work; the guests show their thanks by offering a small gift; she is gracious and offers them back some of their offering. God does the same thing: we offer bread and wine; God gives us back Jesus. We offer Jesus; God says thank you, y'all have some too. And when we "receive from this altar the sacred body and blood" do we put it in our pocket for later? *No, we eat it right then!* That's right! That's how we show thanks at a feast: we eat it all right then! And remind me: what was that Israelite miracle bread called? *Manna!* Yes; could they eat it later? *No, they had to eat it when they got it.* Yes, just like we do when we get our miracle bread. And when Jesus multiplied the bread and fish, did everyone take the leftovers home? *No, the apostles picked up the leftovers!* Yes! Y'all are so smart!

The Holy Tornado

New topic: tornadoes. Tell me about tornadoes. *They blow around?* Yes; where do they start? *In the sky.* Yes, in the clouds. They are powered by the atmosphere; and what happens? *They make a funnel and go down to the ground.* And what happens to small things they might run over? *They get sucked up!* Yes, and plopped back down later.

Look again at the Mass picture, see how it looks swirly toward the top? *Yes.* Well, I like to think of what happens at Mass as a Holy Tornado: God swirls it from Heaven down to our altar, and it carries the angel and the Body & Blood up to the altar in heaven, *zhoop!* Then it sends Jesus' Body and Blood back down for us to eat, *phhhhht!* How long do tornadoes last? *A few minutes?* Yes, and like regular tornadoes, a Holy Tornado is over pretty quick, too. But Masses are being celebrated all over the world, 24/7. Remember Malachi prophesied that "in every place incense is offered to my name, and a pure offering..." So imagine thousands of Holy Tornadoes all around the world, *zhoop, zhoop, zhoop,* connecting heaven and earth for a few seconds each time. Let's draw that connection [under the drawing of the Heavenly Worship]. This is in church...what's this big blocky thing? *The altar?* Yes, like the one in heaven. And an altar is for...*sacrifice,* yes.

And we have this guy...*the priest*...yes, the presbyteros, the elder, like in heaven. And altar servers burn... *incense,* yes, like...*in heaven.* Yes...there we go. And here's the Holy Tornado connecting both altars with the *same sacrifice*, which is...*Jesus.* Yes. That makes sense because Jesus is both man...*and God,* yes, so he fits well into both places.

One last bit and we're done for tonight: this block thing isn't just an altar. What else is it? When the priest says, "this is my body, this is my blood, do this in memory of me" what are we doing in memory of Jesus? *The Last Supper?* Yes, which was...*supper?* Yes, a meal. So the altar is also...*a table?* Yes. And this meal isn't just any old supper...it's like Christmas dinner at my house...*a feast!* Yes. We'll learn about that next week, which is our last class. Your suffering will soon be over!

Praised be Jesus Christ! *Now and forever!* Class over!

Chapter Thirty-Six: Wedding Reception

(Mass 4)

(Rev 4 & 5) Liturgy of the Eucharist: Heavenly worship: incense, angels, New Passover lamb.

Hey y'all, Lent is over, and last Sunday was Easter. So instead of praying an Act of Contrition for Lent, we have an Easter season prayer, which I will sing because it's also a hymn to Mary that's about 900 years old. It tells her to be happy because Jesus isn't dead anymore:

"O Queen of Heaven, be joyful, alleluia.
For He whom you have humbly borne for us, alleluia.
Has arisen, as He promised, alleluia.
Offer now our Prayer to God, alleluia"

Ok, last week in our Mass class we stopped with the priest saying,

"command that these gifts be borne
by the hands of your holy Angel
to your altar on high,"

and discussed that great image of the angel going up to heaven in the Holy Tornado.

Moving forward in the Mass from there, the priest says,

"Remember also, Lord, your servants N. and N.,
who have gone before us with the sign of faith
and rest in the sleep of peace."

Who are these people? *Saints?* Yes. And the priest mentions some of them:

"graciously grant some share
and fellowship with your holy Apostles and Martyrs:
with John the Baptist, Stephen,"

Stephen was the first...? He was stoned to death...*the first martyr!* Yes. Saul saw him get killed. And:

"Matthias, Barnabas,
Ignatius, Alexander,
Marcellinus, Peter,"

Matthias was... he replaced the bad apostle...*Judas!* Yes. And Barnabas? *He was with St. Paul.* Yes, and Peter? *The first pope!* Yes.

And now a group of women saints:

"Felicity, Perpetua, Agatha; Lucy, Agnes, Cecilia, Anastasia."

These saints were all among the first Christian martyrs. And I like Anastasia because her name comes from *Anastasis*, which is Greek for...*Easter!* Yes, it means... *resurrection!* Yes.

And when the priest asks for "fellowship" with the saints, what's he mean? *To be friends with them?* Yes, to be part of the Communion of Saints, who are at Mass with us even if we can't see them.

Tell me, when we think about our sins, do we want God's justice? *No, we want his mercy!* Yes, his forgiveness. That's why we next hear,

"admit us, we beseech you,
into their company,
not weighing our merits,
but granting us your pardon,
through Christ our Lord."

During the Eucharistic Prayer we're kneeling; when it comes to and end, we stand up. When we stand up, what do we pray? C'mon, y'all know this:

"At the Savior's command
and formed by divine teaching,
we dare to say:"

...*the Our Father!* Yes, which comes to us straight out of Jesus' mouth in the Gospel of Matthew. And y'all know this line:

"and forgive us our trespasses, as we forgive those who trespass against us."

Well, right after Jesus finished the prayer the first time, he said, "For if you forgive men their trespasses, your heavenly Father also will forgive you; but if you do not forgive men their trespasses, neither will your Father forgive your trespasses." (Matt 6:14) So, if we don't forgive others...*God won't forgive us.* Right. I expect to spend quite some time in Purgatory burning my resentments away in order to forgive everyone. So even though y'all are way younger than me, y'all may beat me to Heaven, even if I die first as expected. When you zoom past me, say, "Bye, Stratopops, I'll pray for ya!"

Now we get to my favorite part of the Mass. First we say,

"Lamb of God, you take away the sins of the world,
have mercy on us. "

How many times? *Three!* Yes; and who are we quoting? *John the Baptist!* Yes, and we kneel again. Then the priest holds the Body up, which looks like...*bread,* yes, and says:

"Behold the Lamb of God,
behold him who takes away the sins of the world."

And who first said that? *John the Baptist.* Yes; about whom? *Jesus.* Yes, when? *When Jesus came to be baptized.* Yes; where? *In the Jordan River.* Yes, good. This reminds us that Jesus is just as physically present at Mass as he was when John spoke those words at the Jordan River. It's the Lamb of God, it's Jesus. And what's the deal with the Passover Lamb? *You have to eat it!* Right. By the way, what did John eat in the desert? *Bugs!* Yes, tasty when dipped in honey...right, girls? *Ewww!* Uh-huh...boys? *Cool!* Maybe so.

Then the priest quotes an Angel in Revelation:

"Blessed are those called to the supper of the Lamb."

This reminds us we're about to share in the Wedding Feast. Let's look at where this comes from in Revelation, which we already know says a lot about the Heavenly Worship that connects to Mass on Earth. But first let's read a bit from Isaiah that you heard earlier this year: "On this mountain the LORD of hosts will provide for all peoples a feast of rich food and choice wines; juicy, rich food and pure, choice wines. On this mountain he will destroy the veil that veils all peoples, the web that is woven over all nations; he will destroy death forever. The Lord GOD will wipe away the tears from all faces..." Tell me, is Isaiah describing a snack? *No, a feast!* Yes, and all peoples are there, not just the Chosen People. And there's no death or tears, so it must be...*in Heaven!* Yes.

Revelation adds to Isaiah's prophecy: "Then I heard what seemed to be the voice of a great multitude, like the sound of many waters and like the sound of mighty thunderpeals, crying, "Hallelujah! For the Lord our God the Almighty reigns. Let us rejoice and exult and give him the glory, for the marriage of the Lamb has come, and his Bride has made herself ready; it was granted her to be clothed with fine linen, bright and pure." And the Lamb is...*Jesus,* yes. And the Bride is...*the Church,* yes, which is all the nice buildings? *No, it's us!* Yes; and we'll all live in the Holy City, the...New...*Jerusalem!* Yes.

So Jesus marries the Church...why? *Because he loves Her!* Yes. So much that He died for Her. And after a wedding, there's...*a reception!* Yes! So it's a happy feast, but serious, too. And an angel said, "Blessed are those who are invited to the marriage supper of the Lamb...On his robe...he has a name inscribed, King of Kings and Lord of Lords... Then I saw an angel standing in the sun, and with a loud voice he called..."Come, gather for the great supper of God..." So when we eat the feast on Earth...*they're eating the feast in heaven?* Yes.

When I was about your age there was a rock band called Genesis. They wrote a song about the Book of Revelation, which is clever: *Genesis* is the first book in the Bible, and *Revelation* is...*the last one.* Yes. The song is called "Supper's Ready." Is it about eating leftover pork and beans around the kitchen table? *No... is it about the Wedding Feast?* Yes! Listen to the last few lines of the song, which ties together all the stuff you've learned about Revelation [I sing]:

"There's an angel standing in the sun,
And he's crying with a loud voice:
This is the supper of the Mighty One.
The Lord of Lords, King of Kings,
Has returned to lead His children home,
To take them to the New Jerusalem."

So when the priest says, "Blessed are those called to the supper of the Lamb," use your imaginations.

And then we respond to the priest...you know it:

"Lord, I am not worthy
that you should enter under my roof,
but only say the word
and my soul shall be healed."

And who said it first? *The guy who wanted his servant healed...* Yes...who was this "guy"...the popsicle man?
No, a soldier. A paratrooper? *Ha, no a Roman soldier.* Yes, who commanded a hundred men...*a centurion!*
Yes; and he was a pagan; not a Chosen Person.

I really like the centurion. I always have to pray for faith before Communion because it looks like plain-old
flat, dry bread to me. I struggle with doubt even while I believe. But I'm reminded of the faith of the
centurion. He believed Jesus could miraculously heal his servant without needing to visit him; and even
though he was a Roman officer, the centurion was so humble that he didn't feel worthy to have Jesus come
to his house. If a pagan can have such faith and humility then it's not beyond my reach.

This is how the Church uses the Bible to prepare us to receive Jesus at Mass. But you have to know what the
verses mean, and think about them, for it to matter. Think about John and Jesus at the Jordan, the Wedding
Feast, and the believing Roman officer, and why the stories are put together right before Communion.

What's next? *We go up for communion.* Yes, and do we go and grab a fistful of communion hosts? *No, the
priest gives us one!* Yes, just like when Jesus multplied the loaves & fishes: the people didn't *take* the
miracle food: the apostles *distributed* it to them. And when we eat the host, we eat...*the Lamb!* Yes. And we
eat...*Jesus!* Yes. And we eat...no more guesses? We eat *God;* we're God-eaters. Why is that good: to eat
God? *'Cause God is good?* Yes, like eating broccoli, God is good for you, but more than that...imagine I'm a
young hunter in a primitive tribe. If I kill a lion, what part of the lion would I especially want to eat? His toes?
His nose? What was the matter with the lion in the Wizard of Oz? *He didn't have any courage!* Yes, which a
lion is supposed to have. So what part of a lion would a hunter want to eat? *Umm...his heart?* Yes, what
would he hope to gain from that? *To get the lion's courage?* Yes, and maybe his fearsomeness, strength,
speed, and hunting skill. People have believed by eating the heart of an enemy or an animal they could gain
their power. Does that really work? *No.* Right. But with communion it's different: what do we get by eating

God? *His goodness?* Yes, his holiness. Have you ever heard the saying "you are what you eat"? *Yes.* Well, when you eat Jesus you become more like Him, more *of* Him, more holy. And remember the day after the Loaves and Fishes, Jesus said "Truly, truly, I say to you, unless you eat the flesh of the Son of Man and drink his blood, you have no life in you;" so you're doing *exactly* what Jesus expects you to do- truly, truly.

And after you receive communion, how long is Jesus physically in you? *Until your stomach digests, umm, the communion?* Yes, for about 15 minutes. So when you get back to your pew, don't daydream: pray while Jesus is in you. I usually thank God for making this little miracle of the Body'n'Blood available to me, but you can pray however you like.

(Class continues in the next chapter.)

Chapter Thirty-Seven: Arks & Tabernacles

(Mass 5)

Liturgy of the Eucharist part 2, through Dismissal. Balaam's Ass, Isaiah's veil, Letter to the Hebrews

Mass is almost complete now that we have received Communion; in a few minutes the feast will be over. This is a good time to look at how a Catholic church helps the feast take place.

But first, does anyone know who Balaam [on the board] is? No? How about Balaam's Ass [on the board]? (giggles & snickers) No? OK then: Balaam was a pagan who lived when the Israelites were getting established in the Promised Land after their 40 years of wandering in the desert. He was famous for blessing and cursing people, and making it stick. Well, the Israelites had been whipping their local enemies in battle so thoroughly that Balak, the king of Moab, wanted to pay Balaam to curse the Israelites. Balak didn't want to be next on their whipping schedule. Y-H-W-H (don't say it!) told Balaam not to visit Balak, but the Book of Numbers says, "Balaam rose in the morning, and saddled his ass, and went with the princes of Moab."(more giggles & snickers) OK, what's 'ass' mean? *Donkey?* Yes. Now this is your last chance to act like babies when I say 'ass'...ready? Ass. (fewer giggles & snickers) Alright, that was it. No more giggling like 5-year-olds. "But God grew angry because he went; and the angel of the LORD took his stand in the way as his adversary." An angel blocked the way to Moab. "And the ass saw the angel of the LORD standing in the road, with a drawn sword in his hand; and the ass turned aside out of the road, and went into the field; and Balaam struck the ass, to turn her into the road." [I act all this out] "Then the angel of the LORD stood in a narrow path between the vineyards, with a wall on either side. And when the ass saw the angel of the LORD, she pushed against the wall, and pressed Balaam's foot against the wall; so he struck her again." Poor donkey, she's doing Balaam a favor!

"Then the angel of the LORD went ahead, and stood in a narrow place, where there was no way to turn either to the right or to the left. When the ass saw the angel of the LORD, she lay down under Balaam; and in anger Balaam beat the ass with his stick." Now I love this: "Then the LORD opened the mouth of the ass, and she said to Balaam, "What have I done to you, that you have struck me these three times?" And Balaam said to the ass, "...I wish I had a sword in my hand, for then I would kill you." Then the LORD opened the eyes of Balaam, and he saw the angel of the LORD standing in the way, with his drawn sword in his hand; and he bowed his head, and fell on his face." Balaam decided to get himself some humility in a hurry. Trick question: why was Balaam riding the donkey with his eyes closed? *His eyes weren't closed!* No? It says, "the LORD opened the eyes of Balaam, and he saw the angel." Doesn't that mean his eyes were shut? *No, it means he couldn't see the angel until God let him.* Oh. But the donkey saw the angel the whole time...how come? No guesses. Tell me, can we see water wash sins off a baby at Baptism? *No.* Can a saint see it happen? *Yes.* Why? No guesses? Put it this way: why *can't* we see it? *'Cause we're sinners!* Yes, sin makes us...*blind!* Yes! So Balaam couldn't see the angel...*'cause he was a sinner!* Yes; but Balaam's ass could see the angel because...*animals don't sin?* Maybe that's why, the story doesn't say. But remember in one of Isaiah's Christmas prophecies, he said the people of Israel didn't know their master, but the ox and ass did.

Now, back to the feast, listen again to another bit of Isaiah you've heard before: "And he will destroy on this mountain the covering that is cast over all peoples, the veil that is spread over all nations." Are 'all people' sitting under a giant blanket? *No, it's not real.* So what is covering them, what sort of veil is it? *Is it sin?* Yes, at Isaiah's feast the veil of sin will be "destroyed" so people will be able to see God clearly. And if sin is destroyed, where must the feast be? *In Heaven.* Yes.

Now let's look at this handout again, you've seen it before:

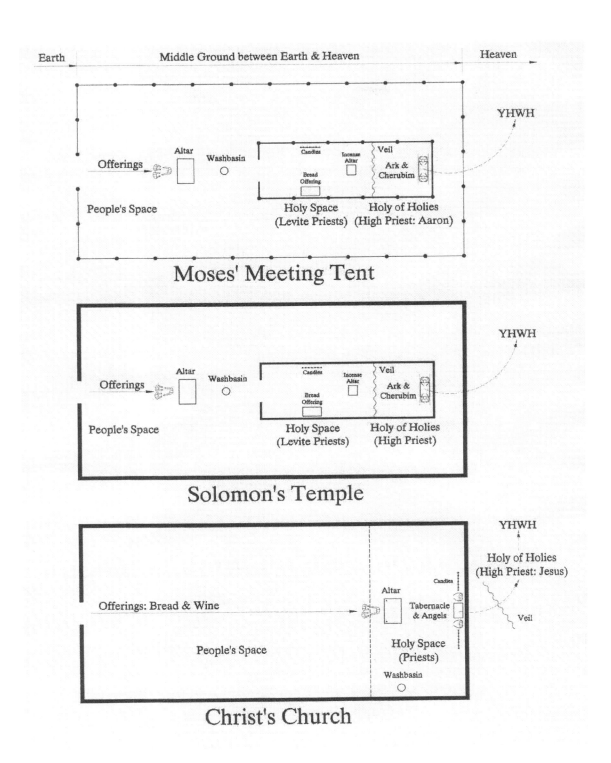

What's the first plan? *Moses' Meeting Tent.* Yes...did Moses design it? *No, God did.* Yes, God gave instructions about every detail of the Tent: "And let them make me a sanctuary, that I may dwell in their midst. According to all that I show you concerning the pattern of the tabernacle, and of all its furniture, so you shall make it." God showed Moses the heavenly pattern of all the stuff that went in the tent, even including little things like the candlesticks. And if God "dwelled" in the tent, then it was...*his house?* Yes, he lived in a tent because his people, the Israelites, lived in tents.

Somebody tell me, what's a tavern? *Is it like a bar?* Yes. Up North, like in Pennsylvania, people will say 'tavern' when we say 'bar'; I think tavern sounds more civilized. Anyway, *taberna* [on the board] is a Latin word for house. Yes? *Why does it have a b?* Because *b*'s and *v*'s sound almost the same in some languages. Somebody digame, como se llama *twenty* in Español? Somebody say *twenty* in Spanish. *Veinte* [on the board]! Yes. See, it's spelled with a *v*, but listen to the sound, please say it again. *Veinte.* Does it sound like a *b* or a *v*? *Kind of in between.* Yes.

So *taberna* means house, and a *tabernaculum* [adding to taberna] is a *little* house, or a tent or a log cabin. Where an English Bible says 'tent,' a Latin Bible will say *tabernaculum.* What word do we get from that? *Tabernacle.* Yes. *We have a tabernacle in church!* Yes, good, we're getting to that. The whole meeting tent was the tabernacle, God's dwelling. Now look at the Holy Spaces where only the priests could go: what separates them? *A veil.* Yes. Is it a real veil? *Yes!* Right, it was a beautiful curtain that prevented everyone from seeing what? *The Ark!* Yes. Only one person could go behind the veil...who? *The High Priest?* Yes. The other priests could tootle around the rest of the Meeting Tent, but they couldn't go past the veil. So who would offer the most important sacrifices to Y-H-W-H? *The High Priest.* Yes; he offered sacrifices for the whole nation, all the people of Israel, right in front of God. Was God there physically? *Well, God doesn't have a body.* Right; but Y-H-W-H's *presence* was right above the Ark, between the cherubim. What's *ark* mean? *A container!* Yes, good. And what was in the Ark? Come on, y'all know this. *Umm...the Ten Commandments?* Yes, and...the miracle bread...*manna!* Yes, a pot of manna; and Aaron's staff. Are those things God? *Ummm, no?* Right; God wouldn't live in a box. God's *stuff* is in the box. But the Israelites had super-respect for that box of stuff.

Now look at Solomon's Temple: it's bigger and nicer and more permanent than the Meeting Tent; but it has the same *pattern* as the Tent. Who designed the pattern? *God!* Yes. Is that a real veil? *Yes!* Right; just like in the Tent. Now look at the Church: tell me about the pattern. *It's the same!* Yes, almost.

In the New Testament there's an Epistle to the Hebrews...what's *Epistle* mean? *Letter.* Yes, so it's a letter written to Jews who had become Christians. I think they might've been worried about not going to the Temple in Jerusalem and sacrificing a Passover Lamb. The Epistle explains to them that it's not necessary anymore, because "we have a great high priest who has passed through the heavens, Jesus, the Son of God...who is seated at the right hand of the throne of the Majesty in heaven, a minister in the sanctuary and the true tent which is set up not by man, but by the Lord." So where is the "true tent"? *In Heaven!* Yes; tell me, *who* is the High Priest in the church plan? *Jesus.* Yes, and *where* is the High Priest? *In Heaven.* Yes, he's the slain Lamb, a perfect Lamb, who offers himself right in front of the Father's throne in Heaven, in the true tent. So the Hebrew Christians didn't need the Temple priests to sacrifice and offer lambs for them anymore. And how long will Jesus be a High Priest? *Umm...forever?* Yes, at least until the Final Judgment in Revelation. The Epistle says we have "a hope that enters into the inner shrine behind the veil, where Jesus [has] become a high priest for ever after the order of Melchizedek." What's the deal with Melchizedek? *He offered bread and wine!* Yes; like...*Jesus!* Yes, at...*the Last Supper!* Yes! But did Jesus offer God $10 worth of bread &

wine? *No, he changed it into his Body & Blood!* Yes, y'all are too smart!

At Mass, can we see Jesus offer himself in Heaven? *No.* Right; now tell me about the veil on the church plan. *It's not in the church!* Right; is it a real veil? *No... it's sin!* Yes, sin veiled Balaam's eyes from seeing the angel, and sin veils us from seeing what's in Heaven. But if we become saints, and free from sin...*then we can see.* Yes. So the visible pattern in a church stops at the veil of sin, and the rest of the offering of the sacrifice takes place beyond that veil, in... *Heaven,* yes which is the *true tent,* not an earthly copy. People have doubts sometimes about believing in things they can't see. In his Epistle to the Corinthians, St. Paul wrote, "For now we see in a mirror dimly, but then face to face. Now I know in part; then I shall understand fully..." So even a motivated saint like Paul would get frustrated by the veil of sin blocking his view.

Now tell me about the Ark in the church plan. *There isn't an Ark, there's a tabernacle.* Yes; what's the difference? No guesses? What's *ark* mean? *Container!* Yes, in this case, a box. And what goes in a box...people? *No, stuff!* Yes. Is Jesus stuff? *No, a person!* Yes, and if Jesus wants to dwell with us in church, would you have him live in a box? *No!* What do people live in? *A house?* Yes, so Jesus...*has to have a house.* Yes, but he doesn't take up much room under the appearance of bread; he doesn't need a full-size *taberna,* but a...*tabernacle!* Yes, a "little house." Why do tabernacles often look like little houses? *Because Jesus lives there!* Yes, as the Bible might say, Jesus *dwells* among his people in the Tabernacle.

Back in the Tent and the Temple days the Jews had great respect for the box of God's stuff. But what should get more respect: God's stuff in a box, or God himself in his little house? *God in his little house!* Yes, so always behave in church with the respect that Jesus deserves. Somebody tell me, what guarded Eden with a flaming sword? *An angel!* No, an angel's a messenger, try again. *A cherub!* Yes, cherubim...fat little Valentine babies? *No, God's bodyguards.* Yes. And later, who guarded the Ark? *Cherubs!* Yes. Where were they? *On both sides of the box!* Yes. Now if the Ark was guarded by *kerubim, near ones,* one on each side, what would you expect for the tabernacle in our church? *It's got cherubs too?* Yes. How many? *Umm... two?* Yes, where? *On both sides?* Yes. *I've seen them!* Honorary son, good for you for noticing them! They're hard to see, but look: [I draw] here's the tabernacle. And here are the *kerubim,* like so, facing each other across the top of the tabernacle, just like they faced each other over the Ark in the Meeting Tent a few thousand years ago.

The kerubim guarding the tabernacle at St. Mary's

Now after people eat a feast, what needs to be washed and put away? *The dishes?* Yes; who does them...the guests? *No, the person who invited them.* Yes, the host or hostess. Well, after Communion, the priest does the dishes. When he's done, Jesus is put back into his little house, and we all sit down. Following a short prayer and any announcements, the priests blesses us and says, "Go forth, the Mass is ended." Somebody *digame* how to say *Mass* in Spanish. *Misa!* Yes [on the board]. It comes from this Latin word: *missa* [on the board]. At the end of Mass in Latin, the priest says

"Ite, missa est" [on the board].

It means "Go, [it] is dismissed." That's where we get the word *Mass*, from the dis*miss*al. And the people say...*thanks be to God!* Yes. Then what happens? *Well, we leave?* Yes, the Mass is over.

And our year of 6th grade Wednesday Sunday School is over too, along with all your misery. I do hope y'all learned a thing or two while y'all suffered so dreadfully. And for the rest of your lives, if you have a question about being Catholic, or the Bible, or the Mass, or whatever, get a hold of me and I'll find you an answer.

Before class is "dismissed" I want to draw one last picture that pulls together a lot of what we learned this year. [I draw] What's this? *The altar.* Yes, which is also a...*table*...yes. It represents...*Mass?* Yes...and here's the priest, who stands in for...*Jesus.* Yes. Now around the Mass I want y'all to name anything you learned that ties into the Mass. *The Last Supper!* Yes, and? A man who offered bread and wine...*Melchizedek!* Yes, and...blood on the doorposts...*Passover!* Behold the Lamb of God...*John the Baptist!* Yes....miracle bread in the desert...*Manna!* Yes...more miracle bread...Jesus...apostles...*Loaves & Fishes!* Yes! *Abraham & Isaac!* Yes! *When Jesus was crucified!* Yes! *Abel!* Yes! *When Jesus made wine at the wedding!* Yes, Cana! And last of all...we learned it tonight...wedding...*Wedding Feast!* of...*the Lamb!* who is... *Jesus!* Yes, good children! [That's not everything of course, but this concluding topic is always limited by the remaining time.]

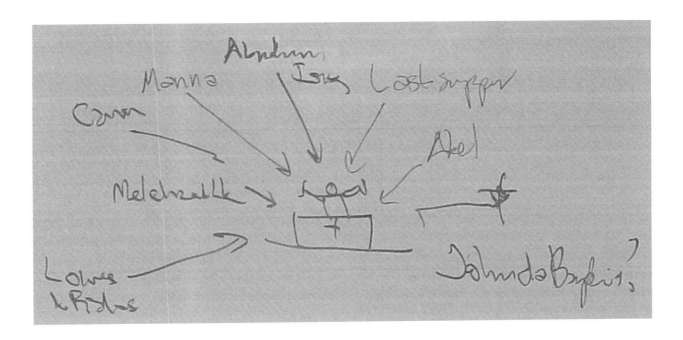

Praised be Jesus Christ! *Now and Forever!*

Class over!

Afterword

Thanks for reading all the way to the end of the book! I hope you didn't suffer any worse than the kids did. And I hope it helps you in your catechetical classroom.

In closing I'd like to emphasize some points that are implicit in the *The Bible Tells Me So*, but may not necessarily be obvious:

The catechist drives the class. Not the textbook, not the lesson plan, not the Bible. You. My image of this driving force is that I'm a wave that the kids surf on. They have to stay on the wave, but it's the wave that provides the energy to lift them and push them forward. Lift and push. But I can't push so fast that they fall off, nor go so slow that they can't stand up. I understand this can be difficult at first. But the more the catechist is motivated to teach the children what he/she knows, the easier it is to drive the class.

You can't cover everything. 30 class periods (if that) is not much time. In my opinion, it's better to drop something from the lesson plan than to go too fast.

Kids need variety. The catechist can read aloud, sing, ask questions, draw and write on the board, provide handouts, direct impromptu skits, use props. Too much of one thing and the kids will fatigue.

Kids love to go sideways. I don't mean that they like to digress (which they do), but that their nimble brains like to connect old knowledge to new knowledge. That's perfect for learning about Catholicism, which is much more a web of faith than a tree of faith.

Kids need to repeat and review. Typically we spend less than 2 minutes at the start of each class reviewing last week's material. Otherwise most review is done on the fly. I think it's best to review at the moment that old information will reinforce new information.

Let the kids do the talking. It's true, I talk a lot in class. But as much as the children can explain something, tell the story, or play parts in an impromptu skit on their own, I let them.

Don't let the kids run a discussion. The catechist runs the discussion, asks specific questions, and decides when to move on. A child never asks another child a question.

Ask lots of questions:

Ask questions constantly; maintain a rhythm of Q&A.
Ask individual students if hands aren't going up.
Adjust questions to steer the discussion, usually forward, but sideways or back is fine as appropriate.

Accept a few wrong answers before simply giving the class an answer.
Answer off-topic questions briefly, and return to topic with a new question.
Build on answers by affirming, repeating, restating, expanding, or refining them.

Use correct answers as the jumping-off point for the next question.

Let momentum carry the class when possible: yes, and... good, and... and then...?

Maintain a rhythm of affection and approval through a flow of small, *earned* affirmatives: yes...yes...good...yes...good children.

Don't read too much at one time. Kids zone out fast if I read more than a paragraph before pausing to ask a question, or draw a picture, or write something on the board. It's important for them to see & hear the catechist read & teach from a Bible held in the hands; but their attention level will determine how much they can listen to at any given point. For example, they can listen to a longer passage at the start of class than they can near the end of class.

Expect a lot. Kids like to think, and love to rise to the occasion. Don't baby them. Emotionally they are children, but their thinking skills are razor-sharp. So I expect them to operate at my level, and I'm rarely disappointed.

Biography

Christian LeBlanc is a revert whose pre-Vatican II childhood was spent in South Louisiana, where he marinated in a Catholic universe and acquired a Catholic imagination. During his middle school years at St. Mary's parish in South Carolina, Christian was catechized under the benevolent dictatorship of Sister Mary Alphonsus, who frequently admonished him using the nickname "Little Pagan." After four years of teaching Adult Ed and RCIA, he returned to Sr. Alphonsus' old classroom to teach sixth grade Catechism himself. This is his eighth year of teaching sixth grade. Married to Janet, the LeBlancs have five children and two grandsons.

Christian is a regular columnist at AmazingCatechists.com, and also posts at his blog, Smaller Manhattans.

Email Christian at chrisleb1@aol.com.

Images

Eve and Mary by Sr. Grace Remington O.C.S.O. Used by permission.

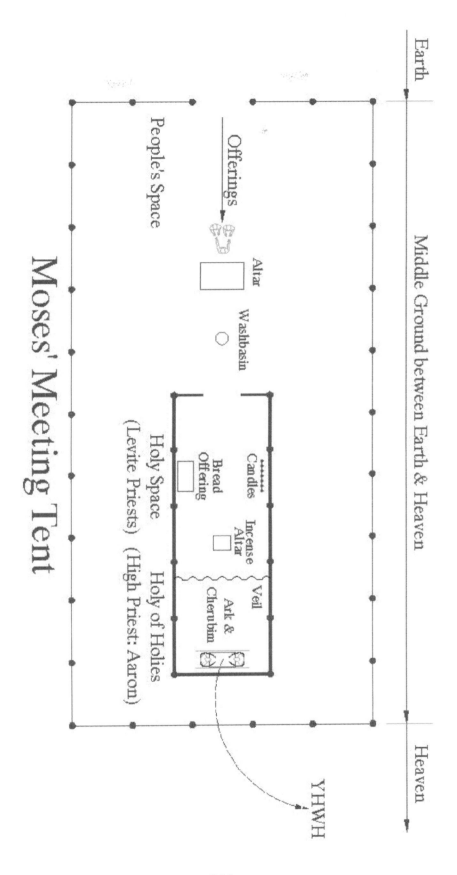

Moses' Meeting Tent

Earth

Middle Ground between Earth & Heaven

Heaven

People's Space

Offerings

Altar

Washbasin

Holy Space
(Levite Priests)

Candles

Bread
Offering

Incense
Altar

Holy of Holies
(High Priest: Aaron)

Veil

Ark &
Cherubim

YHWH

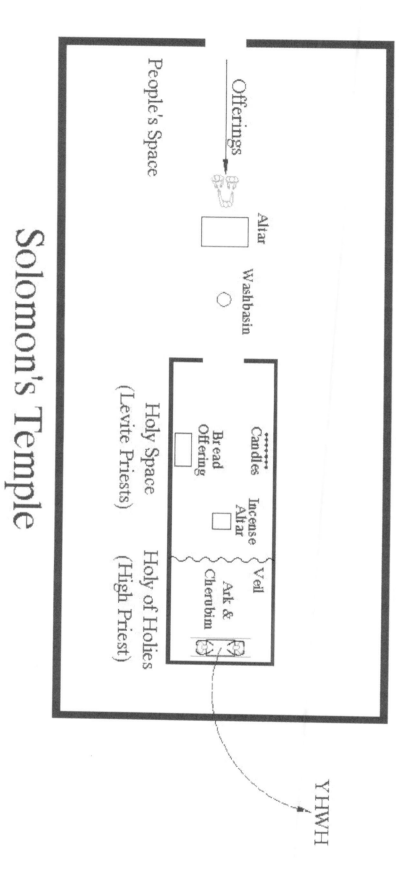

Solomon's Temple

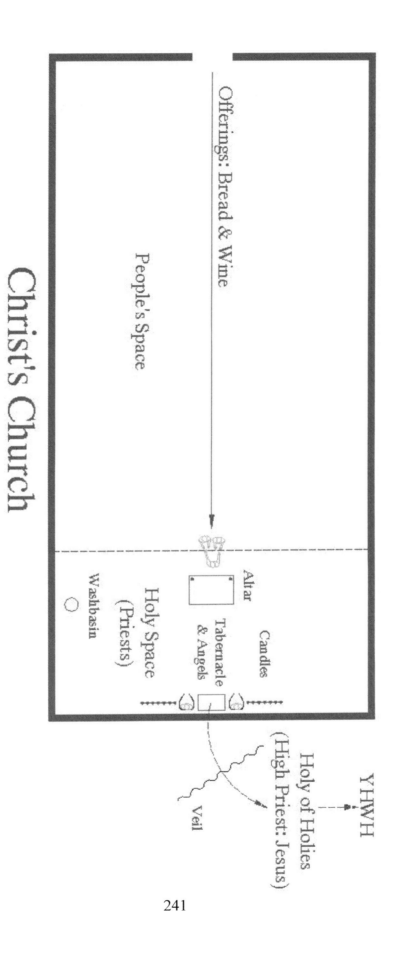

Christ's Church

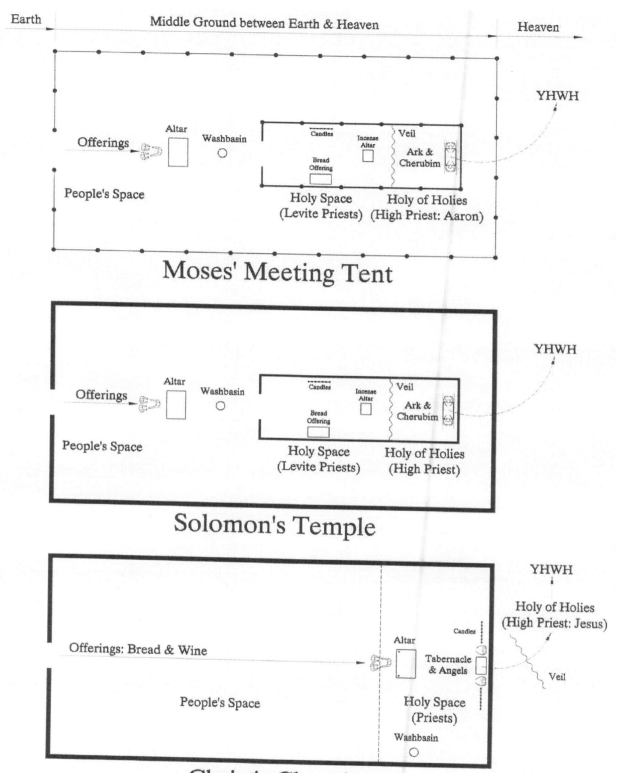

Earth | Middle Ground between Earth & Heaven | Heaven

Moses' Meeting Tent

Offerings → Altar Washbasin Candles Incense Altar Veil Ark & Cherubim YHWH
Bread Offering
People's Space
Holy Space (Levite Priests) Holy of Holies (High Priest: Aaron)

Solomon's Temple

Offerings → Altar Washbasin Candles Incense Altar Veil Ark & Cherubim YHWH
Bread Offering
People's Space
Holy Space (Levite Priests) Holy of Holies (High Priest)

Christ's Church

Offerings: Bread & Wine → Altar Candles Tabernacle & Angels YHWH Holy of Holies (High Priest: Jesus) Veil
People's Space Holy Space (Priests) Washbasin

dead · alive

Eden — Bodynsoul

Sheol — Soul

B.C. | A.D.

Heaven — Soul

New Jerusalem — Bodynsoul

Image by Ariel Agemian. From 'My Mass Explained and Illustrated' by Fr. Joseph Frey. Permission granted by the Confraternity of the Precious Blood

Made in the USA
Lexington, KY
13 August 2014